· RADCLIFFE BIOGRAPHY SERIES ·

The Alchemy of Survival

· RADCLIFFE BIOGRAPHY SERIES ·

DOROTHY DAY
A Radical Devotion
Robert Coles

SIMONE WEIL
A Modern Pilgrimage
Robert Coles

MARGARET BOURKE-WHITE
A Biography
Vicki Goldberg
Foreword by Phyllis Rose

MARY CASSATT
Nancy Hale
Foreword by Eleanor Munro

THE THIRD ROSE
Gertrude Stein and Her World
John Malcolm Brinnin
Foreword by John Ashbery

MARGARET FULLER
From Transcendentalism to Revolution
Paula Blanchard
Foreword by Carolyn Heilbrun

EMILY DICKINSON
Cynthia Griffin Wolff
Foreword by R. W. B. Lewis

CHARLOTTE MEW AND HER FRIENDS
Penelope Fitzgerald
Foreword by Brad Leithauser

Published by Delacorte Press

HELEN AND TEACHER
The Story of Helen Keller and Anne Sullivan Macy
Joseph P. Lash

WOMEN OF CRISIS
Lives of Struggle and Hope
Robert Coles and Jane Hallowell Coles

WOMEN OF CRISIS II
Lives of Work and Dreams
Robert Coles and Jane Hallowell Coles

BUYING THE NIGHT FLIGHT
Georgie Anne Geyer

The Alchemy

RADCLIFFE BIOGRAPHY SERIES

A Merloyd Lawrence Book

Addison-Wesley Publishing Company, Inc.

Reading, Massachusetts · Menlo Park, California · New York
Don Mills, Ontario · Wokingham, England · Amsterdam · Bonn
Sydney · Singapore · Tokyo · Madrid · San Juan

of Survival

One Woman's Journey

John E. Mack, M.D.

with Rita S. Rogers, M.D.

Library of Congress Cataloging-in-Publication Data

Mack, John E., 1929–
    The alchemy of survival: one woman's journey/John E. Mack with
Rita S. Rogers.
        p.   cm. — (Radcliffe biography series)
    "A Merloyd Lawrence book."
    Includes index.
    ISBN 0-201-12682-6
    1. Rogers, Rita S. (Rita Stenzler) 2. Psychiatrists — United
States — Biography. 3. Psychiatry — Political aspects. I. Rogers,
Rita S. (Rita Stenzler) II. Title. III. Series.
RC438.6.R64M33 1988
618.92′89′00924 — dc19
[B]   87-36447

Illustrations by Mark Andres
Designed by Copenhaver Cumpston
Set in 12 point Garamond no. 3 by DEKR Corporation, Woburn, MA

ABCDEFGHIJ-HA-898
First printing, May 1988

The Radcliffe Biography Series

RADCLIFFE COLLEGE is pleased and proud to sponsor the Radcliffe Biography Series depicting the lives of extraordinary women.

Each volume of the series serves to remind us of two of the values of biographical writing. A fine biography is first of all a work of scholarship, grounded in the virtues of diligent and scrupulous research, judicious evaluation of information, and a fresh vision of the connections between persons, places, and events. Beyond this, fine biographies give us both a glimpse of ourselves and a reflection of the human spirit. Biography illuminates history, inspires by example, and fires the imagination to life's possibilities. Good biography can create lifelong models for us. Reading about other people's experiences encourages us to persist, to face hardship, and to feel less alone. Biography tells us about choice, the power of a personal vision, and the interdependence of human life.

The timeless women whose lives are portrayed in the Radcliffe Biography Series have been teachers, reformers, adventurers, writers, leaders, and scholars. The lives of some of them were hard pressed by poverty, cultural heritage, or physical handicap. Some of the women achieved fame; the victories and defeats of others have been unsung. We can learn from all of them something of ourselves. In sponsoring this series, Radcliffe College is responding to the continuing interest of our society in exploring and understanding the experience of women.

The Radcliffe Biography project found its inspiration in the publication in 1971 of *Notable American Women*, a scholarly encyclopedia sponsored by Radcliffe's Schlesinger Library on the history of women in America. We became convinced that some of the encyclopedia's essays should be expanded into full-length biographies, so that a wider audience could grasp the many contributions women have made to American life — an awareness of which is as yet by no means universal. Since then the concept of the series has expanded to include women of our own times and in other countries. As well as commissioning new biographies, we are also adding reprints of distinguished books already published, with introductions written for the series.

It seems appropriate that an institution dedicated to the higher education of women should sponsor such a project, to hold a mirror up to the lives of particular women, to pay tribute to them, and so to deepen our understanding of them and of ourselves.

We have been joined in this project by a remarkable group of writers. I am grateful to them and to the editorial board — particularly to Deane Lord, who first proposed the series, both in concept and in detail. Finally, I am happy to present this volume in the Radcliffe Biography Series.

Matina S. Horner
President

Radcliffe College
Cambridge, Massachusetts

To the cherished memory of Rita's parents

Acknowledgments

We thank Dr. William Davidson for introducing us, and Deane Lord who created the opportunity for our collaboration. Special thanks go to our children, Rita's daughter Sheila and John's sons Kenny and Tony, for their essential contributions.

Anatol Dvorak, our guide in Mogilev Podolskiy in 1981, made it possible for us to find Olya, in whose house Rita and her family were interned. We are also grateful to Nora and Abraham Wiznitzer, Betty Zeiger, Olya and her daughter, and Herta Korn for sharing their memories.

Anna Ornstein, Tess Wise, Joseph Glenmullen, Nancy Kricorian, Robert Jay Lifton, the late Joseph Lash, and Robert Coles read the manuscript of this book and offered helpful comments and suggestions.

Our deep appreciation goes to Laurie Tobyne, Oie Smith, Helen Modica, Michael Davis and, above all, Patricia Carr, for their transcription of tapes and preparation of the manuscript. Rodica Mihalea Liggett helped with certain Romanian expressions. We offer special thanks to our editor, Merloyd Lawrence, whose gentle persistence, dedication, and support enabled us to see this work through. And, finally, we thank our spouses, Sally and Allen, and our children, David, Danny, and Judy, for their devotion, tactful discretion, and patience throughout this journey.

Contents

BALTIC
SEA

Gdansk

Warsaw

GERMANY

POLAND

U. S. S. R.

Kiev

Prague

CZECHOSLOVAKIA

Mogilev Podolskiy

Czernowitz

UKRAINE

Vienna

Budapest

Rădăuţi

BESSARABIA

Dniester River

AUSTRIA

HUNGARY

Iasi

Odessa

ITALY

ROMANIA

BLACK
SEA

Bucharest

Constanţa

YUGOSLAVIA

ADRIATIC SEA

BULGARIA

Sofia

*now MOLDAVIAN S.S.R.

Survival is a collective act, and so is bearing witness. Both are rooted in compassion and care, and both expose the illusion of separateness. It is not an exaggeration, not merely a metaphor, to say that the survivor's identity includes the dead.

— Terence des Pres
The Survivor

Introduction

Walking along a street in Princeton, New Jersey, in November 1973, I encountered a psychiatrist colleague accompanied by a short, energetic woman of middle age with lively, deep-set eyes. The woman turned to her companion and said, in a thick European accent, "And who is this young man to whom I have not yet been introduced?" The companion was Dr. William Davidson, president of the Institute for Psychiatry and Foreign Affairs. The woman was Dr. Rita Rogers, a Romanian-born child psychiatrist. Charmed by her expression of interest, I waited for Bill Davidson to introduce us.

Rita Rogers was in Princeton to present a paper on David Ben-Gurion, the first prime minister of the state of Israel, at a conference on the psychological aspects of conflict in the Middle East. The conference was one of a series sponsored jointly by Princeton University, Dr. Davidson's organization, and the American Psychiatric Association's Task Force on Psychiatry and Foreign Affairs. In her paper, which was one of several psychobiographical studies of political figures connected with the Middle East, including mine on the life of T. E. Lawrence ("Lawrence of Arabia"), Rita wrote of how realistic Ben-Gurion had been about Israel's situation and his awareness, especially after the 1967 war, of the importance of building bridges between Israel and her Arab neighbors.

The Yom Kippur, or October, War of 1973 had ended only a month before, with terrible casualties on both sides. Rita, whose father and many other relatives still lived in Haifa, had traveled to Israel during the war. She found it easier to be there than to worry about that country from California. At this conference, and at a follow-up meeting in Princeton in March 1974, after another trip to Israel, Rita spoke of the trauma of the Yom Kippur War for Israeli society. Many of the young "supermen" of the Israeli Air Force, the invincible jet pilots of the swift Israeli victory over the Arabs in 1967, had been shot down and killed by electronically guided, Russian-made Sam 6 missiles, thus raising a new specter of vulnerability for the Jewish survivors of the Holocaust and the pogroms of Russia. Rita spoke of the despair in Israel and the need to find government officials and generals to blame for the surprise attack that had found the nation so unprepared. Our Princeton group included members of Arab background who spoke of the meaning of the 1973 war for the Arab world and the enhanced national self-esteem that the "good showing" against the almighty Israeli army had provided for Egypt and other Arab countries.

These Princeton meetings on the psychology of Middle Eastern leaders and the Arab-Israeli conflict were the beginning of a fifteen-year association between Rita and me that has resulted in this book. As we talked, I soon discovered that Rita's life dramatized, in the experience of a single individual, the most important themes in our field of psychiatry and foreign affairs. At meeting after meeting, usually concerned with some aspect of the psychology of international conflict, Rita told me stories of her life, beginning with Rita Stenzler, a child in the Bukovina, the northern border province of Romania. I learned of her Jewish family background, her protected childhood in the town of Rădăuți, of the years spent by her family and community in a German transport camp during World War II, and their later homeless wandering in Bessarabia and Soviet-occupied northern Bukovina as the war continued to the west. She told me about her family's repatriation to their homeland on the last day of the war and her escape from Romania soon afterward as the Communist regime began to take power there. We talked of her happy years in Prague as a medical student and her flight to Vienna after the Soviet-backed coup made life in Czechoslovakia unbearable. She spoke of years of poverty and the pain of statelessness in Austria and her search for a country, which led finally to her immigration to the United States in

1953. Above all, we came to understand the power of international events to shape the lives of individual human beings, a connection of which so many Americans seem blissfully unaware.

For me, Rita's life story uncovered lesson after lesson, while for her our collaboration became an opportunity for personal integration. It has given her a chance to sort out, reexamine, and pull together the many strands of her identity and its evolution through war, internment, exile, immigration, marriage, motherhood, and a career in psychiatry. For both of us, exploring her life has led to a deeper understanding of the meaning of survival.

As chief of child psychiatry and clinical professor at the Harbor General Hospital in Torrance, California, which is part of the UCLA Department of Psychiatry, Rita Rogers was responsible for training the majority of the child psychiatrists in the South Bay area of Los Angeles. She is a pioneer in the field of psychiatry and foreign affairs, a member of the Pugwash Conference on Science and World Affairs (one of the few psychiatrists) and many other national and international multidisciplinary groups that address conflicted relationships among nations. Rita is invited all over the world to present her work on psychological mistrust between nations and related topics. As a child psychiatrist she has developed an international reputation through her writings on the emotional vulnerabilities of children and adolescents. In both her chosen fields of research — psychiatry and foreign affairs and child psychiatry — Rita has focused on intergenerational relationships, especially the transmission from one generation to another of historical hurts and grievances. Her purpose in both arenas is to interrupt the cycles of enmity and revenge that result from transmitted suffering.

But this book is not as much about Rita's achievements as it is about the way she transcended personal suffering, converting her experiences into resources from which to draw in her personal and professional life. In this respect Rita's story fits at the center of my own research interests as a psychiatrist and a biographer. I have long been curious about how some individuals, including survivors of the European Holocaust of World War II, have been able not only to survive deeply traumatic histories but to transform those experiences and make them part of a fruitful life of service and commitment. These individuals, like any other survivors of trauma and war, may suffer from one or another scar or neurosis. But psychological conflict as such is not the focus of this book. The emphasis is rather on the surmounting of obstacles, physical and psychological, and how it was accomplished, on the stretching of what is humanly possible, and the determination of one individual in the face of adversity. Our book, by and large, is a success story, the triumph of an individual against the odds and the exploration of the roots of that triumph.

The narrating "I" is John Mack, but Rita insisted from the beginning on active participation. Her insistence on active partici-pation is connected with her attitude toward being in a passive role. Rita has never sought psychotherapy or psychoanalysis as a means of resolving personal conflict, which is unusual for a dynamically ori-ented psychiatrist. As someone whose survival depended on initiative, she finds the potential passivity in the patient role intolerable for herself. Associated with Rita's active stance in life is her attitude toward privacy and personal suffering. Some suffering, she maintains, must remain private and cannot or should not be shared. How she integrates her intolerance of passivity and respect for privacy with her style of psychotherapy will be examined in Chapter 8.

Though this book does not "tell all," a great deal of intimacy is shared, much inner experience that Rita has entrusted to her coauthor and thus to the reader. The creation of the book has not been therapy for Rita but a personal exploration with a friend, a chance to remem-ber, to go back in order to go forward. There has been no effort to smooth the rough edges of character. The pettiness, egocentrism, arrogance, and entitlement that the Nobel Prize–winning writer Elias Canetti has ascribed to survivors[1] are provided here along with Rita's loving, courageous, and heroic qualities.

The Czech novelist Milan Kundera has said, "We will never remember anything by sitting in one place waiting for the memories to come to us of their own accord. Memories are scattered all over the world. We must travel if we want to find them and flush them from their hiding places."[2] When we first talked about collaborating on this book, Rita said that she had never examined the most precious parts of her life, her early years in the Bukovina. Yet she craved to go back physically to the places of her childhood and youth. Her mother died in Haifa in 1970 and her father in 1979, just a few months before our decision to write the book, and Rita longed to return to the places associated with them. So we decided to go back together, psychologically and physically.

Beginning in the summer of 1981, on a journey in which we included her younger daughter, Sheila, and my second son, Kenneth, we traveled to Bukovina, to Mogilev Podolskiy, where Rita was interned during the war, to Prague, to Vienna, and to many places in the United States. This book is based primarily on the memories "flushed from their hiding places" during our travels. Its raw materials were notes and tape recordings of conversations with Rita and others, supplemented by interviews and her own written recollections and observations stimulated by our travels and conversations. When quoting from conversations, interviews, or notes provided by Rita herself, no specific annotation has been provided. I have relied on Rita to supply me with the materials with which to reconstruct her life. Rita has relied on me as a friend, a psychiatrist, and a writer to tell her story faithfully. She, of course, has had many opportunities to read the book in progress and determine if the story is accurately told and whether the interpretations of history and personality, with which she may not always entirely agree, are plausible or at least tolerable.

Difficult periods in our collaboration have required, several times, a renewal of our commitment to see the project through to completion. We have had to contend first of all with the sometimes conflicting psychological forces that are the substance of any biography, especially delicate when the subject is still very much alive. In addition, we have had to confront a problem not fully anticipated by either of us when we began. As we worked together, we gradually became aware of a sharp contrast between our political selves. Our values, fears, and points of view stem from radically different personal histories. Put simply, Rita's is the experience of a wary survivor of Eastern Europe, who has felt personally and directly the impact of war and political conflict over three decades. Mine is the experience of an American of German-Jewish background — curious, open, seeking to be empathic, yet, like most Americans who have been spared the worst effects of international conflict, innocent and, at times perhaps, naive. With much personal struggle, involving a good deal of self-examination and "talking through," we have been able to understand and respect these differences even when we could not altogether reconcile them. Our effort to do so mirrors directly the goals of our work in psychiatry and foreign affairs.

Several stories are told in this book. One is the story of events in Eastern Europe between the late 1930s and early 1950s and their impact on one teenage girl and her family. During this time fascism and anti-Semitism proliferated in Romania, providing a receptive climate for Nazism and Hitler's global ambitions. A 1940 deal between Hitler and Stalin resulted in the transfer of large parts of Romania, including much of Rita's native province of Bukovina, to Russia, only to be followed in 1941 by Hitler's invasion of Russia and the return of these lands to Romania. These were years of war and unprecedented mass killing, leading to the death in World War II of millions of civilians and soldiers in Romania, the Ukraine, and the border territories in between. The defeat of Germany was followed by the ceding to Russia, once again, of the Romanian lands of northern Bukovina and Bessarabia and by Communist takeovers in the late 1940s in Romania, Bulgaria, Poland, Hungary, and Czechoslovakia with a minimum of obstruction by the Western democracies. Only in Austria did internal and external resistance eventually result in the creation of an independent country in 1955.

Rita and her family were directly affected by all these events, and there is a good deal in the story about courage and determination in the face of what seemed at times to be the grimmest possible odds. The location of her native town in a border province of Romania, for centuries a center of conflict, has a particular psychological significance, which we explore. The calendar of events in Rita's life has always been shaped in relation to the timetable of events in Europe. For example, the birth of Rita's second child, Judy, on October 16, 1956, is associated in her mind with the Hungarian uprising, which occurred later that month.

This is also a psychological story or, more accurately, a story of the reciprocal relationship between these outside events and the private, inner world of a person who would one day succeed, in her own way, in helping to affect the international political process itself. It is a story of the capacity for survival: a combination of circumstances, luck, emotional strength, and enduring relationships. Such survival involves transformation, an alchemy that enhances creativity and power. Rita not only endured, she prevailed.

Yet another story is one of intimate family relationships and the way that rich, culturally rooted family traditions can provide a child with confidence, security, continuity, and psychological strength. Whatever the events of our lives may be, our perception of them is determined by how well our parents and community transmitted to us a sense of our basic value. Such a legacy not only increases the chance of survival but may reduce the subsequent personal costs. Rita's Eastern European Jewish community, with its cohesiveness, sense of belonging, and ingenuity, including the culturally given ability to bribe creatively, played an important role in her survival and that of her family and its other members. Rita's frequent efforts to recapture the security and intimate ambience of Rădăuţi in organizations and institutions in the United States, as we will see, have not always been so successful.

This book is also about personal identity, about the struggle of one person to reconcile the multiple strands of her inner, family, ethnic, political, and professional selves. Rita was uprooted at sixteen from a German-speaking, upper-middle-class Jewish family and community in a part of agricultural Romania that had been for a century and a half — until shortly before Rita's birth — part of the Austro-Hungarian Empire. It was, therefore, not surprising that she would find it hard to maintain a sense of herself as a refugee in several European countries and, eventually, in the United States. Rita returns to Eastern Europe whenever she can. "There is something about going to Eastern Europe," she has written, "which is more meaningful for me than the fanciest, most elaborate travel in the West. Maybe it is the color of the sky, the smell of the air, the old buildings, the old radios, the familiar furniture from my childhood, but most of all the people. They dress, look, act, and interact as they used to . . . and yet, of course, they don't."

Rita has always been drawn to people who feel "true to themselves," certain about who they are. She was attracted originally to the Romanian peasants, envying their centuries-old connection with their land and customs. She enjoys being with people who are "authentic" in the sense of being firmly rooted in their geographically established nationalities. Her experience of statelessness, lacking the documents necessary to function or belong, underscored for Rita the value of this rootedness. She married an American who was always "sure of who he was." There is also a paradox here, for the shifting layers of Rita's identity may have given her, along with other immigrants of complex national background, a valuable adaptability, a flexibility and tolerance of ambiguity in situations and in other people that can be an asset in uncertain times.

Finally, and perhaps most important, this book is about human connections and the continuity of generations. Rita's love of children, her caring maternal qualities, which reflect those of her own mother, lie at the core of much that follows. Rita holds close to her the memories of her parents and her grandparents. In Rădăuţi and Mogilev Podolskiy, we visited gravesites to reestablish connection with relatives who had died. It was particularly disturbing for Rita to find the Jewish cemetery in Rădăuți uncared for and in Mogilev Podolskiy to be unable to find the graves of her two grandfathers who had died there. It felt as if the continuity of generations had been broken, for Rita the most painful of human tragedies.

In describing the events that follow, especially in conveying Rita's experience of her years in Mogilev Podolskiy, I feel the need to offer a kind of disclaimer, almost an apology, for there is lacking here the relentless horror that most Holocaust victims, including survivors, experienced. This is partly attributable to the fact that Mogilev Podolskiy was not actually a concentration camp. The so-called transition or transport camp was more like a ghetto, but a ghetto with many of the characteristics of the camps, especially the terror of what might lie ahead. But equally important is the attitude of Rita herself, the way she saw things. There was a great deal of horror, but Rita and her family waged a kind of campaign to preserve some optimism, even joy in life in the camp. Other Rădăuți Jews who survived Mogilev would tell a different story. "I think the Mogilev years did not fully penetrate my sense of reality. . . . The idea that one people, whose literature I loved, was out to exterminate another people did not fully sink in." The hope for the future imparted by her parents in the Rădăuți years — the idea that "good things were bound to happen to me" — seemed to color the surrounding reality, which may have contributed to her psychological, if not physical, survival.

Only forty years later, in the fall of 1986, when a friend in Vienna insisted she watch with her the documentary film *Shoah,* did Rita's denial fully end. The relentless images, and the testimony of those who survived or participated in the destruction of the Jews, brought home to Rita how fortunate she and her sister, Nora, had been to have their parents with them and how terrifying it must have been for her parents to know how little protection they could provide their children. There is no insult to the dead or irreverence intended here to those who were not so fortunate as the Stenzlers. The perspective revealed in these pages, Rita would readily admit, is that of a previously pampered teenager whose parents never stopped repeating the message that she was supposed to survive, a message that in itself may have provided emotional protection.

Anna Ornstein, another child psychiatrist and survivor of the Holocaust, has told of the fine thread of chance upon which her life and her mother's had depended. Shortly after their arrival in Ausch-witz, they were taken by the SS, along with a terrified group of Hungarians, to a building surrounded with geraniums, which they were told was a "bathhouse." Much later they learned that they had been spared because the flow of Hungarian transports had outstripped the capacity of the gas chambers. The opportunity to survive involves luck. The creative transformation of the experiences made possible by that opportunity is the substance of this story.

·

1. Home and Childhood in Rădăuți

Rita Stenzler was born on July 30, 1925, in Rădăuți, an ancient market town in the northern Romanian province of Bukovina. Like most babies in that time and place, she was delivered at home — number 15 Strada Pictor Grigorescu — by a midwife. In 1925, July 30 coincided with Tishah-b'Av, a Jewish day of mourning. Because of the separateness between Jewish family life and Romanian bureaucracy, and because Mr. Stenzler was too busy with the activities surrounding Rita's birth, he did not register her birth until August 5. In any case, in Rădăuți, no Jewish family registered a child on Tishah-b'Av. These circumstances gave Rita's parents the opportunity to celebrate her birthday three times a year — on July 30, August 5, and Tishah-b'Av, whenever it might fall. Throughout Rita's childhood, birthdays remained a special time of celebration, observed from the moment the family rose. "When you woke up in the morning and opened your eyes, you always had to see your gifts right there in front of your eyes." Mrs. Stenzler's cooking, always elaborate, took on a special intensity on birthdays.

But the three celebrations of Rita's birthday could not compare with the one for her sister, Nora, born February 26, 1922. On February 26 everybody was at home and in a mood for celebration; July 30 was when all neighbors, friends, and we ourselves were on vacation. Nora's birthday was a big social event in town, celebrated for "at least a week," with parties given "for this group and that," because "my mother loved good things in life like good parties." Rita perceived her own birthday parties "more as an appeasement: renting horse-drawn carriages to pull my friends and me all over Rădăuţi, resort parties, swim parties, and so on."

The Stenzler home was a highly sheltered world. There was a "plentiful flow and a feeling of permanence, a lack of anxiety in the household . . . no real conflicts, a secure and serene atmosphere, no shattering events. I never saw suffering or illness. I did not see people drop dead. I did not see violence."

Both girls were pampered. "The law of our household was that anything which upsets the children is not good for them. I was terribly spoiled," Rita said. "In winter, Resi, the maid, used to come in to make a fire in the little tile furnace before waking us. The down comforters were held against the warm tile in the evening so that the bed was cozily warm by the time we climbed in. In the morning I used to stick my foot out from under the covers for Resi to put on my shoes and socks. I would not get up until the fire was fully going and it was pleasant. She used to bring me hot milk with chocolate, and by the time I got out of the bed the whole house was shining, with both fire and warmth." The sisters did no housework. "I did not know the word *chore*. Once I overheard my father telling my mother, 'Helene, really, don't you worry about the girls? They don't know how to cook, and they don't know how to clean, and they don't learn these things.' She said, 'I don't worry one bit. They will marry men who will spoil and take care of them in the style to which they are accustomed.'"

The maids were essential to this spoiling, especially Resi, who was to stay with the Stenzlers until the day the family and the entire Jewish community were taken eastward to a camp in the Ukraine. They adored the children and their parents. "The idea of being left with a baby-sitter was unheard of." All the Stenzlers' maids came from the village of Fürstenthal (the "Prince's Valley"), where poor and industrious Germans lived. They were known for their dedication and honesty (Romanian maids were considered less reliable by Jewish families). Each maid stayed with the family until she married. The maids dated firemen and policemen whose credentials Mr. Stenzler would "make it his business" to check out when they came to ask for a maid's hand. "It was considered natural for them to ask my father.

He then would make a trip to Fürstenthal to consult with the maid's
father and give him a report." Mr. Stenzler would arrange the wedding, pay for it, "and we all went on gaily decorated horse-drawn
buggies to Fürstenthal to celebrate the wedding."

One of Rita's earliest memories is of her first trip away from
home — to Fürstenthal with the maid to visit her family. "I wanted
to see her family because she kept telling me stories about them. I
had a very good time, but I woke up in the middle of the night and
realized I was very homesick. The maid had a huge family, and all
of them — her father, her mother, her brothers and her sisters, and
her uncles — got onto horses and a carriage; a whole caravan took
me back to Rădăuţi right then in the middle of the night."

Each summer the family journeyed to Vatra Dornei ("the hearth
on the Dorna"), a popular spa by a river in the Carpathian Mountains.
"It was like a pilgrimage," with rows of suitcases gathered on the
train platform. "Papa would join the family on weekends. The idea
of basking lazily in the sun didn't appeal to him too much. I remember leaning out the train window during the ride to Vatra Dornei,
with the train whistling — the way it whistles only when one goes
through the Bukovinian mountains — and seeing the water rushing
down from the mountains with a single log on it and a peasant
standing on that log — that's how trees were transported down the
mountains." On the way, they would often stop in Cîmpulung,
another mountain resort, where Mr. Stenzler's sister Minna lived with
her husband, Jaacov, and their four children. Unlike the chubby
Stenzler girls, Minna and Jaacov's children were thin, so their parents
would "send them to my mother's in the summer to fatten them up.
It never succeeded. But I used to get envious when my mother would
run after Schella — one of the children — trying to get her to eat a
piece of chocolate. Nobody ever had to beg me."

In the heart of Vatra Dornei is a beautiful park, stretching up
from the river and town through evergreen forests and meadows.
Bathhouses with hot springs and a tower, in which one could drink
the special mineral water from the mountains, are at the base of the
park. The family would stay at a villa in town. Rita's memories are
full of gaiety: colorfully dressed, well-to-do families who came for
their holidays from the towns and villages of Bukovina and other
provinces; music, dancing, and lavish food in the many outdoor
restaurants with their white tablecloths.

When Rita and I traveled back to Vatra Dornei in July 1981 to retrace the scenes of her childhood, it was still a resort, but frequented by working people brought in groups for their vacations from the state-run industries in towns and cities. It was shabby, and litter and trash were everywhere, especially in the bathhouses and the tower. Although beer could be bought, food was scarce, and we were fortunate to be able to buy *mamaliga* (a Romanian staple made of cornmeal mush and topped with sour cream or cottage cheese) at the Villa Syndicat, one of the few local restaurants that was open. The management also proudly produced some peach drink from Bulgaria, kept "fresh," we were told, by a special Bulgarian process of "preserving it in the bottle."

Illness was very rare in Rita's childhood. Rita had a bout of diphtheria while the family was on holiday in 1929; it was the only serious threat to her health as a child. She became delirious from a high fever. When Rita was three, she was taken to the eye doctor. "My mother told me that I was diagnosed as being nearsighted and in need of glasses. I remember leaving the doctor's office, which was in his home in Czernowitz. There was an impressive stone stairway, and I threw my first pair of glasses down it. They got smashed and my mother declared, 'I don't like you to wear spectacles.' Neither did I, obviously, so I didn't wear glasses and I didn't see." In school this meant that Rita had to sit in the first row. Even at the university she would not wear glasses. (In the United States, later in life, Rita started using contact lenses, which did not have the same stigma for her.) Rita's childhood intolerance of myopia extended to other children who were similarly "defective." One day she reported to her mother that she did not like Hilda Abraham. "Hilda wore glasses, was nearsighted and cross-eyed. As far as I was concerned, Hilda was no good."

On our trip to Romania, we journeyed by train from Bucharest through the Moldavian Soviet Socialist Republic to the Ukraine. Rita found it difficult to change her contact lenses in the inadequately lighted train bathroom. At the Soviet border we were searched in our compartments at 4:00 A.M. by Russian customs inspectors, and Rita was shaken by the experience. Later, when the train slowed without apparent reason, she remarked sardonically that the engineer was slowing down to make it easier for her to change her lenses. I realized that she had felt doubly vulnerable: the weakness of her vision blended with memories of dehumanizing government treatment evoked by the customs search.

But Rita never let the burden of poor vision daunt her. Many times I have seen her hold pages close to her face, straining to read, even with contact lenses. She takes tennis lessons, and her teacher marvels at her determination on the court. He knows that the ball can appear as little more than a blur. In the late 1970s, by which time her father had grown totally blind from glaucoma, Rita's vision in the better of her two eyes was threatened by a cataract. In January 1981 she underwent surgery to have it removed. Talking with her in the hospital before the surgery, which turned out to be quite successful, one could not tell that she was facing the possibility of almost complete blindness.

Along with poor vision Rita also experiences a high degree of difficulty with spatial orientation and has a poor sense of direction, but she turns this handicap to her advantage. Porters, friends, colleagues, and even strangers are inevitably at the ready to rescue her from hapless straits. The secondary advantages of this failing were evident to Rita at a young age. She remembers a scene in Vatra Dornei. "I had walked up the well-groomed hill to collect wildflowers and got lost. Suddenly I found myself in a meadow where the grass and flowers reached up to my chin. I remember not searching for a way back. Shortly after I realized that I was lost, I heard my mother call me. '*Riterl, Ritonzka, wir kommen*' [We are coming]."

A lack of concern about money added to the atmosphere of security during Rita's childhood. Mr. Stenzler's huge textile business, with a wholesale store on the main street in the center of town, brought a feeling of permanence. Even as small children, Rita and Nora could go into the various stores in town and get whatever they wanted without paying, for "father had accounts with all the storekeepers. I never thought about money. Nobody ever talked to me about money, and I never heard conversations about money."

Mr. Stenzler traveled frequently to the textile factory at Arad, in Transylvania, in which he was a partner, and to Bucharest. "I hung on his tales about these grand cities. To him and us, they were the 'far west,' at least as occidental as one could get in Romania. He would come home from the trips loaded like Santa Claus with packages and packages and packages . . . dolls and clothes and things like that." In Rădăuţi there were daily visits to the several sweet shops. "I used to eat coffee ice cream with whipped cream every day . . . I was very fat." When Rita was twelve, her mother was hospitalized in Vienna because of fibroid tumors. Four people from two families moved into the house to look after the children, even though the maids were there. Nevertheless, "my sister felt responsible for my happiness. She would come to me and say, 'Ritula, I want to take you to have coffee ice cream. You haven't had it yet today.'"

Beyond comfort and security was the sense of joy about living radiated by Mrs. Stenzler. "My sister and I thought she would have permitted us anything as long as it was fun. Once we said that if she heard we had been faithless to our husbands she would probably ask, 'Do you have fun?'" She was always in the house when the girls came home from school. "I would walk in the gate, and she would come out with her hands full of dough, or whatever . . . She would walk to meet me, always with a sparkle in her eyes. This was so in Israel." Rita describes herself as "very naughty," but remembers no harsh punishments or scoldings.

In the garden at 15 Pictor Grigorescu stood a cherry tree under which Rita sat as a small child, "telling my dolls stories about the wide world I had not seen." One day it was time to start kindergarten. "There were children I had never seen before. I did not like the dirty fingernails and things like that and complained that the children were dirty. My mother came to the school and agreed. But I probably used that as an excuse because I longed for my mother, my dolls, and home. I was not a very clean or fastidious child, and my beloved dog rolled in the Rădăuţi mud." The next day Rita did not return. The kindergarten teacher came to the house "for a fact-finding visit and found me under the cherry tree with my baby carriage stuffed with dolls." She said to Rita's mother, "I think your daughter is right. It is much more pleasant to be here than in my kindergarten." The teacher and Mrs. Stenzler agreed that Rita was better off at home and "that was the end of my kindergarten career. Nobody ever talked to me about going back. Besides, I was surrounded by friends to play with. That is how the 'pleasure principle' operated in Rădăuţi in those years."

Rita's dearest friend was Mikki Drimmer, who had been too young to start kindergarten. Mikki's sister, Nini, and Nora were girlfriends. The girls' mothers had been intimate friends, and *their* mothers had been closest friends — "We were the third generation." The next year, when it came time to start first grade, a new "crisis" arose. Mikki, whose birthday came in October was, according to the local rules, not old enough. "You were supposed to be six years old by September." So she was not permitted to go. Mikki cried for many days that she needed Rita, and "I cried that I needed Mikki. My father and my grandfather were very instrumental when the laws needed to be changed in Rădăuți. I don't know what was done, but suddenly Mikki joined me in the first grade."

Another problem arose because Mikki and Rita were among the tallest children in the class — "something that disappeared later in both of us" — and were therefore seated in the last row. Rita, whose nearsightedness kept her from seeing the blackboard, had to be moved to the first row. "But Mikki has to sit with me," Rita insisted. Dr. Drimmer, Mikki's father, and Rita's father again appeared at the school "to demand that Mikki be seated next to me in spite of the protests of the children behind us who could not see the board. Shamefully I must admit that I did not feel guilty. There was not an ounce of social consciousness in me."

When Rita was a small child her father would bring her dolls from his journeys to the West, and she began to collect them. Rita grew up with a series of German books, starting with *Nesthäckchen und ihre Puppen* (The Youngest and Her Dolls) and *Nesthäckchen als Grossmutter* (The Youngest as Grandmother). "Particularly in vogue then were Curt Mahler's romantic novels. All the heroes and heroines were from aristocratic backgrounds and carried pretentious names like Udo von Axelrod. As a result, all my dolls — I still had twenty-one when we were deported to Mogilev even though I was sixteen years old — carried aristocratic names and had intricate family relations. Only my first Russian doll, a *babushka* with twelve babies of diminishing size nesting in her tummy, had a Romanian name. And so did all her children, Papusa, Printesa, and so on."

Rita's grandfather Zaziu, as a good Chassid and Orthodox Jew, was forbidden to look at, or acknowledge, any artificial likeness of human beings ("Only God could do that"). "So dolls were forbidden. One day my father brought me the most magnificent doll from Bucharest. She was child-size and wore a splendid green silk dress with a matching green hat. Since I was living in a kingdom, this doll, the most splendid, immediately became Queen Sylvia — Sylvia was probably the heroine I was reading about at the time or perhaps related to a piano piece I was practicing for an audition, the Pizzicato Concertino from the opera *Sylvie*. Anyhow, my doll Sylvia was grand

and my father rejoiced in my joy. Zaziu did not look at her, but with a chuckle would inquire every day how Queen 'Slyvia' was doing. I think he mispronounced her name for the same reason he did not look at her."

Later in her life, Rita continued to collect dolls, as embodiments of the uniqueness and preciousness of men, women, and children all over the world. She picks up new dolls wherever she travels and has assembled an extraordinary collection. Her living room shelves look like the United Nations. "People who are special to me still bring me special dolls from special places."

Rădăuţi in the 1930s before the rise of fascism was, for Rita, a circumscribed world of certainty and plenty. Promenading in the lovely town park and watching people arrive and leave from the train station were important entertainments. Rita also went to market with the maids and later with her friends. Every day the villagers would come to the large cobblestoned marketplace to buy butter and fresh ricotta and other cheeses wrapped in big green leaves. Friday was the special market day. Before 5:00 A.M., when the selling began, processions of horse- and donkey-drawn carriages and carts would clog the tree-lined roads leading into town. The peasants, dressed in brilliant home-sewn and embroidered blouses and trousers, brought earthenware, *catrintzas* (embroidered material wrapped as a skirt), chicken, geese, tomatoes, cucumbers, fruit, delicious-smelling vegetables, and nuts. At the height of the growing season buckets of corn on the cob were sold at each corner, as well as baskets of peaches, apples, pears, and other fruits. At the market the vendors sat on carpets and beckoned potential customers to buy their clothing, foodstuffs, and other commodities. It was a great social occasion, a time for bargaining, storytelling, and testing of wits.

When Rita and I returned to Rădăuţi, the market was still held on Friday, and much of the peasant color remained. But goods were scarce, fresh vegetables and fruits virtually absent, and the peasants seemed depressed emotionally as well as economically. Yet bargaining and wit were still in evidence. Rita and her daughter Sheila spied a beautiful *bondita*, a hand-embroidered leather vest, fringed with lamb's wool. Rita bargained for it in Romanian. Once a price was agreed upon, Rita went with Sheila to change money at the bank. When they returned a friend of the seller's was wearing the vest and the seller announced with a straight face, "I sold it." Rita quickly entered the game. "How dare you wear my bondita!" This banter was a routine and pleasurable — perhaps essential — dividend of the transaction.

Gypsies added a note of exotic excitement in Rita's childhood. They rode into town in covered wagons with skinny dogs and dirty, neglected children — "with gorgeous big, black eyes" — running behind the wagons. All kinds of lore and mystery clung to these people. It was said that if one puts a money purse on one side of a newborn boy and on the other side a violin, then depending on where the baby reaches first, he becomes a thief or a violinist. A Gypsy boy supposedly always reaches for both simultaneously and, therefore, becomes both a thief and a musician. For us children in Rădăuţi, the arrival of the Gypsies at their temporary camps above Pictor Grigorescu was frightening and exciting. They loved children and were said to steal and sell them. This added color to our family romance fantasies. We could pretend to ourselves that we were really a prince or princess, stolen by the Gypsies and purchased by our parents. The fact that their children ran around naked until about age ten was captivating for us *wohlerzogene gute Bukowiner kinder* [well-bred, good Bukovinian children]. On summer evenings, we used to sneak out toward their campsites and, shivering with excitement and fear, watch their frenzied dances by the fire. Maybe the Romanian song *"Uite aşa aş vreau să mor* [Look, this is how I want to die] *Cu ţiganul lingă mine* [With the Gypsy by my side] *Cu ţiganul şi cu tine* [With the Gypsy and you]" was written by someone who still felt his childhood excitement while hiding to watch the Gypsies dance.

"I can never hear a Gypsy song without remembering the flicker of their campfires, the heartbeats of my girlfriend Mikki and me as we hid in the bushes. We were in our nightgowns because these clandestine escapades were carried out after we were supposedly sound asleep in our beds. The cozy nursery with its warm white and pink linen was so wonderful to fall asleep in after 'escaping' from the Gypsies."

To be a child in Rădăuţi in the 1930s also meant ice-skating at night, hayrides through the countryside, swimming by a mill in a river that ran through Dorneşti, a little village nearby, and of course, parties at home with friends, family, and lots of good food. Rita's father adored music. "He was a wonderful dancer with a splendid ear for rhythm, and whenever a tune was on the radio we rolled up the carpet and he danced with us girls."

Between Nora and Rita there were inevitable jealousies. In Rădăuți, such feelings were overt and expected. The rivalry between the two sisters was diluted in part by their differences in build, natural abilities, and predominant interests. "Nora and I looked alike, but she was taller and more slender; I was very chubby. She was a wonderful figure skater; I skated only fast and often. She played the piano beautifully; I practiced diligently, but never did the piano sound as soft and tender as under her fingers. Nora was beautifully dressed and kept her clothes neat and tidy; my clothes got easily messed up and untidy."

The relationship of Rita and Nora with the family dog reflected their contrasting personalities. He was a mutt, "a street potpourri," given to Rita by a boy in the town. She named him Leandi, after the Greek hero Leander, and he acquired several nicknames such as Leanderrucu, Rucucucu, and Prince Leandi, a reference to a reputedly royal (Polish) ancestor. Leandi followed Rita everywhere, and when he could not find her he would park himself in front of the *Meth konditorei*, a local patisserie, confident that she would show up sooner or later. She would receive messages — "Leandi is waiting for you." Leandi was not particularly clean. "He bounced in the mud in Rădăuți and would greet me exuberantly when he found me, jumping on me. Nora would cross the street and hide from Leandi when she saw him sitting in front of the konditorei. Leandi would run across the street — there was only one car in Rădăuți — and, to Nora's consternation, jump up on her, mud and all. Leandi was a big dog. Nora felt that I put him up to it. Maybe I did!" On the night when the Stenzler family was taken away by the Germans, a peasant came from a nearby village to take Leandi. The dog got away and ran all night until he found the train where, "covered with sweat and saliva, he lay exhausted at the train station and howled."

Nora and Rita always dressed alike. "My mother would take us to the dressmaker, where we would select a pattern. I always wanted Nora to select hers first and then I would insist on having the same. She hated this. She did not want me to be dressed like her. It never looked the same because she cared for her clothes so well." According to Rita, Nora tended to be soft-spoken and did not usually stand up for her rights. "Whenever she had to straighten something out, I had to do it, like returning something to the store or telling somebody off. When she started dating, which she did relatively early, I had to invent excuses and cancel the dates she did not want to keep."

Mikki and Rita terrorized Nora and her friend Nini. "We spied on them, and when we heard of their doing anything our parents were not supposed to know, we blackmailed them. We appeared at the parties they went to and insisted that they ask their boyfriends to dance with us, otherwise we would tell this and that. I used to memorize conversations we heard between them and their friends, love letters they had received, and threaten to recite these at embarrassing times."

Rita excelled in school. "I took and loved private lessons in languages. Nora did not, and she skipped them. I would deliver notes to her boyfriends, telling where and when she would meet them instead of taking French, English, or whatever lessons. Then she would meet me at a prearranged place and we would come home together as if we had both attended the lessons." As Nora grew prettier and began to dress fashionably, Rita sensed "a tinge of envy in the teachers' voices."

From early childhood Rita experienced "an almost sensuous joy from learning," particularly reading and languages. The talent for languages was one Rita shared with her father and, to a lesser extent, her mother. After his wife died in Haifa in 1970, Mr. Stenzler stayed with two Hungarians who maintained their privacy by speaking Hungarian. Their privacy lasted only three months, because Mr. Stenzler, then in his late seventies, learned to understand and speak Hungarian. Love of books was tied intimately to her mother's enjoyment of reading, especially in German, and to the exciting glimpses of the world outside Rădăuţi to which Rita was exposed as a child through the stories and gifts her father brought back from his travels. Languages, too, became her bridge to worlds outside the family and the Rădăuţi community.

Rita's mother encouraged her to read and learn not so much through insistence upon their importance as by example and support and the creation of a warm home atmosphere surrounding the school experience. "When I came home from school my mother ran from the summer kitchen to catch my stream of reports as I opened the gate, entered the garden, and told of my school experiences. I don't remember what she said or whether she had time to say anything, but I remember her hugs and embraces. Some decades later in Israel, on my visits from the United States, she would furtively kiss me the same way on my eyelids, on my shoulder, and so forth. When I would come back from a walk to her apartment at 51 Herzl Street, she would spot me from her balcony the same way she had spotted my return from school on Strada Pictor Grigorescu three decades earlier. I never returned to an empty house in Rădăuţi from 1925 to 1941 or to an empty apartment in Haifa during my visits between 1953 and 1970.

"My mother treated my reading more respectfully than my homework. I can't remember her ever asking me if I did my homework. Quite the opposite. She would come in and suggest that I had done enough, and she worried about nearsightedness. But when I read she walked on tiptoes, and when she walked by she would only pat my hand or give me a passing kiss on the cheek. I read Lion Feuchtwanger, Ibsen, Zola, Baudelaire, and Voltaire. I read German, French, and Romanian, and always things which were above my head and understanding . . . Finally at night my mother used to come into the children's room to beg me to put out the light and to put away the books so we would get rest."

Many of the readings were in German. Through these, Rita developed warm feelings about Germany and the German people. "The memory of reading these books in my cozy *Kinderzimmer* is also mixed with the smell of freshly baked sweets."

The memory of reading Schnitzler brought other associations. Mrs. Stenzler had a much younger friend who apparently did not have a very good marriage. This woman, a Mrs. Beer, "shared her confidences with my mother on their walks, and I used to be asked to walk in front whenever the conversation became really interesting. My mother was reading a book by Arthur Schnitzler at the time, and I used to read along — clandestinely. Whenever anything really sexy came up Schnitzler would substitute for words with '. . .' My fantasies about what Mrs. Beer was reporting to my mother became strangely entwined with Schnitzler's book."

Other nostalgic literary moments linger in Rita's memory. Nora had practiced a Chopin *valse* for a recital "while I was reading *The Rise and Fall of the Romanovs*. It was spring in Rădăuţi, and I was deeply involved with the fate of the Romanov families. That particular Chopin waltz, the czar's family, and the mysterious tragedies and enigmas of Russia have remained forever joined in my consciousness. There was another piece Nora practiced, "*Fruhlingsrauschen*" (Spring Whistles) by [the Norwegian composer Christian] Sinding. While she practiced that I remember reading Romain Roland."

Rita attended four years of public school, which was like an

American elementary school, after which the children took an entrance exam in order to be accepted into the *liceul* [high school]. Rita attended the girls' Liceul Elisabeta Doamna. The entrance exam was "tough, and only bright and privileged children passed it. The liceul covered eight years of study. After four years, one had to pass a *matura mica* (little baccalaureate) in order to continue at the liceul.

"There was a lucky match between my natural endowment and what was cherished and appreciated in that part of the world at that time." "Teachers were always a very important part of my life," Rita has written. Her memory of her teachers, including an eccentric spinster who taught French and had as a pet a fly to whom she spoke during class, is warm and detailed. "While in elementary and high school I was always best in academic subjects and worst in athletics." She is convinced that if she had grown up in the United States three or four decades later and gone to an elementary school here, she would have been tested because of her lack of spatial orientation and competence in "all technical things" and been "called, interchangeably, hyperactive or suffering from minimal cerebral dysrhythmia." She might then "have gotten placed in some classes for the educationally handicapped, my teachers might have recommended Ritalin, and my pediatrician might have prescribed it, though my mother would not have accepted such recommendations. Anyhow, in Rădăuți I was safe from testing, and nobody knew about Ritalin there. While my language teachers were thrilled with my talents and diligence," she observed, "my piano and music teachers were impressed only with my diligence. My gym, tennis, ski, and all athletic teachers were always impressed with my fundamental lack of talent and lack of ability. The only asset I had and still have for these physical athletic endeavors is determination and perseverance."

Betty Zeiger, Rita's Hebrew teacher, spoke to us with enthusiasm when we visited Rădăuți about what a "formidable" pupil she had been from an early age. Rădăuți's school system during those years rewarded rote memory. "I was blessed with an excellent memory — my father possessed the same faculty until his death at eighty-seven, when, blind, he used to give me all the telephone numbers of friends and family members during my visits to Israel." In elementary school, memorizing poems was considered important, and Rita received a good deal of acclaim for that. During the 1970s, when Rita visited her aunt Schewa in Montreal, she proudly reported to Rita's husband that as a four-year-old child at the ceremony celebrating the birth of Schewa's twins, Jacki and Riita, Rita had recited a poem of seventeen stanzas.

Equally important, however, were Rita's qualities of imagination and the powerful reinforcement and encouragement she received at home and from the community. "I traveled all over the globe in my mind. I knew nobody who had traveled in those days. But I could put into that world whatever I wanted to. It was a mishmash of books and dreams, and all could be switched and changed to fit the needs of the moment. My teacher of religion, Professor Stein, had a doctorate in theology from Berlin, and when he taught class I felt that he was lecturing just to me. Maybe he truly did, since nobody else paid attention. I once wrote a composition about Moses. He liked it so much he read it in the 'big synagogue' on Saturday. My father, who very seldom went to the synagogue, happened to be there and he was delighted. Of course, the few who did not hear about my composition from Professor Stein heard it from my father." This feeling of guaranteed success permeated Rita's years in Rădăuți and contributed powerfully to the self-assurance that would prove so valuable for her later survival and endurance.

Rita's favorite teacher was Mrs. Foreanu, who taught Romanian language and literature. "She had big black eyes, pulled her hair back in a bun, wore beautiful clothes, and stood right in front of me at my bench with her sparkling eyes fixed directly on me. She would read Eminescu [Mihail Eminescu, the great nineteenth-century Romanian poet] poems with gusto. I can still recite them. Sometimes she would turn to me and say, 'Now, Stenzler, will you tell us what the main idea is?' Once, in front of the class, Professor Foreanu said, 'If I were to have no other reward for lecturing than Rita Stenzler's eyes, that would be reward enough.' The only negative experience with Professor Foreanu happened one day just before the bell rang for recess, when we wanted to rush out of the class and Professor Foreanu said, 'By wanting it to be five minutes later than it already is, you are rushing to your death. You have wished five minutes of your life away.' The whole class froze dead with fear. I expected her to say 'Not you, Stenzler,' since she always treated me as extra special. But she did not say it."

As Rita grew older, there seems to have been a never-ending succession of lessons, in and out of school. "I went to school from eight to one and home for lunch from one to three; then from three to five there was school again. And then I could come home again and eat. Mutti used to have special food for me. Then I went to my private lessons — piano lessons, French lessons, Hebrew lessons, English lessons, and for German literature I had a special teacher. Between lessons I ate generously." The only worry was that the lessons would interfere with having fun. "My mother would say, 'When will you have time for ice-skating?'"

Rita took piano lessons from age six until she was sixteen. Her musical knowledge, if not talent, would later prove to be a lifesaver during a dangerous encounter with Soviet authorities. The music lessons were "unconsciously fired by sibling rivalry, since my sister Nora was a talented pianist." The best thing about Professor Hanons, the girls' piano teacher, was her two "very handsome" sons. "For recitals we would play in eight hands on two pianos, Nora and the older son, Traian, and me with Liviu, the younger. I never could decide which of the two I liked better. Not being Jewish, they were fascinatingly different. When I walked in for my piano lessons, I would catch smells from the nonkosher *goyische* kitchen. The aromas of mixing meats with sour cream, contrary to kosher law, remained associated with the thrill of playing with Professor Hanons's sons."

Even before fascism and then Nazism gained ascendancy in Romania, there was a sharp religious and cultural division between the Jewish and Christian populations in Rădăuţi. For the Jews, Christian households — and particularly Christian places of worship — were taboo. "My Catholic girlfriends always used to bless themselves when we walked by," Rita explained. "I grew up very much under the impact of the forbidden cross." Christian friends would take Rita to the Romanian Orthodox churches on special days, such as the king's birthday, or on the many national holidays. She did not tell her family of these visits, especially not her grandfather Zaziu. Rita loved the dark beauty and musty smell of these churches and their painted murals that blended the exploits of Romanian national heroes with biblical episodes. The experience of the mysterious became particularly powerful when the worshipers crossed themselves or during the resonant chanting of the monks with the church congregation.

The schools also conducted religious services. The children would stand up when the teacher entered the classroom and began the morning service with a prayer. The Jewish children recited the prayer, but "not quite all the way." When the other children crossed themselves, the Jewish children did not, "so we were standing up half participating and half not." For several days during Lent the teacher would recite *Hristos* — *a înviat, adevărat a înviat . . . cu moartea pre moarte călcînd* (Christ has risen; Christ has truly risen . . . stepping with death on death). The Jewish pupils had to recite this as well. Lent coincided with Passover, and the whole Christian population believed, Rita's classmates told her, that on the Seder evening "we would drink the blood of a Christian child." Later she learned that this medieval myth, based on a perversion of New Testament passages, was still widespread in Eastern Europe.

There was one Christian child, Lucica Dumitriuc, with whom Rita was especially close. Lucica was outspoken about the stories her parents told her of what Jewish families did at Passover, and Rita told her what was said in her home. "In our home it was never said that the Christians were nonhuman. There was no bitterness, no undercurrent of hostility. The worst accusation that my mother held against non-Jews was the same as she held against many Jews — that they didn't read."

As was the case for many Jewish families with strong attachments to German culture, Christmas was among the times of family excitement, celebration, and gift giving. The maids would slip into the children's room with gifts they bought with money given to them by Mr. and Mrs. Stenzler. Sometimes ("Mutti knew") Mr. Stenzler brought home (but not into the house) thin-sliced ham. The children would eat it in the garden, holding this *trayf* (nonkosher food) on pieces of paper. Rita had a particular fascination with Christmas trees, and each year the maids slipped a little one into the house.

In 1950, in a letter to Rita written on Christmas Eve from Israel, where she had arrived only six weeks before, her mother Helene wrote of the meaning of Christmas to her. "It is Christmas Eve tonight. When you two were small children at home, the maids made for you, with our permission, Christmas trees. We did this because we wanted you to feel close to this holiday which brings happiness to a world full of children."

On the day before the Jewish population of Rădăuți was deported, Lucica told Rita of a rumor that Hitler was intending to send the Jews to Madagascar. "Lucica tried to tell me that there were nice orchids and roses growing in Madagascar." In 1981 we visited the street in Rădăuți where Lucica had lived. Her house had been transformed into an orphanage. Lucica's had been one of the more prominent and wealthy families. To escape imprisonment and death, which had been the fate of many of the men in such families under the

Communist regime, they had gone to Bucharest, where they could disappear into relative obscurity. A neighbor showed us a 1937 picture of Lucica, Rita, and their twelve-year-old classmates. We also heard that Lucica had never again set foot in Rădăuți after the Communist takeover in 1947.

In this proper, small-town environment, adults maintained a standard of privacy and decorum. Sexuality was surrounded by secrecy and information was gained only through hidden initiatives. Early teenage experience was more vicarious than actual. Of her parents, Rita said, "I don't think I ever saw them kiss, or anything. It was a very discreet, 'kosher' household. My mother was always fully dressed and doors were kept closed."

The house at 15 Pictor Grigorescu had an attic where the Passover dishes and other special articles were kept. Rita made frequent "unauthorized expeditions" there. One day she discovered a hidden diary her mother had kept when she was Rita's age. "I read breathlessly. I can still see the pages in front of my eyes . . . Mutticuta loved the world at large, although she knew it mostly from her books and fantasies." The diary was a beautiful leather-bound book with entries in an elegant Gothic handwriting. Some concerned flirtation with a visitor "from I think the Middle East. Perhaps it was Ankara, Turkey, but I'm not quite sure. The remarks were intermixed with quotations from Goethe, particularly from *Die Leiden des jungen Werthers* (The Sorrows of Young Werther)."

Rita's thirteenth birthday party was the only one that eclipsed Nora's. It became "the official, first mixed social gathering of the children my age." Eleven girls and twelve boys were invited, among them two boys named Auslander from next door. They were too shy to join the girls gathered in the Stenzlers' garden and were discovered peering through a hole in the fence that separated the Auslanders' yard from the Stenzlers'. Nora and her girlfriends did the mixing and helped the boys find the courage to ask the girls to dance. As gifts, each of the boys made doll furniture for Rita's collection.

The high school in Rădăuți had strict dress and conduct codes. Pupils were required to wear school uniforms even when off school grounds. Dating was not permitted. Mrs. Stenzler opposed these rules. "She cherished buying Nora exquisite clothes and arranged short trips to the nearby city of Czernowitz, the former capital of Bukovina, and longer ones to Bucharest so Nora could date and wear fashionable clothes." In 1939 when she was seventeen, Nora received her first fur coat, a gray Persian lamb with matching hat and white leather boots. Nora had a boyfriend, a second cousin, Soniu Shiffris, who had a degree in chemical engineering from Belgium. Nora and Soniu would meet in Bucharest under the chaperonage of relatives there. One day while eating in a restaurant, Nora and Soniu were seen by the liceul principal, who happened to be in Bucharest for the day. She came over to the table and insisted that Nora take the first train back to Rădăuți. "A big scandal ensued, and the school insisted on expelling Nora for a week because she was out of uniform and with a date. This was the only time my mother went to our school. Parent-teacher conferences did not exist in Rădăuți. When a problem arose at school my father had gone. This time my mother went, uninvited, and gave the school faculty a lecture on how it is more important for seventeen-year-old girls to enjoy beautiful clothes and dates than to wear bleak, black uniforms and associate only with girls — the girls' liceul and boys' gymnasium had only two dances a year when it was legitimate to dance with each other."

The world outside Rădăuți intruded little into the life that Rita, Nora, and their friends experienced. Between the two world wars the community and its population were constant. "I didn't know about people coming and going, or immigrating or emigrating. A big stir in Rădăuți was created when an American family, for some strange reason, came to live there. That was probably the most 'external' event that I saw in Rădăuți during my childhood."

An exception was the romantic activities and adventures of the Romanian royal family. King Carol II himself came to Rădăuți to conduct maneuvers. Army officers were housed throughout the town and two generals stayed at the Stenzlers'. The girls had to give up their room to the officers and move to another one temporarily. They curtsied politely when they saw the officers at the house or in the street. Rita recalls that the house was suffused with "a smell of fancy perfume and tobacco" while the generals were there.

King Carol's scandalous liaison with the beautiful Jewess Magda Lupescu provoked much local excitement. Carol's son, Michael, had become regent in 1925, when he was only four years old, and Rita, Nora, and their friends, together with the rest of the country, had watched him grow up. Michael was much beloved by the Romanian people. Rita treasured the certificates at school with his picture on it. Once he came to a nearby village during the royal maneuvers and Rita and her schoolmates went there to join in the ceremonies. The villagers danced the hora, the Romanian national dance later appropriated by Israelis, and Michael, Rita remembers, was the best dancer. "I danced along in the square with the villagers and other schoolchildren. In our minds I am sure each and every one of us danced with Michael."

As Rita approached her teens, the first harbingers of political change began to touch Rădăuți. News of communism and fascism reached politically conscious people only slightly older than Rita. Even calls for Zionism were heard in the Jewish community, although the dream of a homeland in Palestine was not part of Rita's or Nora's consciousness during these years. In the 1930s in Rădăuți, it was the male cousins (girls, "of course," were not involved in political issues) on her mother's side, idle dreamers drawn to lofty causes, who drifted toward Zionism. They joined various Zionist youth groups: Shilo belonged to Hashomer Hatzair, a left-leaning organization that emphasized tilling the earth and transforming Jews in the Diaspora from tradespeople to peasants; Norziu belonged to Betar, a rightist group which advocated that Jews have to fight to obtain *Eretz* (the original land of) Israel by any means; and cousin Avrumabe belonged to a moderate Zionist organization, "the name of which I think I never knew because Avrumabe was himself so moderate and self-effacing."

"Rumors about communism during the 1930s were mysterious and romantic, coming from the USSR and from intellectual circles in Paris." One who introduced these ideas to Rita and Nora was Arthur Klang, a friend, at times a boyfriend, of Nora's, whose mother had died when he was little and whose father was unemployed and supposedly undependable. "Arthur was tall, blond, chewed his fingernails, read Rilke with passion, and once left behind a battered edition of Freud's *Interpretation of Dreams* — my first encounter with Freud's writings — which I read in hiding and did not understand a word of. I returned it to him clandestinely by slipping it into his knapsack. Arthur Klang talked about communism and wrote poetry for Nora. Nora hid the poems from me in her doll buggy. I used to memorize them, then replace them under the doll mattress. Then I would recite them to Nora and Nini so that Mikki and I could blackmail our sisters into taking us along to dances." Arthur Klang talked of injustice, workers' rights, and imprisoned Communists. But for Rita, his poems, his anguish, and "the romanticism of the big neighbor, the USSR," were all rather vague, becoming, like the sound of Nora practicing a Chopin waltz, "strangely intertwined with the fate of the Romanovs."

During an earthquake that occurred around this time, communism rolled tragically close. News reached Rădăuţi that young men imprisoned for their Communist sympathies died in their cells, since nobody had let them out. Nevertheless, "I think there was not enough anger in me," said Rita, "and in those who were very close to me, to embrace communism. I had no social consciousness, had not been raised with any pretense at egalitarianism, and the sole attraction of communism was the otherness of it. I think I was more attracted to its being Russian than by its cause. For me it was mixed with Russian folk melodies, which I adored and still do, with dreams of Russian steppes and troikas, with the sound of this melodious language which I so love, and with the earthiness and realness of the Russian people."

Rita's romantic images about communism were to encounter harsh reality in 1940 when northern Bukovina, which included Czernowitz, "the flower of Bukovina," its cultural center, was presented to Stalin for signing a nonaggression pact with Hitler. Some young Communists from Rădăuţi crossed into northern Bukovina, while a bigger contingent fled south to Rădăuţi. Bruno Auslander, the neighbors' son, was one of those who crossed into northern Bukovina, not because of communism but because he had a girlfriend in Czernowitz. "Since he was seventeen and not aware of how intransigent Stalin's border concepts were, he never realized that in the USSR one can enter but not leave. Poor Bruno! He did not get back until the 1960s, with a Russian wife."

After Stalin's annexation of northern Bukovina, many family members and friends in Czernowitz were rounded up and transported to Siberia. The father of Nora's boyfriend Soniu, known as Uncle Shiffris, had been a furrier. Nora's Persian lamb coat was in his establishment, in summer storage, when the Russians occupied Czernowitz in June 1940. In the summer of 1941, when German troops moved eastward and invaded the Ukraine, Hitler gave northern Bukovina and Bessarabia back to Romania. "Nora's fur coat returned to Rădăuţi while Uncle Shiffris and his wife were already dead in unmarked graves in the tundra of Siberia."

Fascism, and soon Nazism, entered Romania from Austria and Germany. It penetrated into Rădăuţi and the Bukovina less subtly than communism. The ground had been prepared as early as the 1920s by a native fascist movement, founded upon Romanian nationalism, Orthodox religion, and anti-Semitism. In 1927, Corneliu Zelea Codreanu, a young lawyer with a dramatic personality, named the movement the League of the Archangel Michael, and in 1930 renamed the organization the Garda de Fier, the Iron Guard. By 1937, the movement was strong enough to receive over 16 percent of the vote in national elections. In response, King Carol dissolved parliamentary government in February 1938 and established a royal dictatorship led by a right-wing coalition under Octavian Goga and Alexander C. Cuza, a wealthy peasant who lived on the outskirts of Rădăuţi. "I remember his house because of its classic Bukovinian style, with a portal of entry." Codreanu and thousands of Guardists were arrested in November, and Codreanu was murdered in a forest near Ploeşti. Despite this temporary setback, the Guardists remained popular and by the end of 1940 had assassinated many active and former national leaders and lesser opponents, including four premiers.

Those who listened most attentively to the call of fascism were fundamentally different in background, aspirations, and cohesiveness from those to whom communism appealed. "Fascism was embraced by young, fiercely nationalistic, ethnic Romanians who exchanged their civilian garb, and in some cases national peasant costumes, for the brown shirts and brown trousers of the Garda de Fier." The involvement of such groups in the Bukovina brought fascism ominously closer. Rita remembers when she first saw the Hitlerian salute of the Iron Guard. Soon Guardists began marching into Rădăuţi to beat up Jews, whom they labeled the cause of all the miseries of the Romanian people. Alexander Cuza "hosted these visiting groups and led them through the streets of Rădăuţi on wild rampages. I remember seeing the horse-drawn buggies roll down Horodnic Street, where all my grandparents lived, and I can still feel my goose pimples, heartbeat, fear . . . and some fascination."

Hitler's occupation of Bohemia and Moravia in March 1939 and the invasion of Poland in September brought Nazism still closer to Rădăuţi. Early in 1940, Carol sought reconciliation with the Iron Guardists and the support of Germany, which was not immediately forthcoming. In June 1940, the Soviet government, after consultation with the Germans, demanded the cession of Bessarabia and, as mentioned, the northern part of Bukovina, which had a large Ukrainian population. Meanwhile, Hungary, with Hitler's support, pressed

Carol for the cession of Transylvania, which was given to Hungary by the Vienna Award of August 30, 1940. Within a few months Carol had given up one third of Romania's territory. Shortly after the Vienna Award a new government was formed under Marshal Ion Antonescu, a supporter of the Iron Guard. Carol, completely discredited, was forced by Antonescu to abdicate and left the country with Madame Lupescu, crossing the Yugoslav border after his train was machine-gunned by Iron Guardists.

Michael ascended the throne but was confined to Sinai, a royal resort north of Bucharest, and had little power. Antonescu led the country, relying on the Iron Guard, which now became the ruling party. Horia Sima, its leader, became Antonescu's vice premier. Antonescu soon allied Romania with Germany, and in October 1940, a German military mission arrived in Bucharest, which was to grow to 20,000 men by January 1, 1941. In November 1940, Antonescu visited Hitler in Berlin and entered into the Tripartite Pact with Germany and Hungary, an agreement that recognized Hitler's "New Order" in Eastern Europe.

The arrival in Rădăuți of refugees from Czechoslovakia and Poland, who fled east and south into Romania in 1939, exposed Rita for the first time to the impersonal power of governments. "The first Czech refugees, whom my mother and I encountered on a train, profoundly molded my impression of Czech people and my feelings about governments — all governments — who made refugees of their own and other peoples . . . In our compartment was a young couple. They told us that they had fled Czechoslovakia because of Hitler's deal with Chamberlain. I remember nuzzling up close to my mother because of the fiery hurt in these refugees' eyes. They asked, 'Do you know how beautiful Prague is?' At that time I did not. Then the woman looked straight into my eyes and said, 'Do you know what it is like to flee one's country, one's loved ones, one's language, customs, songs, and dances?' We did not know then, but learned soon after. The man added, in his limited German, 'Do you know what it is like to speak in a language one does not know very well?'"

Both of Rita's grandmothers died in Rădăuți during the winter of 1938–1939, "before the big trouble," and were buried in the Jewish cemetery there. During the family's internment in Mogilev, Zaziu Wohl once said, "It's nice Judith got to die in Rădăuți."

✳

After the invasion of Poland the war came right into the Stenzler household when several retreating members of the Polish officer corps, aristocrats, entered Rădăuți seeking refuge from the Nazis. Although they were committed anti-Semites, only the Jewish houses were good enough for them to stay in. One of them, Otto, came to live with the Stenzlers for six months, maintaining his aristocratic pretensions throughout his stay. Mr. Stenzler found a job for him in a local pharmacy.

The sheltered, idyllic childhood of Rita and Nora had come to an end. "I remember when in the coziness of our living room in Rădăuți I first heard the blasting oratories of the Führer." His speeches, "and the thousands of voices of German people shouting 'Sieg Heil,' penetrated our sheltered lives. That one man's voice, incentive, and paranoia could destroy the harmony, the shelter, and safety of Rădăuți, and my apparently secure existence, was a lesson never to be forgotten. I had never heard such an inhumane, terrible voice. I remember one particular evening when everybody was sitting around the living room. There was tenderness and cheerful activity, joking, and a warm feeling in the family. Suddenly on the radio, which I can see today in front of my eyes, Hitler's blasting voice came through, penetrating my being and piercing all feelings of security I had had until then."

Rita can also remember the first time she saw uniformed German officers. "We were shopping and my mother was chatting with a girlfriend of hers. I saw uniforms, Wehrmacht uniforms, three stocky officers." Her mother's conversation with the friend stopped abruptly. "I reached up to my mother's hand. My mother put her arm around me, as if anticipating that she would have to shelter me from Nazism from then on. I felt — and I can feel it now more than forty years later — as if the pavement of the Rădăuți street trembled under the boots of the German SS officers. Until then I'd heard the Führer and his plans for us Jews only on the radio. I stole a quick glance at the officers, both frightened and fascinated. It was such an overwhelming experience that I turned my face from it immediately and hid it in my mother's dress. I can still smell the comfort of her familiar perfume."

In 1939, visits from relatives who had immigrated to New York stopped abruptly. Every year at Passover and other occasions, two uncles — one Rita's mother's brother, the other her father's — who had immigrated to New York between 1910 and 1912, would come to Rădăuţi. Rita had particularly enjoyed the visits of her father's next to youngest brother, Itzik, who was "Shajculica's [a diminutive for Shaje, her father's name] biggest problem. Father shipped him off to 'find himself.' As soon as Itzik arrived in New York, where he became Irving, he worked only until he had enough money for a one-way ocean liner ticket back to Paris. Aboard ship and in Paris he had a wonderful time. Then, when he ran out of money, he would come home to Rădăuţi, and my father would send him back to New York, again with a one-way ticket. I used to love Uncle Irving's visits. He would burst into the children's room, make me close my eyes, and shower me with tiny American candy bars and lollipops, unknown in Rădăuţi. I never see a lollipop without thinking of Uncle Irving. Well before Uncle Irving's arrival, perfumed postcards from his girl-friends would flutter in. They were in English, French, German, Italian, and I adored them and the fantasies they evoked. Curiously, I never remember my father yelling or being angry at Uncle Irving. I suspect that Uncle Irving did some surrogate acting-out for my father. For me the strangest thing about Uncle Irving was that he used to get an American newspaper, thick and heavy, take out a section with cartoons, lie down on the floor with them, and laugh. I had never seen cartoons, much less a grown man lying on the floor laughing. I remember inviting my classmates to view the spectacle."

In 1939, Mr. and Mrs. Stenzler had planned to go to a World's Fair in New York. Relatives had sent them tickets to encourage them to come. But "Father changed his mind because he was worried about leaving my sister and me, and all the family who depended on him." Despite the ominous political signs, Mr. Stenzler did not make plans to immigrate to New York with his wife and daughters. Although he was ordinarily a realist, and unusually perceptive about foreign affairs, "Father also, I think, did not believe, or did not want to believe, that Hitler's plan would succeed and reach out into 'his' Rădăuţi." At another level Rita suspected that her father really knew what was coming. "But he was not a quitter. He could no more leave Rădăuţi, with all that it meant to him and what he meant to it, than he could leave his aged parents, his brothers, sisters, and their families, who all depended on him financially, socially, and to a certain degree emotionally. He could not just pack up his wife and children and go to the United States. It would have been contrary to all that he stood for."

Rita knew the Germans of Bukovina through the family maids,

some classmates, and neighbors, as Rădăuţi was the most "German" town of the Bukovina. "Suddenly in 1940, the Germans disappeared from our midst. First the young men took off. In the summer of 1940, they supposedly went to summer camps, but actually they were taken into the military service in preparation for the war against Russia. The fittest among them, particularly when they fulfilled the Aryan race ideal, were taken into the SS." In the 1980s, in Cambridge, Massachusetts, Rita read in a German history a long list of fallen Bukovinian Germans. She could hardly believe it when she saw the large percentage of Rădăuţi Germans who had entered the SS, many of whom were killed on the Eastern Front. "I remember our German neighbors packing — they could take everything with them. Our maid did not leave. I never heard any conversation about her leaving. Maybe she considered herself as much part of us as we considered her."

After Antonescu's alliance with Hitler became firmly established in the autumn of 1940, the situation for Jewish families in Romania grew worse. Laws were passed severely restricting the rights of Jews. They were not allowed to travel outside the town or to sit on park benches. Every Jew had to wear the Star of David, and Jewish children were forbidden to attend the high school. As no person Rita knew in Rădăuţi had felt the need to deny being Jewish, these laws were both humiliating and difficult to evade. "I remember my mother sewing the yellow Star of David for me and then pinning it on my left chest between kisses and caresses."

The Iron Guard under Sima became restless for vengeance against those who had opposed them. In collusion with the Antonescu government, they increased their atrocities against the Jews and others considered to be their enemies. On November 27–28, sixty-four political prisoners were murdered in a Muntania jail by the Iron Guardist police; the noted economist and ex-minister for the National Peasant Party, Virgi Mageara, was killed in Snagov Woods on the outskirts of Bucharest; and ex-prime minister and world famous historian, Nicolae Iorga, was murdered at Strejnica. At about the same time, another mass killing was committed in Iaşi, about one hundred miles from Rădăuţi. In one night all Jewish males were rounded up, put into a cattle wagon on a train with no destination, and suffocated there.

✳

One day in late 1940, Mr. Stenzler came home covered with blood. At first he said he had had an accident. Finally, under pressure, he admitted that he had been beaten up by hoodlums from nearby villages. In fact, he had been attacked on the street in Rădăuți by the Iron Guard because he was a Jew. "I remember the afternoon like today. He tried to keep himself upright in spite of his pain, and upon entering our yard dispatched the maid to Zaziu to prevent him from walking on the street because of the marauding Iron Guard. While my mother and sister and I washed off the blood, he kept reassuring us that this was really nothing. That afternoon fascism and Hitler reached into Strada Pictor Grigorescu 15. As my mother's sister's and my tears mixed with Papunzika's reassurances, we all knew it was the end of an era. If my father was vulnerable to hooligans, then Rădăuți was unsafe. Today, in New York, Los Angeles, and other cities where citizens often get mugged and robbed, an incident like this would not mean what it meant in Rădăuți. I had never heard of a robbery there. Doors were unlocked day and night and muggings did not exist. For Shaje Stenzler to be attacked by hooligans, beaten in his town, on his own street, meant the beginning of the end."

Shortly afterward all Rădăuți males were forced to spend the nights from sunset to sunrise on one street. "That sounded very ominous, particularly since news about the massacre of Iaşi had reached us. We trembled every night till morning, and Christian maids and friends circulated throughout the night between the house where my father had taken his father, father-in-law, brother, brothers-in-law, and grown-up nephews and our house. Christian maids were told to leave their Jewish employers. "Our Resi never wanted to hear about that. She had red eyes from crying night and day and just did not know who she should worry more about, *der alte Herr* [the old gentleman, Zaziu], or *mein Herr* [Papunzika]." Despite these persecutions, Mr. Stenzler continued many of his regular activities and kept his store open.

Rita was the last Jewish child to attend the Liceul Elisabeta Doamna. After the law officially forbidding Jewish students to attend the high school was passed in 1941, many of the parents kept their children home. Other children were forced out by being given so low a grade at matura mica that they did not meet the requirements to remain. But this did not work in Rita's case, as she had already done so well on this and other tests that she won a national French competition administered to the best students in all the liceuls by French professors from the Sorbonne. Her prize was a trip to Paris, where, of course, she could not go because of the German occupation of France.

When the family realized that Rita was the only Jewish student left in the school, there was an argument. Mr. Stenzler thought that Rita should stay home, but her mother insisted that she enjoyed learning and should continue at school. One day in 1941, the director came over to Rita's French teacher and whispered something in her ear. The teacher then went to Rita and said, "Stenzler, you and I are not welcome in this school anymore," and left the room with Rita. The windows of the classroom were open, and the students watched with silent curiosity as the teacher, crying, walked out the front door of the school and accompanied Rita all the way home. The hurt of having, finally, to leave the school was mitigated by the support of the teacher and the principal. "I also knew that my father felt that I should not attend school when other Jewish children could not and that my mother would see to it that I continued to study privately."

On June 22, 1941, the Nazi army, with the troops of Germany's Eastern Europe satellites, including thirty Romanian divisions, invaded Soviet Russia, passing through northern Bukovina and Bessarabia. Hitler attempted to persuade Antonescu to annex a strip of Ukrainian territory to the east between the Bug and Dniester rivers, which was labeled Transnistria. Although administered by Romania during the war, Transnistria was never made part of Romania, which had no ethnic or territorial claims to it.

The pace of atrocities in Bukovina quickened after the invasion of Russia. Left-leaning Jews were rounded up and taken away. Frightening stories about the concentration camps began to be heard in Rădăuţi with increasing frequency. In July 1941, a favorite uncle, Moishe Wohl, Rita's mother's brother, was arrested in Rădăuţi. He was a socialist and, like the rest of the Wohls, "lived with only one foot in this world . . . The rest of their being was suspended somewhere between romantic dreams and the world of books. One day I saw Moishe being marched through the streets of Rădăuţi with a sign in front and back saying that he was a traitor. I loved Uncle Moishe and I remember the pain of seeing him marched on a chain." Uncle Moishe was to die of cancer in Mogilev Podolskiy. In September, the younger brother of Shaje Wohl and his family, living in Maramureş in northern Transylvania, disappeared. This brother had been mayor of the town, and the families had often been together in Vatra Dornei at holiday times or in Rădăuți at Passover.

In spite of the growing restrictions, Rita visited, before Yom Kippur, with teenagers "in the home of friends 'from the wrong side of town.' My parents disapproved of the parents of these boys and girls. At that party I smoked my first cigarette. Smoking was forbidden on any Saturday, especially on the Saturday before Yom Kippur, when one cleansed one's slate for a new page in the Book of Life. When we were deported shortly afterward, I was convinced — and still am in some hidden corner of my existence — that I brought on this catastrophe with my severe transgression. This feeling of guilt is entangled with a memory of the first visit Zaziu made to our house on a Saturday, a day when he never came by, because our house, with maid and activities, was not strict enough for him in terms of Sabbath observance. On that Saturday before our deportation, the house was full of young people and activities not befitting the Sabbath. On the train to Mogilev I remember thinking of Zaziu's angry face." It was the only time Rita remembers seeing him angry.

When the U.S. consulate sent a car for the American family in Rădăuți, to return them to the United States, the sense of danger grew intense. On October 13, Lucica arrived with a message that "something was going to happen" to the Jews. That afternoon Mrs. Stenzler insisted that Nora and Rita bring to the Stenzler home the Jewish spinster teacher of English and her old father and spinster sister. "When Nora and I asked them to come to our home they said, 'No, we'll stay home.'" Soon after this they killed themselves.

That night the Romanian police and soldiers rounded up the Jews and took them to the railroad station. When they came to the Stenzler home there was no chance for the family to take much with them. Helene took only a single doily and a figurine. Rita managed to hide a tiny baby doll in her pocket. The family went with the soldiers to get the two grandfathers. Shaje Wohl wore the dress of a Chassidic Jew. At the station there was pandemonium. The soldiers were pushing people into waiting cattle cars and parents were being separated from their children. Rita and Nora began to cry, fearing they would be left behind. Mrs. Stenzler, who had never shown qualities of leadership or self-assertion, underwent a dramatic change of personality. "Mutticuta's grandest hours were during that horrible night. We arrived at the train station. There was chaos, a frightened crowd shoved and pushed by soldiers into trains. They separated husbands from wives, mothers from children. We arrived huddled around our two old grandfathers and suddenly Mutticuta took over. She ordered us to the side of the train station hidden from the soldiers. We were anxious to get into the train, probably because we were frightened to be separated from the community. Mutticuta, though, had a different agenda. She, who had never worked a day in her life, had never belonged to any organization, suddenly was in charge of reuniting small children with their parents. She knew every Jewish child in town and with firmness got the soldiers to open the cattle cars, called the name of the child left on the platform, and placed each one with its parents. The soldiers obeyed her because of the unambivalent authority in her voice. Only after each child was re-united with its parents for that horrible journey did she rejoin us, and we got on the train."

When the Stenzlers finally boarded the train, their car was less crowded than others, filled only with "the remnants." As the doors were closed, they had no idea where they were going. But there was no panic. "Father calmed everyone." Of each rumor Mr. Stenzler said firmly, "That's not true." When someone asked, "How do you know?" he replied, "I know." Later, he admitted he had had no idea. Just before the train was to leave, a carriage drew up and a gynecologist was taken off the train so that he could deliver the baby of the mayor's wife. Some men opened the doors of the windowless cattle wagon and asked Mr. Stenzler to sign papers giving away his house and store and especially the factory in Arad. "I won't sign anything," he said, and handed back the papers. They did not force him. Rita found his refusal reassuring.

As the train pulled away from the station, Resi's loud sobs could be heard above the noise of the engine, blending with Leandi's howls of despair. "Resi's crying and Leandi's howls have accompanied my every memory of that night, forever."

2. A Jewish Family in the Bukovina

Like an abrupt pain, I felt homesickness: for home, for the Bukovina, where I had loved this hour just before darkness so much that I had always run out of the house and into the countryside, into that abstract, lilac-colored light. Its lower part would be a whirr with flitting bats and smoky with the dust of darkness, while the night wind wafted the fragrance of hay from distant meadows into my face; and before me the enormous source of night, where, toward Galicia, the flat earth fanned out to melt cosmically into the heavens.

— Gregor von Rezzori[1]

But Bukovina was different. All these years I had told my family how very different the Bukovina is. For years I had compared in the negative all other mountains in the rest of the world with the gentle *paysage* of the hills from the Bukovina. And now when I saw them they seemed lovelier than ever. They blended with each other, with the sky, and with the people. They were more beautiful than my memories.

— Rita S. Rogers, August 1981.

In the Carpathian hills, 30 kilometers from Rădăuţi at the end of a long alley lined with ash, chestnut, and fir trees, stands the walled monastery of Putna. One exterior wall within the monastery bears this inscription: "The highly praised prince of the whole country of Moldavia, I, Stephen Voivod [local feudal ruler], son to Bogdan Voivod, had this monastery built and erected, to dedicate to the Virgin, under Archimandrite Ioasaf, in 6987 [1491]."[2]

For five centuries Putna monastery, built by Stefan Cel Mare (Stephen the Great), the Moldavian national hero, has been a symbol, not only for Bukovinians and Moldavians but for all Romanians, of their never-ending struggle for unity and independence from outside invaders. In 1981, Rita, her daughter Sheila, my son Kenneth, and I attended the morning service at Putna on the four hundred seventy-seventh anniversary of Stefan Cel Mare's death. Religious ritual blends with secular adoration as the bearded, black-robed monks and priests sing the liturgy and chant stories and legends of the time when Stefan defended Christendom from the infidel Turks, while the church bells ring their accompaniment as they have for centuries. The last part of the service is held in Stefan's tomb room, with each person in the congregation holding votive candles. Great loaves of bread and large cakes are brought in by the monks in a ritual that is both a feast and a Eucharist-like offering to Stefan's spirit. There is little in this passionate, down-to-earth service that seems stern, severe, or ascetic, and the participation by each worshiper creates a powerful sense of connectedness and community.

The same mixing of Christian and earthly — princely — worship can be seen in the murals on the outside walls of the other Bukovinian monasteries built by Stefan Cel Mare. Scenes from Revelation and other New Testament books, along with the exploits of Stefan Cel Mare, are depicted in red, blue, and gold. The battles of Stefan and the other princely voivods of medieval Moldavia have a special meaning to the people of this region. For four hundred years they experienced a struggle not only to secure the independence of their lands but to preserve the freedom of their faith in the face of the Moslem power from the East. This struggle, which is vividly presented to every Romanian schoolchild, did not end until the capitulation of the Turkish armies to Romanian and Russian forces at Plevna in November 1877, leading to the establishment of Romanian independence in the following year.

The region known as the Bukovina, which means the "land of beech trees," lies in the northern part of historical Moldavia. Since the end of World War II, when Stalin made permanent his wartime seizure of the northern part, the Bukovina has been divided between Romania and the USSR. The Romanian sense of national identity has been heightened, if not created, by the threat of Russia — and later the Soviet Union — to the East. Romania, though populated by large Slavic minorities, has passionately refused solidarity with its huge menacing neighbor. Southern Bukovina, Transylvania to the south and west, and Oltenița, Walachia, and Dobruja to the south and east form the present state of Romania. The northern portion of Bukovina, including Czernowitz, the region's most important city, has been absorbed by the USSR into the Ukraine. The splitting into two parts of their traditional land remains a painful wound for the Bukovinians. A bank clerk in Rădăuți said to Rita in 1981, with tears in his eyes, "They took away the heart of Bukovina."

The wooded hills and mountains and steep narrow valleys of the Bukovina are separated from the West by the Carpathian mountains. Toward the East it was and remains open and vulnerable. "Maybe this is related," Rita says, "to a state of mind of Bukovinians: they concentrate and look with fear toward what is happening in the eastern part of Europe and fantasize and aggrandize about what happens west of their beloved mountains." Much of the countryside is farmland, with houses set on gentle hillsides, among fields of muted green, gold, and brown. The Bukovina does, however, have a mountainous backbone. "Rocky peaks did loom here and there from the green ones of the forest Carpathians, and the poetic gentleness of the flowery slopes was all too deceptive in obscuring the wildness of the deep forests in which they were embedded," wrote Gregor von Rezzori, a novelist of Italian background who grew up in the Bukovina.[3]

Because of its geographic position in relation to the Dniester, Prut, and Seret River waterways, which were important trade routes connecting the Ukrainian, Balkan, and Mediterranean regions with Poland and the Baltic lands to the north, the Bukovina has at times acquired a strategic importance disproportionate to its small size and population.

All people feel a special connection with their land of origin. Yet for Rita and other natives of the Bukovina there seems to be something more, some special feeling of pride, a sense of particular prestige. One might try to explain this in terms of the beauty of the countryside, the uplifting example of the national hero Stefan Cel Mare, a higher standard of living, the superior level of culture or education that many Bukovinians have achieved, or the 143 years during which the Bukovina was a part of the Austro-Hungarian Empire. The explanations seem unsatisfactory, but the feeling is real and convincing. In 1986, for example, Rita and her husband were taken to a New York airport by a cab driver from Romania. After Rita mentioned that she was from Romania, he asked which part she came from. "When I told him Bukovina, he gave forth a long stream of names of the great poets — Eminescu, Alexandri — painters, historians, and politicians — I think he must have even added a few non-Bukovinians to the illustrious list. He then asked, 'Does your husband know what a special place Bukovina is?' The driver was from Dobruja."

The power the Bukovina holds for its people is expressed in poignant ways. On our journey from Bucharest to Suceava, the landing point and district capital of the part of Bukovina now inside Romania, the pilot of the Tarom (Romanian Airlines) twin-engine plane pointed out the sights along our route and told the passengers the history of the Bukovina, interlaced with a poem or two by Eminescu. Rita asked to see the "travelogue" she had so enjoyed over the loudspeaker. The pilot said he had no travelogue and showed her his handwritten notes in which he had recorded the personal thoughts he enjoyed sharing with his passengers as he was flying to the province of his ancestors. "Then I knew that it was going to be all right to come back to the Bukovina, where I had not been since 1947 and had not lived since 1941. The pilot's notes were a reassurance that certain feelings had survived everything that had happened in this part of the world."

Throughout its history, Bukovina has been a classic border area. Although the battles over its land have been better recorded since the formation of the Moldavian state in the fourteenth century, the territory of Bukovina has been disputed since ancient times. From the period when the Roman Empire in the west was being overrun by Germanic tribes to the north, the region that came to be known as Moldavia endured a series of invasions by Nomadic tribes from Central Asia and later by Slavic peoples, Poles and Ukrainians, who settled in the region. Huns, Avars, and Magyars were followed by Pechenegs, a Turkish people, and by the Great Mongol invasion of 1241, which was particularly devastating to Moldavia. Until the fourteenth century, Moldavia remained a primitive region at the edge of Byzantine and Kievan Russian Christendom, fought over by numerous peoples but part of no stable state or empire.

In 1359, Bogdan, voivod of Maramures, led a successful revolt against the suzerainty of Louis the Great, king of Hungary, thus establishing the principality of Moldavia with frontiers on the Dniester and Danube rivers. It was during this period that St. Nicholas Church was built in Rădăuți. By the end of the century Moldavian suzerainty had passed to Poland, with whom the voivods entered into binding military alliances against the Hungarians and the Teutonic knights to the north.

In the early decades of the fifteenth century, the Ottoman Turks penetrated into Walachia, Transylvania, and finally into Moldavia, leading to the capitulation of the principality to the Turkish sultan, Mehmed II in 1456. The stage was now set for the emergence of the legendary hero of Moldavia, Stefan Cel Mare. Over the next half century, until his death in 1504, Stefan Cel Mare resisted the Ottoman advance and scored a brilliant sequence of military victories against the Turks, Poles, and Hungarians. He strengthened the princely authority and created a prosperous and powerful Moldavian state.

After Stefan's death, Moldavia again came under Ottoman domination, and over the next two and a half centuries its lands were disputed among Poles, Austrians, Turks, Ottomans, and finally, the emerging power of czarist Russia. The period of Ottoman domination left a residue of anti-Turkish prejudice and fear that carried into the child-rearing behavior of parents in the twentieth century. Rita remembers that when children were naughty they were threatened with "if you don't behave the Turks will get you." This was particularly effective with little boys who had learned about the eunuchs who guarded the sultan's harems.

When Rita's parents grew up in the Bukovina, it was still a province of Austria. The Austrians gained possession in 1774, when two cavalry regiments entered the region and attached it to the empire. The justification for occupying Bukovina was entirely strategic. Austria feared Russian power and expansion and openly stated its need to have direct, uninterrupted contact with other parts of the empire, especially Transylvania and Galicia. Russia, grateful to Austria for its help against Turkey, did not interfere, and in October 1775 this area of little more than 10,000 square kilometers, which would be Rita's homeland, became a border outpost of a different empire. Austria defined the region's boundaries and called it the Bukovina.

Austria — later Austro-Hungary — sought not only to enlarge its territory for "defensive" purposes but also to bring the elements of Western culture and civilization to these neglected areas. Empress

Mother Maria Theresa, who ruled jointly with her son Joseph II, had some misgivings about the treatment of this region. "In Moldavian affairs," she said, "we are totally in the wrong and hardly with honor."[4] Despite her misgivings, during the nearly a century and a half of Hapsburg occupation the Austrians sought to suppress the emotional currents, language, and religious and cultural institutions through which Bukovinians experienced their ties to Romania. Colonists from Germany and Austria streamed into the towns and rural areas of Bukovina, and the Hapsburg monarchy provided them with benefits that included land, houses, freedom from taxation, and the support of their cultural institutions. Protestant minority dissidents were encouraged to enter the region and supported in practicing their religion freely. Austria even encouraged the political and national aspirations of the Ukrainians of Bukovina at the expense of both the native Romanian population and the Russians.

The Austrian occupation resulted in the lasting influence and absorption of Austro-German language and culture by Rita Stenzler's ancestors and other Jewish families of the Bukovina. German became the native tongue for the upper- and middle-class Jewish families, many of whom were educated in the German-speaking schools of the empire. The non-Jewish Romanian population of the Bukovina also seems to have gained a feeling of superiority, owing perhaps to a higher living and cultural standard developed under Austro-Hungarian rule. At the same time, according to the Bukovinian historian I. Nistor, "one hundred and fifty years of Austrian domination left no durable creations in Bukovina. All the monuments of Bukovina are the work of the native Rumanian spirit."[5]

At the beginning of World War I, thousands of Bukovinian Romanians refused to enlist in the Austrian army. In 1916, Romania, under the influence of her English-born, westward-looking, liberal Queen Marie, changed sides and joined the Allies against Austria-Hungary and Germany. Many Bukovinians joined the Romanian cause in the hope of liberating Bukovina from Austria and uniting the region with the Romanian kingdom. Nevertheless, the emphasis given to steadfast national feeling in native Romanian historical texts obscures the torn allegiance that many Bukovinians, especially those among the educated classes, experienced during World War I. Shaje Stenzler was himself briefly inducted into the Austro-Hungarian army but soon released because of his poor eyesight. Two of Rita's mother's brothers fought on the side of Austria-Hungary. Many Bukovinians died in the service of the empire.

After the defeat of the Axis powers, a General Congress of Bukovina was convened at Czernowitz on November 28, 1918, to declare the union of Bukovina with Romania. The Motion of Union contains these stirring patriotic lines: "Considering that the Bukovinians nevertheless did not lose hope that their hour of salvation, awaited with so much terror and courage, would one day strike, and that the heritage of their ancestors, divided by unjust frontiers, would be completely restored by the reunion of Bukovina with the Moldavia of Stephen . . . Bukovina, within its ancient frontier extending to the . . . Ceremus and Dniester [rivers], is unconditionally and forever united to the Kingdom of Romania."[6]

The four years of war, which included frequent Russian occupations, left the Bukovina a desolate wasteland. Ruined villages and towns were filled with rubbish, while roads and bridges were impassable. Public services were disorganized, and starvation was widespread. In some districts deprivation and misery led the population to violent rioting. In 1918–1919 there was a frightening interregnum between the withdrawal of Austrian authority and its replacement by effective Romanian national and local administration. Gregor von Rezzori was a child of about five during this period. In his ironically titled novel, *Memoirs of an Anti-Semite,* Rezzori recalls the situation. "As a child in the Bukovina, within walking distance of the Dniester River, beyond which Russia began, he [Rezzori writes of himself in the third person] had been awakened in the night — the Austrians had marched out, the Romanians had not yet marched in; people were afraid the Bolsheviks might attack or at least maraud; hordes were already passing through the countryside and plundering the military depots."[7] Rita, shielded by her mother's penchant for emphasizing only life's "happy and good things," heard little of all this, although she did learn of the severe influenza epidemic that ravaged the Bukovina and much of Europe and the United States at the end of World War I.

After the formation in 1920 of Greater Romania, which included Transylvania, Bessarabia, and Bukovina, the history of Bukovina becomes inseparable from that of the Romanian nation. Despite the critical importance for our story of the brief period between the world wars — less than two decades — it is a time still so close to us psychologically, so emotionally charged, and so susceptible to varied ideological interpretations that it is particularly difficult to evaluate.

While recovering from World War I, a weary Romanian population began an experiment in parliamentary democracy in conjunction with a monarchy descended from the Hohenzollerns, which the nationalist leaders had imported from Germany in the middle of the previous century. In 1923, a national constitution was voted into existence, and through the decade of the 1920s Romania experienced a remarkable period of economic growth, including considerable industrial development and active international trade. "Rumania was a rich land in those days," von Rezzori wrote. "Sausage and ham, pastries and pies, flowed into the house in vast quantities."[8] At the same time, a cultural flowering took place in Romanian education, literature, art, music, and science.

The victory of totalitarian forces in Romania in the 1930s has been attributed to the failure of the liberal and peasant parties, dominated by a newly created middle class and by wealthy landowners, to extend the privileges of democracy widely enough, to share wealth sufficiently, or to institute adequate land reforms. Corruption, illiteracy, and bribery — always blamed on the Turkish occupation — continued to flourish. But powerful economic and political forces outside of Romania, especially the worldwide economic depression of the early 1930s, the rise of fascism in Italy, Nazism in Germany, and bolshevism in Soviet Russia, also led to the failure of the short-lived Romanian effort at parliamentary government, especially as it received very little support from the democratic countries. It is true that Romania produced its own crop of fascist thugs and developed a particular virulent home-grown culture of anti-Semitism. Nevertheless, it was the play upon the social currents that were indigenous to Romania by outside economic, political, and ultimately, military forces that proved decisive in aborting the creation of Romanian democratic institutions. In Rita's words, "What always flowed in Romania was not only pastries and pies, but also flowers and songs, twinkles and tenderness and passions, good and bad. But what was completely missing was any durable structure of democracy."

For Rita Stenzler, the events described in this brief history were part of her inner being. She learned about them not only in the schoolroom but also through local stories and myths and visiting the lovely monasteries in Carpathia. Rita knew at an early age that she was growing up in a border region over which soldiers of a multitude of loyalties and nationalities had fought from the beginning of recorded time. Although the conflict into which she and her community were personally to be swept was perhaps the most deadly the world had ever seen, it was for the Bukovina but the most recent in a sequence of wars that had taken place on Moldavian soil since the time of Bogdan of Maramures and before. For Rita, there could never have been any question about the power of international events to affect the emotional life and inner sense of identity of the individual. Foreign affairs could not be kept separate from private life in the psychiatry that this Romanian Jewish native of the Bukovina would later practice.

✳

Nineteenth-century German texts describe the Bukovina as *bunt* (many-colored), referring to the many nationalities it contained. One author, in 1876, listed among the permanent inhabitants Romanians, Ruthenians, "Israelites," Germans, Magyars (Hungarians), Poles, Great Russians, Slowaks (*sic*), Armenians, and Gypsies.[9] Later texts refer to the presence of Hutuls and Greeks.[10] In 1930, there were in the Bukovina 380,000 Romanians, 236,000 Ruthenians — a Slavic people ethnically akin to but culturally distinct from Ukrainians — 92,500 Jews, 75,000 Germans, and 70,000 Hungarians and assorted peoples of twenty-three other nationalities.

Rita compares the polyglot nature of the Bukovina with Los Angeles, where she lives now. "I am certain that there are many more national groups living in Los Angeles. But there was a difference. In L.A. all the different immigrants want to be Americans. In the Bukovina, each of the different groups was separate and wanted to remain that way. They and their children had their identities, which they considered superior, and did not wish to merge with other groups. For me, they were fascinating because they were different, a little bit dangerous, and I had little contact with them. From the shelter of a very secure home life, I glanced furtively but with great excitment toward these 'other' people."

In the thirteenth century, Jews began settling in Eastern Europe. A history of Moldavia mentions them for the first time when Prince Stefan the Younger (1517–1527) chased them away for the protection of the other people.[11] Another prince, Peter the Lame, did the same thing in 1579. Prior to 1769, when the Russians occupied Moldavia for five years, there were said to be only two hundred Jewish families in all of Moldavia. When Austria took over the Bukovina in 1775, the Jews gladly placed themselves under the more tolerant Austrian administrative protection. As a result, Jews migrated into the Bukovina from Poland (Galicia), Russia, and other parts of Eastern Europe. It is likely that Rita Stenzler's forebears entered Bukovina in the period of active Jewish migration during the early and mid-nineteenth century. By 1900 Jews were the third largest national group in the Bukovina.

While nineteenth-century textbooks differ in their description of the many nationalities, depending on whether they are written by Romanian, German, Hungarian, Ukrainian, or other authors, they agree in their derogatory description of the Jews. The Austrian general Gabriel Freiherr von Soleny reported to the court in 1779 his determination not to let "that insect," as he referred to them, rise in the Bukovina. "The Jew," he stated, "in no country had so much wealth and freedom and paid so little [taxes were only 5 percent per year]: Everybody wants to settle in the Bukovina, which I will never accept or tolerate."[12] The nineteenth-century historian Bidermann accuses the "Israelites" of pouring into the Bukovina in the expectation of finding in the land "a second Canaan."

With the growth of the Jewish population in Romania, especially in the Bukovina and other parts of Moldavia, anti-Semitic feeling grew in intensity. According to British scholar of Romanian history R. N. Seton-Watson, writing in the early 1930s, "The theoretical equality 'allowed' to Jews in Romania was rendered illusory by a host of restrictions." Although free to exercise their religion, Jews "remained in certain respects citizens of second rank."[13] Seton-Watson, downplaying the role of prejudice, regarded the situation as "essentially an economic problem, in which the Jews showed their economic superiority, their greater agility and an alertness and, it must be added, their greater readiness to work."[14] The rabbis in the Jewish communities were counselors, advisers, and judges and handled many administrative matters involving their parishioners. Some had a special place in the larger community. Those from Sadgora and Viznitz were considered "miracle" rabbis because of their reputation for wisdom and special knowledge of human nature.

Overwhelmingly represented in intellectual professions, the Jews maintained a strong sense of cultural superiority, which, in Rita's words, reached the level of a "grandiosity stance." This feeling has a number of sources. "We were much more educated, cultured, hygienic, and sophisticated than the non-Jews from the Bukovina, the majority of whom were peasants. Our grandiosity was enhanced by the tenderness, servility, and respect with which the Romanian peasants and German maids treated us. We were the doctors, lawyers, merchants, and so forth. We spoke and read different languages; we played the piano, traveled, read, and knew about the rest of the world." The police, teachers, clerks, and city officials were Romanians, most of whom came from other parts of the country, or were the sons of wealthy land-owning families who had received some education. "The Jews were an island by themselves. They spoke German — only the uneducated Jews spoke Yiddish. They looked down on the Romanian peasants. They hummed Viennese operettas, read German classics, and were successful businessmen, except for the poor who lived along the Toplita, a little, stagnant stream. The wealthy supported these poor Jews and that made them feel good."

Paris was a second focus of cultural identification for the Jews of Bukovina. Rita remembers the hot late spring afternoon in 1940 when news reached Rădăuți that Paris had fallen to the Germans. She was walking with her cousin Schella, after whom her youngest child, Sheila, is named. (Schella died in childbirth while Rita was pregnant with Sheila). "I shall never forget the personal pain we experienced upon hearing that 'our' Paris fell. Paris was our *cité lumière*. To understand the vehemence of our Paris allegiance, one has to be familiar with the flirtation and indeed passion which educated Romanians had for Paris. First of all, it created a connection for the Romanian people with their 'romance' brothers and sisters in the West for whom they felt affection, closeness, and love. Unfortunately, the tie to Paris is also represented a defensive wall toward the 'barbaric Slavs' from the north, east, and south, who really surrounded Romania."

The Jews of Bukovina looked down on the Jews of Romania proper or "old" Romania — Bucharest, Muntania, and the rest of Moldavia — which was referred to as the Regat. Jews from the Regat were "not our caliber." They were thought to be poorer and lacked German culture. They came from stetls of Eastern Europe, as, in fact, had some Bukovinian families, spoke Romanian or Yiddish and no proper German. Indeed, no higher praise could be given a Romanian Jew than the words "He speaks beautiful German."

This thicket of prejudice in Bukovina extended in many directions and contained intricate hierarchies. "The Transylvanian city dwellers considered themselves very Western because they were west of Romania." All Bukovinians, Jews and non-Jews, looked down on the inhabitants of some of the poorer villages. Just outside Rădăuţi was such a village, Vicovul de Jós. "If you wanted to offend someone you would say, 'Ah, you are from Vicovul de Jós,' that is, a nobody. Among the Jews of Bukovina those from Czernowitz liked to think of themselves as very cosmopolitan and their city a suburb of Vienna, even though "the Viennese did not quite accept them that way." The Viennese used to call the Bukovinians *zugereiste,* someone who has "traveled in." Some roots of World War II can be seen in this tangle of ethnic hatred.

Yet there was also an affinity among the peoples of Bukovina, Jew and non-Jew, which might yet have permitted them to live together successfully if destructive outside forces had not upset the precarious balance. Part of this affinity was the shared experience of survival. Romanians, like Jews, had centuries of experience in learning the skills and adaptations necessary for survival, one of which was the talent for bribery. Rita summed this up succinctly. "Romanians loved being bribed, and the Jews from Romania were good at bribery." In the ghetto at Mogilev, bribery became an essential element of survival. "Bribery is not a good description. To be good at bribing demands a certain flexibility and largess — at a moment's notice. And by the ones to be bribed also. There has to be the right timing."

Of the 800,000 Jews who had lived in Romania in 1930, only 25,000 remained in 1985.[15] Approximately half survived the war. Of these, the majority left to escape the cultural, economic, and political persecutions and deprivations of communism. Many immigrated to Israel after the formation of the Jewish state in 1948, where they constituted the largest national bloc in the country, about 10 percent of the population. The Jews of the Bukovina, Bessarabia, and the Dobruja district suffered the hardest fate. The Soviet Union, which occupied Bukovina in 1940, began deporting Jews and non-Jews in a purge that was already in progress when the German invasion began. The area then lay in the path of the German armies on the Eastern Front. Of the 160,000 Jews who had lived in these three regions, fewer than 50,000 survived.[16]

In 1981, we found little remaining of the Jewish community in Rădăuţi. The cemetery was overgrown and the synagogue locked, neglected, and rarely used. The story of the Jewish survivors in the late 1970s has been lovingly, though sadly, told by Ayse Gursan-

Salzmann and her husband, Laurence Salzmann, in their photographic essay *The Last Jews of Rădăuţi.*[17]

✳

Of all the nationalities of the Bukovina, the German people evoked the least curiosity from the young Rita. They were the most similar. "They spoke the same language as we did. Their houses were clean and well kept, and they were reliable, hardworking, and dependable, as we were. It was the strangers who fascinated me. Their national costumes, food, songs, and dances were tempting, foreign, and thrilling. For me in the little safe nest of the Bukovina, these others — the Hutulen, Ruthenians, Lipowaner, Hungarians, Gypsies, and Romanians — were the outside world, outside the Jewish community of Rădăuţi. The Germans were close to our own world until the day Hitler's voice on the radio penetrated our living room."

The other peoples of the Bukovina had their own villages, communities, and land. The Hungarian village of Hadikfalva (Dorneşti in Romanian) was close to Rădăuţi. Rita and her friends walked to Hadikfalva to swim or were picked up by peasants who took them there in horse-drawn carriages. "The Hungarians were cheerful, loved to sing and dance, and wore their national costumes and probably were more Hungarian than the Hungarians in Hungary."

The Poles, in Rita's memory, were especially religious and politically conscious. "They used to greet each other often with '*Pada do nog*' [I fall to my knees], at which occasion they would bow so low that their hats would strike their knees. The gallantry of their hand-kissing, their elegance and pride, and their enthusiastic response when non-Poles joined them in their anthem '*Jeshe Polska ne Sginjela*' [Poland Has Not Gone Under Yet] have remained deeply imprinted in my memory."

Northern Bukovina was home to a large population of Ruthenians — a Latinized form of "Russian" — a Slavic people of the western Ukraine and Galicia who fled to the Carpathian region to escape the Turks, Tatars, and Russians in the seventeenth and eighteenth centuries. In the Austrian Empire the Ruthenians were tolerated, especially after 1596 when the Orthodox church of the western Ukraine united with the Roman Catholic church. The Ruthenians of Bukovina surpassed the Romanian peasants in agricultural diligence and skill, using horses instead of the oxen behind which the Romanians strolled leisurely.

In Rădăuți during Rita's childhood there lived a group of Ruth-enians called *Hutuli* (*Huzulen* in German) by the Romanians. They are strikingly handsome people, thought by legend to have Cuman (a nomadic East Turkic people) blood. The Hutulis lived in a valley near the Galician border. They were known for their physical prowess, daredevil stunts, and artistry. The men adorned their hats with tin ornaments, peacock feathers, and flowers. The women painted ex-quisite Easter eggs, using light-resistant vegetable colors. Their na-tional dance was the Arkan, in which sticks — part of their costume — are thrown in the air and caught high above the ground. In the early 1800s, the Hutil women were considered the common property of all grown-up Hutil men, who would welcome strangers by offering them their women. All the Hutuli, male and female, young and old, are good on horseback. They ride small, quick horses, which are also called Hutuls. In Rădăuți there was a special *herghelie,* a horse ranch of Hutul horses. The Hutuli were profoundly superstitious. Milk, for example, was handled only by men for fear that witches might take the milk from the cows.

The Hutuli were mountain people. Their greatest skill was in cutting trees in the mountains and piloting the logs down the rivers while standing on them. Rita used to see them shooting down the river, standing tall and handsome in their colorful garb. "I have never spoken to a Hutul, but I can still feel the excitement of seeing these mysterious people on their logs going down the river. On their horses, they were woven into a thousand dreams, fantasies, and legends."

Among other exotic people in Rădăuți were the Lipowaner, blond Slavic people who came to the Bukovina in the seventeenth century from the East because of Russian persecution related to a doctrinal dispute with the Orthodox church. They opposed all killing, and therefore refused direct military activity, instead performing services such as cleaning streets. They did not permit their herds to be counted because they believed that once counted a cow would lose its milk. They also did not permit their children to be immunized, and many of them carried smallpox scars. Rita remembers "the sight of the Lipowaner in their bright kerchiefs riding into town in their troikalike carriages filled with vegetables and fruits on their way to market or coming to the house with baskets." They were links to the mysterious Slavic world to the east.

As noted earlier, for Rita the most mysterious and fascinating of the peoples of Bukovina were the Gypsies. Originally from the north of India, the Gypsies streamed into southeastern Europe during the Middle Ages. Because they adopted many habits of the Romanian people, including elements of their language, they became known as "Romanis," and their native language, which included Asiatic, Armenian, and European elements, is called Romany. All efforts to settle these unusual nomadic people, including those by the present Communist regime, have failed.

In the eyes of Rita and her family, the authentic people of the Bukovina, the ones who really belonged, were the peasants or *tărani*. "They wore their national costumes for everyday life, spoke their own language, and seemed to blend with the earth, the gentle lush mountains, the streams, the harvest, the songs and marvelous folk dances. They merged with their own land and were not dreaming of where and when they would go elsewhere." She recalls the slow, dignified way the peasants walked, the tall robust men from the mountains, and the "old, old men with faces which looked like wood carvings and white long hair under their *caciulas* [fur hats]. Earthy smiles revealed poorly kept teeth. Hospitality seemed to shine from the peasants' good-humored eyes. When you entered a house you were immediately welcomed with *dulceata* [preserved fruit] and a glass of ice cold water. You could never refuse. It was understood that people would deprive themselves to be able to serve their guests lavishly." We experienced the native Bukovinian hospitality when we visited. With each person we met there was an extra warmth, an eagerness to help, greetings of "May you live long" or "God be with you," a wonderful spirit despite the poverty and harsh conditions.

As children, Rita and her friends loved to go to the peasants' homes. Most of them lived in small huts with tiny windows called *colibas,* like those their ancestors had lived in for generations. "I used to get goose pimples whenever I entered a Romanian peasant's house. You usually found an old man sleeping, even during daytime, on the *cuptor* — a sort of high ledge next to the oven. This habit was considered inconceivable and hazardous by my family. The peasants' devotion to their past gave the soothing feeling that they and all things will last forever." This sense of permanence drew Rita to Moldavian native history. She identified with Romanian legends, felt the people's hurts and aspirations, and knew every battle and the triumphs and misfortunes of each prince.

Here, too, it was the "otherness" that especially attracted Rita. The peasants spoke of things she had never heard about at home, in a language her parents did not use. Instead of bread they ate *mamaliga* — warm in the mornings with milk, cold for lunch and carried in the many colored *traista,* an oddly shaped knapsack made of homespun wool, and in the evenings with butter, goat cheese, and sour cream — "My favorite way of eating mamaliga." Peasant women made clothes for the family and spun wool at home as in ancient times. When members of a family could not manage to make the clothes they needed by themselves, a *claca,* an evening of communal work, would be organized. Other girls and women from the neighborhood were invited to the house to do the work while the young men contributed music, dances, and pranks.

Rita loved to recite Romanian ballads filled with references to nature and was deeply affected by the music of the people. Romanian music and dancing, permeated by longing, expresses a dreaming people's soul. The most heartbreaking and authentic Romanian song is the *doina.* "There are doinas for different occasions, but the doina is always sad and melancholic and transmits the cravings, the sufferings, and the dreams of a people who have been blessed with a beautiful land that was always craved by others. I knew many doinas and they seemed to accompany the historical facts I was studying; there was Stefan Cel Mare riding into battle or kneeling at an altar; and there was Mihai Vieazul (Mihai the Brave) uniting Muntania and Moldavia.

"In my daydreams, King Michael appeared dancing the hora, as I'd once seen. A real hora gets many spontaneous improvisations, usually provided by the male dancers with cheerful four-sentence calls. To me, the exuberance of a hora or *sărba* cannot be translated to another nation or language. My father, who had a wonderful ear for music and rhythm and who loved to dance, enjoyed Romanian horas and sărbas, and when we heard one on the radio, in a village square, or in a house, he would immediately engage Nora and me in a lively dance. I felt that even though he had glorious memories of his youth as a citizen of the Austro-Hungarian Empire, his love of life and natural zest made the throbbing of the Romanian soul through their songs irresistible to him."

Rita loved the Romanian holidays and celebrations and was powerfully affected by the rituals of the Eastern Orthodox church. "My grandfather's love of his own tradition and lack of venom against other religions and traditions made me venerate others who believe. I remain fascinated by Romanian, Greek, or Russian Orthodox priests who have beards like my grandfather's and are dignified and venerable as he was. This strange, forbidden belief had many more trimmings, including more scents and sounds than Jewish Orthodox services. You must remember that, as a girl, I could never sit downstairs during Jewish services. But when I went with my school class to the Romanian Orthodox church, I was able to sit close to the service."

Pagan rituals also fascinated Rita. "I knew that a peasant woman, after delivering her baby, kept a broom at the door as a protection against evil. The new mother did not leave the house for forty days until she went with the child to church and the priest permitted her entry. The baby always wore a thread around its neck or wrist and everybody who admired the infant had to say '*Ptiu, ptiu! Să nu-i fie de deochi*' (May it be protected from the evil eye)." When peasant women would say something laudatory about Rita to Resi, the maid, or to her parents, they would add the obligatory "*Ptiu, ptiu!*" The preoccupation with the evil eye was ubiquitous and penetrated the Jewish households and the lore of other minorities in the Bukovina. "It offered both an explanation and a solution to all catastrophic events of one's life. One could blame whatever had happened on the evil spirit instead of accusing oneself or others or lingering over the question of responsibility. The simple solutions — a red thread, a broom at the door — drew people together. The evil eye had to be avoided and fought off by all. The same threads and primitive solutions tied one to the community."

The most important landmark in Rădăuţi was the train station in the center of town. Nobody could ever be bored there. Someone with nothing to do could always go to the station to watch the comings and goings of the passengers. If that was too dull, one could exaggerate or invent comings and goings. Listeners would reciprocate, and the stories became more interesting with every telling.

Children had a special place in Rădăuţi. "They knew who they were and what they could and could not do. Parents did not, as a rule, beat children. Sex abuse? I don't know, since one never heard either the word *sex* or *abuse*. Rădăuţi was not a magnificent place but rather a spot which permitted the good and the bad parts of human beings to show their true colors. In Rădăuţi one did not call old age the golden age, but we rose in respect for the old because they might not have much other fun in life. In Rădăuţi one did not call retarded children 'exceptional.' I remember one girl on the Horodniker Strasse who, in retrospect, looked defective. We referred to her as suffering from the English disease, probably because England was far away and we did not know much about it."

When Rita was growing up, the population of Rădăuţi was about 20,000, of whom about 8,000 were Jews. The town seemed isolated then, "a special platform for dreaming about the world at large." It was a place of cobblestoned streets and horse-drawn vehicles. There was only one car, which belonged to the mayor, perhaps two or three telephones, few radios, and no television. Before the ravages of fascism and Nazism shattered its protected tranquillity, this quiet town seemed to be an ideal haven in which a child could grow up with a sense of both emotional and physical security.

In addition, Rita could feel that she belonged to an extended family connected with a well-defined ethnic group. When Rita returned, the townspeople's expectation of belonging was still there. At the marketplace a peasant asked her, "*A cui esti?*" (Whose are you?) He wanted to know the name of her father, for in Romanian villages people were identified that way. "How can I translate the feeling of belonging when a peasant of my native town asked that question? I felt small, young, and connected because of it. Here one did not know of anomie and alienation. One belonged. For us, the displaced people from all over the world, it means something to be asked '*A cui esti?*'"

In 1807, three Jewish families were listed in the tax register of Rădăuţi.[18] In 1830, the Jews launched their own synagogue with a newly found Talmud Torah. Soon thereafter land for a cemetery was acquired and many more Jewish families settled there. By 1914 there were 6,000 Jews, more than 40 percent of the population. Chassidism, with its tradition of passionate yet joyful Orthodoxy, had a strong influence on Jewish life in Rădăuţi, especially the Viznitz, Bojan, and Sadgora dynasties. The Viznitzer shul was begun by followers of a rabbi from the Ukrainian town of Viznitz.

Judith Wolf, Rita's maternal gandmother, came from a prestigious Polish family, and Rita believes that both the Wohl and Stenzler grandparents came to the Bukovina from Poland. Srul Wolf, Judith's father, was a devout Orthodox Chassidic Jew, much adored by Rita's mother. Toward the end of his life he went to Palestine to die. "He

Rita's grandmother Judith Wohl with Rita's mother, Helene,
and her uncle Shmuel Abe

Rita's grandmother
Judith Wohl

Rita's maternal
grandparents, Judith and
Shaje ("Zaziu") Wohl

Rita's grandfather
Shaje Wohl

Rita's mother and
father, Helene and
Shaje Stenzler

Rita at
seventeen months

Nora, nearly five,
and Rita, seventeen months

Rita at
thirteen

did the best thing a religious Jew can do, to be buried in the Holy Land." Rita's mother remembers the day in her early childhood when the family escorted him to the train station for the journey to Bucharest, the Romanian port of Constanța, and then Palestine. "My mother used to tell me with a quiver in her voice about the scene at the train when the family went to see her beloved grandfather off. I think this particular story of my mother's set the seeds for my profound love for my own grandfather Shaje ("Zaziu") Wohl."

The Wohls were dreamers after lofty causes, book lovers unable to make a living. In the family it was said that "the lights never went out at the Wohls'," as they interpreted poetry and debated issues all night and slept late in the morning. None of Rita's mother's six brothers ever worked in Romania. When two of them went to the United States, they took jobs. According to Rita's cousin Shilo, her grandfather Zaziu was a *shoichet,* a ritual slaughterer of animals. In particular, it was his job to cut the throats of chickens, but he was too soft-hearted and didn't do this work. Therefore, Rita's father had to support him for much of his life. Shaje Wohl was a pious man who dressed in Chassidic garb — long black caftan, black hat — and had a long white beard and sideburns. "But his most gorgeous adornments were his warm, sparkling eyes."

Shaje Wohl was much respected by the Jewish community in Rădăuți as a religious and spiritual leader. He was known for his wise judgment, and people came to him to settle all sorts of disputes. "Nobody would have sued, gone to lawyers, or to court. They came to Shaje Wohl. He would say what should happen, and that is how it happened. He would listen to both sides and usually did a little psychotherapy, I think, and that settled it." At the same time Shaje Wohl was not practical or scientific. "He never believed the earth was round. There was no need for justification of anything. The way he felt was what counted, and everyone and everything else fell into place."

Zaziu was the anchor of Rita's childhood. She grew up feeling that she was his favorite among his fifteen grandchildren, which she attributed to the special feeling he had for his daughter, her mother. The Wohls, Shaje and Judith, after whom Rita's first daughter was named, lived in a small house with a big, old-fashioned kitchen filled with wonderful aromas and another big room with two small beds. The house was crammed with huge old Hebrew religious books, which Shaje Wohl read all day. There was also an extra dwelling, a sort of gazebo, for the holiday of Succoth. On Friday evenings Shaje Wohl wore festive clothes and a fur-trimmed hat and walked about his house singing a welcome to Queen Shabbat. Then he would welcome all his children and grandchildren, each of whom had a special glass for reciting the Kiddush, a blessing for the fruit of the vine. This was their introduction to wine and alcohol in general. Before the children could say it, Zaziu would say the prayer as the mothers held the glasses to their lips.

"We all gathered in Zaziu's home at each of the holidays, and he and the house looked, sang, and dressed differently for each occasion. On Passover, for the Seder, we were all there. But I sat next to him, my beloved Zaziu, and sang with him each of the melodies from the entire Haggadah. His eyes beamed with joy as we intoned and sang the old melodies with him or recited the Exodus from Egypt." Rita was raised to feel that she deserved the best things in life, and she enjoyed the preferential treatment Zaziu lavished on her. "I can still feel the specialness of being his chosen one, his lack of pretense at being fair. I knew very well that in a Chassidic home at Pesach — and all the time — the oldest and youngest male were supposed to play first fiddle. That my Zaziu preferred my mother and father to all his children and in-laws was so clear and not disguised that I felt fully entitled to be his favorite grandchild."

At Chanukah Zaziu told the grandchildren that if they looked at the candles long enough they could see the whole story of the Maccabees. He told this legend and others, and Rita could see all those events taking place right before her eyes. On Yom Kippur Rita and Nora would pick up their grandparents at the synagogue — "Not the big, fancy synagogue in Rădăuţi but the little Viznitzer shul." Zaziu always recited the last prayer of Yom Kippur, *Nilah*. "We would stand with an apple in our hands, waiting for his prayer to end and the shofar to blow before being permitted to bite into our apple after a twenty-four-hour fast. Grandfather, weakened by his day of fasting, would walk out erect, wait for his wife, Judith, to descend from the women's section of the shul, and then shake hands with everybody from the congregation, wishing them a happy new year. And we would stand by him, worried about his health and proud of his bearing. Grandfather Zaziu was the holidays, the religion, the wisdom, the background."

Rita visited Zaziu and Judith almost every day and kissed her grandfather's hand when she entered the house. Gentleness and dignity seemed to emanate from him until his last day in the camp at Mogilev. "He belonged to two worlds. With tolerance he belonged to his humble world of Rădăuți. When in this second world, the suffering world of belief, one could almost see in this tall, handsome man a royal pride. He read incessantly and would comment philosophically on all aspects of life. He was my real university. There was joy in his eyes when I understood something and a tolerant smile when I talked about my dolls and my goyische habits." Being Jewish in Rădăuți was easier than in the United States. Because the communities were so separate, Rita felt she was in a majority rather than a minority. "Our world was Jewish. Zaziu was the embodiment of what Jewish Rădăuți stood for: dedication to tradition, to life, and to the book." As her grandfather read the Talmud and its great yellow pages, Rita would ask, "Grandpa, when will you finish the book?" He would reply, "When I am on the last page I shall start again on the first page in order to understand better. I find something new each time I read it over."

Two independent memories of Zaziu were provided by a childhood friend from Rădăuți and a cousin. The friend, Burschi Schachter, a resident of Kibbutz Shamir in Haifa, said, "Shaje Wohl was a concept, not just a man." Burschi described the quiet tone of voice and wisdom with which Shaje Wohl spoke. "You can't imagine what kind of man he was and how he was respected."

Cousin Shilo remembered one occasion when Zaziu said to him, "You must go into town with me to see Berl Rath [the father of Mr. Stenzler's secretary and owner of a large store]. As they reached the man's store, Zaziu walked past it three times. Shilo asked him, "Why don't we just go in?" Zaziu explained to him that he was following his custom, as a very orthodox Jew, of showing respect for those he visited by giving Berl Rath time to put on his hat.

Once in the store, Zaziu told Berl Rath about a good Jewish man who was planning to give his daughter in marriage, but who needed help, meaning money. Rath unlocked his cash register, which was a safe, turned his back, and said to Zaziu, "Reb [a respectful form of address] Shaje, help yourself." Shilo was impressed by the powerful trust Rath had expressed, for he did not simply hand Zaziu a certain amount of money but assumed that Zaziu would know what was needed and take just that amount.

When Shilo asked Zaziu, "Why did you take me along?" the old man replied, "I wanted you to be a *schitov* in a mitzvah" [a partner

in a good deed]. He probably also wanted Shilo to benefit from the
example.

While Grandfather Wohl was a pious man, his son-in-law, Rita's
father, was not religious at all, and their home was quite relaxed.
When Zaziu visited, however, special care was taken. Even the maid
became an expert on Jewish law and knew that as a Christian she was
not permitted to touch the wine in Zaziu's presence. "It was a gentle
pantomime which nobody ever talked about or needed to explain.
My Zaziu never drank or ate anything in our home, since he knew
that although it was kosher, it was not *his* kind of kosher."

Rita remembers Grandmother Judith as tiny, submissive, very
hardworking, and supposedly meek. She had a great deal of energy,
but never spoke up in front of her husband, whom she adored. It was
her role to preserve the Jewish home. In her own subtle way, however,
she encouraged Rita's thirst for learning. Judith herself, in keeping
with her Chassidic orthodoxy, was not supposed to read, although
she did read the Jewish calendar and Sholem Aleichem stories, snick-
ering with pleasure as she went through them. Her marriage had
been arranged, and Judith had known nothing about her fiancé before
the wedding. Heavily veiled as she approached the *chuppah,* the Jewish
wedding canopy, Judith was not supposed to see the groom until the
completion of the ceremony. One of the women who led her said,
"He is very tall." That was all she knew about her groom until the
ceremony was over.

Each day Rita would find Judith, whom she called Baba, at
home, dressed in her wig and kerchief, her hair having been shaved
in the traditional Chassidic manner. Rita remembers her adoring eyes
and sense of fun. At mealtimes Judith never sat at the table but ate
at the stove while serving her husband and sons. But on the Sabbath
eve Judith was treated differently. "On Friday nights our hardworking, tiny grandmother was treated like a queen. She wore festive
clothes, lighted the candles with passion, and was treated with rev-
erence. Her role was to preserve a Jewish home, and Friday nights
she was a *balabuste* [lady of the house] who had prepared her family
and home for Queen Shabbat." The children saw the difference between the way Zaziu treated his wife on Friday nights and at other
times. "Everything was different on Friday nights. Gone were all the
squabbles, activities, and preoccupations of every day. Friday night
everything and everybody looked and felt different. Everybody, children and grandchildren, knew where they were going to be on Friday

night, and they knew how Friday night was going to be. There was a moratorium on all human unpleasantness. Security reigned and tenderness prevailed."

At Judith Wohl's funeral in Rădăuţi in 1939, Rita sat next to Zaziu in a horse-drawn carriage. He held her hand from the time they left home until the ceremony was over. "This was the first death I had known, my first encounter. We sat without words." In 1981, Rita discovered that the Wohl house was gone, and we could not find Judith's tombstone in the cemetery, as later we would not find Zaziu's in the mass grave in Mogilev Podolskiy. "But they were both imprinted in the memories and existence of their grandchildren and hopefully some of what they had stood for has been implanted into their great-grandchildren."

The Wohls and the Stenzler grandparents shared the same house. The Wohls apparently rented from the Stenzlers, who lived on the floor above them. Thus Rita's mother and father actually grew up in the same house. While the Wohls read and debated or slept, "the Stenzlers were early to bed and up at dawn to do a day's work." Shaje Wohl and "all of Rădăuţi used to say that his best real son was his son-in-law, Rita's father. Although his son Shaje had built houses for Shaje Wohl's sons, Chaskel Stenzler, Rita's paternal grandfather, treated Shaje Wohl, who was only two or three years his senior, with great respect. He addressed him as Reb Shaje, while Shaje Wohl called Chaskel Stenzler only by his first name.

Chaskel and Rosa Stenzler did not hold as great a place in Rita's life as Shaje and Judith Wohl. They were referred to as "the other ones," and she knew them less well. There was no pretense of equality. Once a week, dutifully, "after a stopover at Zaziu's," Rita visited the other ones. This was "a performance." They did not ask about school as Zaziu did. However, although the paternal grandparents did not have the same standing, no comparisons were made. "There was a place for everyone."

Both Rita's father and mother felt that they were "winners" among their respective brothers and sisters. Shaje Stenzler was the second son and third child in a family that, though not wealthy, was from "the right side of the street." Born in Rădăuţi on February 15, 1892, Shaje Stenzler was by far the most successful member of his family. His success appeared to come from several sources. He had style and a strong, vigorous appearance, especially when he was young. Among his four brothers and two sisters Shaje was the only one who made a good living. He was always burdened by responsibility for all his brothers and later for his brothers-in-law as well.

At the same time his two younger sisters, Minna and Schewa, were, in Rita's memory, "loving, tender, and motherly toward him." Shaje's older brother, Leon, was handsome and tall. "He had done a dashing stint in the armed forces of Austro-Hungary, a status which was an anomaly for Jewish young men in Rădăuți." Shaje bought Leon a print shop, Tipografia Stenzler. Everybody in town knew that the print shop belonged to Rita's father, and she was proud that the report card pages used at the school, which she never failed to point out to her classmates ("even though, because of my severe nearsightedness, I could really never read it myself"), carried the tiny credit PRINTED IN THE STENZLER PRINT SHOP. The perception of Shaje Stenzler as the most successful member and the leader of the family was enhanced by his conduct in Mogilev and lingered on even after he was blind and widowed in Israel.

The official German designation for the fathers of children from Jewish upper-middle-class families was Papa. "In our family this became *Papunzika*, an endearment which was not German, Romanian, or Yiddish, but imported from the Polish neighbors to the north. The termination *unzika* for males and *onzika* for females was a Slavic custom.

"I called my father Papunzika most of the time when I referred directly to him, but in my mind as a child and later on as an adult I called him Shajulica, his name, Shaje, with the Romanian diminutive *ulica* added. Romanian people add tender diminutives to names and people, blending their Latin origins with the warmth deriving from being so firmly embedded in Eastern Europe. I can still hear his chuckle when during his blind years I addressed him in this fashion." Rita's father was much more worldly than her mother. He read the newspaper daily — when he was blind it had to be read to him — and listened to the news, which did not exist for her mother. "She listened only to news about her children and their friends."

Shaje Stenzler had spent his youth as an apprentice in the textile industry in Vienna, which was his favorite city, and his tales about it have remained forever intertwined with Rita's own Viennese experiences. "I can never attend an opera performance at the Grand Opera House in Vienna without remembering my father's story about his last evening there before the Putsch [the Nazi takeover of Austria in 1938]. He was attending a performance of Rossini's *Barber of Seville* and had to catch a train that night to return home. As he walked into the foyer before the end of the opera, an old usher approached him and said, 'It is sinful not to hear an opera in this house to the end. God knows when you will hear an opera again.' My father, who was usually not obedient, went back to his seat. The usher had been right. It was the last opera he would ever hear in any opera house."

Rita's mother was born Helene Wohl in Rădăuți on June 8, 1894. Her birthday was celebrated both on June 8 and July 8. "I don't know exactly why there were two dates for her birthday, but since *Mutticuta* loved all good things, birthdays and parties, especially, we celebrated her two birthdays." *Mutti*, a diminutive of the German word *mutter*, is what upper-class and bourgeois German and Austrian children called their mothers. Some Jewish children who were raised by mothers educated in the Austro-Hungarian Empire called their mothers Mutti. To this Rita added the Romanian female diminutive *cuta*. "In my mind she always was and always will be Mutticuta."

Rita's mother was the second youngest of eight. For all practical purposes she was the only daughter, since her one sister, Ruchel, was very emancipated and left Rădăuți at the age of sixteen or seventeen, when Helene was only five. Ruchel did not like life there. Around the turn of the century, in a most unusual step for the time, she set off alone for New York to find adventure and a new life, breaking her father's heart. The family sat *shiva*, a period of ritual mourning, usually observed after someone dies, for her for one week and then declared her "nonexistent." Ruchel lived with a man named Silverman, a journalist, for a "trial period" of one year, after which they were married. Rita was curious about Tante Ruchel and asked her grandfather if she had died. He replied, "No, she's in that horrible country, the United States," a sentiment that Helene came to share for this and other reasons. Wanting to reestablish a connection and make peace with the family, Silverman corresponded with Helene, signing his name in big block letters. Helene, who was a prolific letter writer, sometimes wrote back. On four occasions the Silvermans sent tickets to Rita's mother to come to the United States, but each time she sent them back. "She could not bear the emotional hardship such a trip would have imposed on her parents, who had already lost one daughter." Rita came to think of her mother as the only daughter of her Wohl grandparents. Yet whenever Rita did something that "fell from the pattern" or brought her into disfavor, she was told that she looked like Tante Ruchel by her mother's friends. Tante Ruchel died in the 1940s, so Rita never knew her. The Silvermans had two children, whom Rita met once in New York when they were adults. She has not stayed in touch with them, even though she liked them and Mr. Silverman a great deal.

As the only remaining daughter, Rita's mother became even more special to her parents. She also helped look after her brothers, even though all but one was older than she. Helene had witnessed the anguish of her parents not only when they "lost" their other daughter and two sons immigrated to the United States, but more important, she shared their suffering when one by one each of their sons went off to World War I. Although they were all fortunate enough to return, Helene developed a lifelong hatred of war and a desire for daughters. She also explained that having six brothers and being the "only girl" made her feel that she had had enough of boys. Rita and Nora grew up with the sense that their mother never wanted sons, a great contrast with other mothers of the time. "That she was ecstatic about having us she never let us forget, from the day of our arrival till her death. She showed it through her smile, her words, her caresses, her gifts, her embraces, her letters, and her celebration of everything that had anything to do with us."

Mrs. Stenzler lived in the world of her children and her home. "The rest of the world was 'there,' on the outside. Mutticuta loved the world at large, but she knew it mostly from her books, dreams, and fantasies." Her books were German and she devoured classic German literature. She also loved music and knew a repertoire from Strauss, Kalman, and others, with all the words, which Rita, too, came to know by heart. "As my father's wife, Mutticuta lived an indulged life. She slept late, read half the night in bed, arranged beautiful big meals, went for walks — promenading — chatted with us and her friends, and always had maids to do the menial work."

Helene's feeling for children and continuing protective impulse toward Rita herself is captured in a letter she wrote in 1968 or 1969. She had just come across a letter of Rita's, written eight years earlier after the Rogerses brought their older children (Sheila had not been born) to visit their grandparents in Israel. "I still see in my mind the sweet tender face of this boy [their son, David. The incident she describes occurred when he was five] with his innocence as he held tightly on to my hand in the fish market as he saw how one kills a fish and cuts it into pieces. Then he broke one of the good glasses because the soda bottle in the refrigerator gave him so much joy that he continually pressed it. I was not at home when it happened, and when I got back he was brokenhearted and told me all about the accident and I laughed and comforted him. Little Judy [the Rogerses' second child] reminded you in October: 'Do you remember Dave got a spanking from Grandpapa for the broken glass?' 'God forbid,' Papa replied. 'Do you think I would have done that to my dear, sweet boy?' Until this day, Papa speaks about David's good-natured dear face. Even though he could no longer see during our last visit, and he only felt and touched him, it is possible for Papa, when he is very calm and very interested in the children, to know each one of their features. He defended himself and said, 'Maybe I told him not to open the refrigerator by himself.' Muttika [Here she calls Rita "little mother"], now that it's winter, do you still travel to Washington? I kiss you all. Mutti and Papa."

Logic and exactness did not burden Helene. She had a simple code: love and happiness should be indulged in and the rest avoided by all means. To her children their mother's world was a place meant to be enjoyed. "There were two kinds of people: those who loved her children and the others, who did not count. Her brown eyes were moist with joy and love whenever she looked at us — and she always looked at us. Whenever I see a baby or a toddler, and I get it to smile back at me, I feel the warmth of my mother's smile inside. It is there for good, for always and ever in all the smiles of young children."

Many years later, in Israel, Mrs. Stenzler would sometimes follow little girls on the street just because she enjoyed seeing them. There was something about her face, her smile, and the interest she conveyed to these little girls that fascinated them. She loved little girls, she told Rita, "because they remind me of you two, Nora and Rita." Mrs. Stenzler also loved the children's friends in Rădăuţi, and the house and yard was always full of them. She would fix huge trays of sandwiches, "gorgeously decorated, and serve us by the hour without ever complaining or counting. She never believed that one builds character through suffering."

Four weeks before her mother's death, Rita saw a lovely green dress "which looked like Mutticuta" in a Palos Verdes fashion shop. She bought it and a matching pin in the shape of a green parrot, sent it air mail, and Helene received it a week later. "After opening the package, she put it on, ran downstairs, and got a photographer to take her picture on Herzl Street, sent it to me air mail, and one week before her death I got this lovely picture of her in the dress I sent, looking twenty years younger than her seventy-five years." The picture still sits on Rita's desk.

In Rădăuți, Rita and Nora's parents set the example of what was good for children. If Mrs. Stenzler let her children go someplace, that was the thing to do. "She trusted us implicitly. Kids in school used to tell me when they wanted to go on an excursion. They would report that their parents had asked, 'What do Mr. and Mrs. Stenzler say? Can you go?' My mother was the authority. If I reported that she said we could go, then everybody could go." Yet Helene had a sharp sense of where danger lay, which became particularly evident in Mogilev. She was not without anxiety in Rădăuți, but she did not impose it on her children. "I remember when we went skiing or hiking, or on dangerous trips, she would never tell us she was worried. But when we got home she would say, 'The best moment of the whole trip is when you come back, because then I know you had fun and nothing happened to you.'"

Shaje Stenzler had had his eyes on Helene from childhood, but she favored another suitor, Summer Wolf, who was Shaje's best friend. Shaje, therefore, was constrained from pursuing her. Uncle Summer, the son of one of Judith's brothers and thereby a first cousin of Helene's, was an unsuitable partner according to Jewish law. Despite his concern, Zaziu seemed to approve the match, and it was expected that Summer would become Helene's husband. Early in World War I, when Helene was twenty, Summer was on the Russian front and entrusted Helene to Shaje. It was learned during the war that Summer had died in Russia. At that point Shaje, who also loved Helene but had deferred to Summer, asked Shaje Wohl for permission to marry Helene. Zaziu was delighted, as he was fond of Shaje Stenzler, approved of him as a son-in-law, and had been troubled by the genetic unsuitability of Summer.

After the war was over, it was learned that Summer Wolf had survived and he returned to Rădăuți. He had feigned death in order not to be taken prisoner on the battlefield and walked across Russia, including part of Siberia. By this time Rita's parents were betrothed and the engagement could not be ended, as in the Jewish religion an engagement is a promise, and promises cannot be broken. Summer moved to Bucharest but remained a beloved member of the family. As we shall see, he was to play an important part in its survival during World War II. When I asked her how her father and mother got along with each other, Rita once remarked, "He treated her very 'queenly,' in part because he had taken her away from his best friend, but more importantly because he loved her dearly, particularly all her weaknesses." She treated him with respect and devotion. "When he became blind she made him feel that she completely depended on him, including asking him daily for money. In his seventies, after her death, he confided to me, 'As long as your mother was alive I did not really know that I was blind.'"

Rita's parents and grandparents possessed many qualities that proved to be valuable in enabling the children and other members of the family to overcome the horrors of the war years. Rita has written of the "radiant humanliness" of her parents, which was more pronounced than ever during the deportation of the Jews of Rădăuţi, and the "resilience of mind over body" of Zaziu during the same time, "so that my belief in mankind was strengthened rather than shattered." Above all, there was the "nonegotistical way of loving" Rita's parents displayed in relation to each other and toward their children.

The way of loving that Rita describes is hard to define yet essential to the building of a sense of self in children. It is different from self-sacrifice, which is focused on the needs of the sacrificer and exacts a price from its beneficiary, restricting her through guilt and obligation. What Rita's parents illustrated is something different, an ability to take genuine pleasure in a child's realization and fulfillment of herself on her own terms, without the imposition of the parents' ambitions or needs, including the transmission of their private fears. This ability is vital in building a child's self-esteem. Moreover, as we will see in the pattern of Rita's life, it may provide a more important preparation for dealing with later challenges to survival than an emphasis on mastering various adversities in childhood and early adolescence.

In order to be able to ask Zaziu for Helene's hand, Mr. Stenzler had a house built in a comfortable section of Rădăuţi, near the center of town and his textile store. It was a large, single-story, painted wood and stone building, plaster-covered, and fronting directly on the street. Here Rita and her sister were born and lived throughout their childhood and adolescent years. There were summer and winter kitchens and a well-stocked wine cellar, a pantry, outhouses, a dining and family rooms, a spacious veranda, and a cozy children's room, the Kinderzimmer where Rita and Nora slept and lived. As there was no refrigeration, potatoes and other vegetables, fish and chicken, were stored in the cellar to keep them cool. The house was furnished with carpets and other fine things Mr. Stenzler brought back from his travels. There were chandeliers in the living rooms and the space-heating furnace in the main family room, which reached from floor to ceiling, was covered with tiles Shaje had brought from Czechoslovakia. Next to the house was the large garden where Rita played under the cherry tree.

Shaje Stenzler provided generously not only for his immediate family but for countless relatives who benefited from his largess when he returned from trips to Bucharest and other cities. "He was a giver, so it was understood that he would make arrangements for everyone, which helped to give me a feeling of leadership." So many holidays were celebrated that Rita could not always keep track of them. "Everything became a holiday, even small things. Everything became a big, wonderful event."

A sense of security derived from both the structure and order provided in the family and by the Jewish community of Rădăuţi. "Things were stratified and very clear. There was a great deal of respect for authority, and everybody's role was clearly emphasized. Adults were addressed in the German thou form, or the Romanian *dumneavoastră* (the thou voice)."

The sense of pattern and family closeness was strong at meal-times. "There was never a rush. In the United States children are rushed. Do this! Do that! We need to be here; we need to be there. There was no car waiting. There was no gasoline. I don't remember clocks in the house." In the morning they drank hot milk and chocolate while the rooms were getting warm. Then the girls each took two packages to school, one for *pauza mare* (the great recess), consisting of bread, butter, meat, and cheese, and the second, for *pauza mică* (the little recess), containing fruit and sweets. The main meal began at 1:00 P.M. and lasted until 3:00 P.M. It consisted of five courses: appetizer, *tuica* (a clear brandy, like slivovitz), soup, the meat course, and a compote for dessert. Wine was served regularly. After school, at about 5:00 P.M., there was bread and sweets, followed later by a very light supper. Considering the quantities of food the children were given, it would be difficult for a young girl to keep from becoming quite plump, which was considered a sign of well-being and good care. "I don't recall ever having heard the word "diet" in Rădăuţi.

"There was nothing perfunctory about the midday dinner. Father would come home around noon. He might pass through the kitchen with his hands up, as if this were a territory in which he had no jurisdiction. Two or three extra seats were always kept available at the table for unexpected guests who might arrive." It was also a time when friends and those who needed Mr. Stenzler's help or favors knew they could reach him. "There was never a question of how many people were coming for dinner." At the table Shaje was gallant, pulling out chairs for one or another of the women. The table was set with sparkling linens and silver and the various courses were served from many small glasses and dishes. "The whole atmosphere of the house conveyed the feeling that one would welcome guests and they, the guests, always came." Among the guests the children always felt that "ours were the most welcome ones." There was in the Stenzler household between the two world wars a "dedication to plentifulness" and a largehearted responsibility for other people.

3. Mogilev Podolskiy

"The journey from Rădăuţi to Mogilev is clouded in my memory," Rita wrote in 1981, six weeks after she had returned to Mogilev Podolskiy with her daughter, my son and me, traveling by train from Romania through Bessarabia. She had chosen a route that she thought followed the one the cattle train had traveled from Rădăuţi, through the border town of Siret, through Czernowitz, to Vinnitsa and the Ukraine. "Whether in 1941 we went from Rădăuţi to Mogilev via Siret I don't know. The train in which we traveled made no station stops and we, locked in the cattle cars, could not have seen them."

The Stenzler family was fortunate to have been in a car that, containing the last stragglers to be loaded, was less crowded than other cars, in which people suffocated to death. Some who were able to committed suicide. Ominous rumors spread among the occupants, "but we had no idea where we were going." The greatest fear was for the well-being of the two elderly grandfathers. Shaje Wohl, however, remained the calmest of all, praying continuously, seemingly unconcerned. His behavior and Shaje Stenzler's quiet authority had a stabilizing effect on the others.

Somewhere in Bessarabia the train stopped to let people go to outhouses. Local villagers tried to bring water to the cars, but the guards drove them away. During this stop a rumor spread among the passengers that the Germans would kill any Jew found with valuable possessions. Rita's father had brought along jewelry that he had put aside for his daughters. She remembers her father saying to her sister, "Norica, someday your husband will buy things like that," then throwing the jewelry into an outhouse. "We thought then that my father had thrown all the jewelry away. Many years later, when Mutti and Papa lived in Israel, my mother surfaced with a ruby ring for Nora and a jade ring for me." They had both belonged to Helene's mother and she had somehow managed to hide them on the train and throughout the war. Helene's ring has been passed on by Nora to her daughter, Michelle, "and I have added one in order to have a ring for each of my daughters, Judy and Sheila."

Mogilev Podolskiy is an industrial town on the east bank of the Dniester River in the southwestern Ukraine. Across the river to the west is Bessarabia, or what the Soviets now call the Moldavian Socialist Republic. The town sits on a narrow plain between steep, high bluffs carpeted with green meadows and dotted with houses that face one another across the river. Surrounding Mogilev is a fertile region with many fruit orchards. Beets, maize, potatoes, rice, barley, and other cereals are grown locally, and there are several sugar refineries in the town nearby. Granite is quarried in this region. A famous mineral spring flows not far from Mogilev Podolskiy; it was named Regina after a girl suffering from an abdominal illness who was said to have been cured by its healing powers. Well-known Ukrainian writers have come from this region, as, we heard, did one Voronovitsa Mojaisky, a famous inventor of flying machines.

After traveling for two days, the train suddenly stopped and let out all its passengers in Ataki, a town across the river from Mogilev. "The mud in Ataki and in Mogilev is the clearest memory of our arrival," Rita said. The family trudged through it in their heavy coats, carrying their few belongings with them.

Ataki was a town with a predominately Jewish population, and the Germans had just burned it to the ground. Still-smoldering fires created an eerie landscape, and the stench of corpses hung over the ruins of the town. On the white walls of several buildings Rita saw, written in blood, the words "We are the last of the tribe of Levi." According to a German report, 113 Jews had been "liquidated" for resisting "removal" to the ghetto in Mogilev Podolskiy.[1]

The German soldiers pushed the huge crowd of Jews from the Bukovina and other "undesirables" from the rest of Romania toward the river, where they were forced to stand, sinking into the deeper mud along the bank. There, the soldiers began to throw the Chassidic Jews, identifiable by their curling sideburns, or *payes*, and special garb into the river to drown. Terrified members of Rita's family formed a circle around the two grandfathers to protect them. Suddenly, in the midst of the pandemonium, Zaziu disappeared. "We were convinced he had been thrown in the river." But then a German officer came to the group and called out, "Family Stenzler, I have a message from the old man." The officer said that Zaziu had approached him and said he could not travel on the Sabbath — it was Friday evening before the first star — "so he asked me to take him across and I did." Zaziu, standing tall and upright, with his extraordinary dignity and authority in his voice, had evidently been able to persuade the German officer not only to take him across the river but also to tell the others what had happened. The Stenzler family was then taken across the river, which was swollen and very rough that night. "We found Zaziu sitting on a stone. Wearing his *tallis* [prayer shawl], he was praying as if nothing had happened." The family huddled together on the Mogilev side in the mud and rain until morning, while the others waited in Ataki. For Rita and Nora, seeing Zaziu "keep his priorities straight" before the enemy conveyed optimism and a sense that inner dignity could survive any outer circumstance. Her identification with Zaziu's compelling authority was an important source of strength for Rita in Mogilev and in all the years to follow.

While waiting with her family for the crossing of the Dniester, Rita had been searched by a German officer. "He found one illegal possession: a tiny baby doll with a pacifier. She was the youngest of my doll family. Though I was sixteen years old, I'd hidden her in my pocket — she was in a pillow, swaddled, as was the custom in that part of the world. When the officer found her he tossed her into the river. I don't remember whether I cried or not, but I know that even now I cherish my doll collection and get much joy from looking at them, arranging them according to how I am feeling."

Even while they waited in the mud of Ataki, Helene wished "to have a little sign from home. She had brought along doilies and a Dresden figurine and served us something to eat, filling up a doily. She made believe she was setting a table on a crate and placed as a centerpiece the tiny figurine she had managed to hide."

The largest number of Jews expelled by the Romanians from the

Bukovina and Bessarabia to the Ukraine was sent to Mogilev Podolskiy. In September 1943, more than 13,000 Jewish "refugees," mostly
Jews like the Stenzlers, evacuated from the Bukovina, were there.

Mogilev Podolskiy was a transition camp from which the prisoners were distributed to other places, most to extermination camps.
"Mogilev was never supposed to be a permanent camp. We were all
supposed to be dispersed. Trains were taking off to all the other
camps." Because the SS had planned it as a temporary dispersal site,
it had no camp buildings, no barracks with surrounding barbed wire.
It was organized as a kind of ghetto. When they arrived, the Stenzlers
and the other Romanian Jews, with some Ukrainian Jews who were
placed with them, were dispatched to existing buildings and open
areas in one section of the town and kept under guard by Romanian
and German soldiers who patrolled the streets.

Rita recalls that in the first months in Mogilev she and her
family were moved about a great deal. They were put in parks,
courtyards, and large public buildings — schools, cinemas, dance
halls, army barracks, and grain warehouses along the railroad. Sometimes as many as forty would be packed into a single room. The
population was moved about in large groups. "I remember the groups,
not the contact within them. I remember always the worry about the
grandfathers." Rita worried especially for her beloved Zaziu. "It was
always a matter of sheltering him and having him in our midst."

"The first winter of 1941–1942, when we were herded together,
was the coldest and the most bitter of all. In that winter people died
all around us from typhus and other diseases. There were corpses
lying on the streets." Fifty or more people died each day from typhus.
"Illness was very rare in my childhood. I was never in a hospital in
Rădăuţi. Illness invaded my consciousness only in Mogilev Podolskiy.
Typhus was endemic in the Ukraine, but it decimated us, the newly
arrived inmates of the camp. Since the disease was transmitted by
lice and we were new to lice and they to us, my memories of the
winters of 1942 and 1943 are memories of lice and corpses on
Poltavska Street [the street to which the Stenzlers were later moved].
I remember like today when Nora and I spotted a louse on Mutticuta's
forehead. We did not tell her about it, but for twenty-one days —
the incubation period for typhus — we tiptoed to her beside at night,
Nora and I bumping into each other, to watch for symptoms of
typhus."

Rita's cousin Buschku Rachmuth, a young physician, was also in the camp, and she and Nora consulted him when they were frightened that their mother would get typhus. Buschku came each day to look at her. "For most of the people around me, whom I had known in very different positions," Rita recalled, "there seemed to be no bearing of what they had done before on what they were doing in the camp. But I remember Buschku. I was very sick in the camp also. I had typhoid, not typhus. He came to treat me. At the beginning he had no medication. But he would make rounds and go to see everybody from Rădăuţi every morning." The example of Buschku's value in the camp, when so many others seemed to be helpless and unable to do anything useful, was one of the influences that led Rita to choose medicine as a career.

In the camp Zaziu seemed unconcerned, occupied with his religious rituals and a few books he had either brought on the train or obtained from Ukrainian Jews. "What happens here doesn't matter. It must have a rhyme or reason," he would say. Then Herman, his favorite son, "one of the most intellectual in the family," died of typhus a few months after their arrival in Mogilev. After Herman's death, Zaziu quoted a Hebrew saying, "A father is not supposed to survive the death of his son." He lost his desire to live after Herman died, and three weeks later Zaziu, too, was dead. As far as anyone could tell, he had not developed typhus. Perhaps, as Zaziu himself implied would happen, he died of a broken heart.

Despite this great loss, the family carried on. In this "abysmal freezing winter, crammed in a deserted, unheated movie house in Mogilev with all our campmates infested with lice and disease," said Rita, "there was a desire for survival and a conviction that one was entitled to survive." Rita had saved a small book about Nijinsky. She managed to get a candle and read by its light until the candle burned to the end. "I had learned by then the luxury of make-believe and refueling through fantasy. I think I walked through more Parisian streets during that bitter first winter in Mogilev than I ever walked through in Paris when I finally got there."

Anna Ornstein, now living in Cincinnati, has described how fantasy helped her to survive emotionally in a concentration camp to which she was taken from her home in Hungary. Each day, she was marched with other inmates from the camp at Parschnitz, in northern Czechoslovakia, to a train for the trip to a factory an hour away where they turned out copper parts for airplanes. On the way back she looked forward to a fantasy she savored during the march from the station to the camp.

In the center of the fantasy was a window that belonged to a small house in Parschnitz. I had become attached to the window and every night I was looking forward to seeing the house, to see "my window." The house faced the street that took us back to the camp. The window was set directly under the eaves of the roof. The roof came down in a sharp angle, common in one-family homes in Central Europe. The small room I imagined belonged to the window appeared to be snugly tucked under the roof. My attention was drawn to the window because of the curtains. The curtains were white and pulled to the sides, framing the window in the shape of a soft V. I had an elaborate fantasy about the room. It had a highly polished wooden floor with some simple homemade rugs. The narrow bed was directly under the eaves. It had clean sheets with the faint smell of soap, a pillow, a down cover. Next to the bed was the night table with a small lamp and books piled on it. A larger and much brighter lamp was on the writing desk that stood in front of the window. There was also a chest of drawers filled with clean underwear, warm sweaters, and socks. The wallpaper was also white and had tiny red, blue, and yellow flowers. In the spring I put geraniums in the window; in the winter, a small bird feeder was sitting on the windowsill.

I saved the fantasy for the march back to the camp, as if I could permit myself to enter the room only when my window came into sight. Putting myself into that warm little space made the labor of walking, in someone else's shoes, hungry and totally exhausted, just a little bit easier to bear. Once inside the camp, as we stood in line for the spoonful of thin soup, the fantasy died. It could not survive the pushing, the shoving, the noise, the hunger, and the cold. The next day, as if I were in love, I looked forward to seeing the window again.[2]

Each day at Mogilev Podolskiy, Jews were rounded up and "transports" were sent to "other places," usually death camps. "One would wake up in the morning and find a whole street gone." The Ukrainian Jews were particularly cruelly treated and rapidly disappeared. They were unprotected by the special relationship which the Romanian Jews could sometimes establish with the Romanian guards, especially by bribing them.

Despite the "Romanization" of the Transnistrian colonies, however, conditions were grim and remained so. "In the town of Mogilev," the historian Raul Hilberg reports, "crowded to the hilt, a Jewish leader wrote a frantic letter on January 6, 1942, to a Zionist officer in Geneva, stating that of 12,000 people, 5,000 were being fed in a public kitchen with a piece of bread, and that sixty were dying daily. Thousands of Mogilev Jews had typhus, and the mortality rate among the sick was 30 percent."[3] Nevertheless, conditions were better in Mogilev than in some of the other ghettos or camps in which Romanian Jews were interned. Hilberg describes, for instance, two concentration camps run by the Romanians in Transnistria: "Several thousand Jews were incarcerated in Picziora (Peciora), a place in which hunger raged to such an extent that inmates ate bark, leaves, grass, and dead human flesh. The other camp, Vapniarca, was reserved for about 1,000 to 1,400 Jewish political prisoners, many from Old Romania, as well as younger single people. Vapniarca was the site of a unique Romanian nutritional policy. The inmates were regularly fed 400 grams of a kind of chick-pea (*Tathyrus savitus*), which Soviet agriculturists had been giving to hogs, cooked in water and salt mixed with 200 grams of barley, to which was added a 20 percent filler of straw. No other diet was allowed. The result manifested itself in muscular cramps, uncertain gait, arterial spasms in the legs, paralysis, and incapacitation. About a third of the Jews died and most of the remainder were killed."[4]

Among the members of the Stenzler family, as with everyone in Mogilev, fear grew that they would be sent away. "Everyone was looking for a way to stay in Mogilev. Suddenly we heard that there was a foundry where they poured iron to make replacement parts for tanks and all kinds of things." Production at the foundry was organized by an engineer named Jaegendorf, described by Hilberg as "an energetic chief of the Jewish Colony."[5] Men who were successful in obtaining work in the foundry, including skilled engineers from the Romanian Jewish population, received a white arm band, which pronounced them "necessary for the Wehrmacht." Families of these workers were usually not sent to other camps. "I wanted to have that band on my arm. I looked around at my surviving grandfather, father, my mother and my sister. I considered myself the only one in my family capable of working in a foundry."

Rita tried to figure out how to become a foundry worker. Without telling her parents, she went to the man who ran the main factory. She lied about her age, telling him she was twenty-two when she was not yet seventeen. She said she had been a foundry worker for many years. He said, "Tomorrow morning we'll see. You'll show me what you know about foundry work." With the help of a Ukrainian boy, she then found the master foreman. "He was a huge old Ukrainian man with a big white mustache who looked exactly like a walrus." He had worked there for several decades and had little sympathy for the Germans. "I explained my desperate situation in a few Russian words and told him that the next morning I had to appear as a foundry worker." He responded with a conspiratorial smile and said he would teach her the trade in one night.

The foundry was closed at night. "He slipped me in. He was a man of very few words, but he showed me everything." At the foundry, workers made forms in sand into which molten iron was poured. Once the iron pieces had cooled, they were sent to another part of the factory for polishing. After showing her how to make the forms, the old master did one more thing. "He rubbed sand into my hands and under my fingernails so that I could present myself as a mere worker." The next morning she appeared for work, passed inspection, was hired and given the white arm band. She also received pants, made of potato sacks, to wear, one ruble (still the official currency in the Ukraine), and soup and bread every day.

When Rita returned to her parents twenty-four hours later, wearing her sackcloth pants, the story of what she had done came as a complete surprise. Thinking back on this episode, which probably saved her family from deportation and death, Rita observed that her initiative in becoming a foundry worker had motives other than obtaining the permit for the family to stay in Mogilev. "There was also the desire to again stand out in the community, since I would be the first girl to work in the foundry. It would make me again numero uno, as I had been in school. Much was also due to my age. I was a teenager and the foundry breakthrough was a way to be independent. I did not tell my parents until after I succeeded, a pattern I continued when I left Rădăuţi for Prague, Prague for Vienna, and Vienna for the United States. When I got married, I first did it and then told them." In a letter to Rita nine years later, written during the festive and joyful time that followed Nora's wedding in Haifa, Helene recalled "this lucky miracle" of "your being accepted to the *turnatorie*" (foundry).[6]

At times her adolescent bravado led Rita to take unwise risks. One day a high-ranking German officer inspected the foundry. As she was its only female worker, he stopped to ask her to show him her palms. By this time she was proud that her hands looked like those of a worker, rough and chapped, with broken fingernails. The officer was pleased and asked her to show him the products of her labors, the parts for tanks they were making. As he asked for this he said, *"Soll das werk den Meister loben"* (May this product praise the master), a verse from Schiller's poem "die Glocke." Impulsively she gave the next line of the poem, *"Doch der Segen kommt von oben"* (But the blessing comes from above). This was a dead giveaway, and he turned to the others and said, "This girl is no Ukrainian factory worker." Nothing came of the episode but, without any identifying documents, Rita, through her rash behavior, was jeopardizing the relative security she had so recently won for herself and her family. In this instance, and others that follow, we see a paradoxical side of Rita's nature. Her youthful determination and bold risk taking, so important to her survival and that of others in her community, seem at times to have been accompanied by an element of personal entitlement or even foolhardiness that could prove to be dangerous for family and friends.

There was a single toilet with a long urinal for all the foundry workers, and the introduction of a female presented a new problem. The morning after she started work, Rita went to the factory headquarters to speak with the chief engineer. "I told him there was no toilet. He said, 'There's a simple solution. You don't have to be a worker at all. You could be a girlfriend of one of the German officers, like the girls who work in the offices.'" Then she would be able to use the girls' bathroom that the secretaries used. "I said, 'That won't work.' He said, 'Definitely not?' I said, 'Definitely not,' and he handed me the key to the girls' bathroom." The Ukrainian workers applauded when she showed them the key, "because they knew about this dilemma. That was the first big victory."

"I started my smoking career in that foundry," Rita said. At the lunch break the Ukrainian workers stood around a stove to keep warm and to cook potatoes in the coals. The workers smoked *machorka*, a rough-cut tobacco that they rolled in coarse newspaper and lighted. "I remember it clearly. One of them — I can still see his cap — handed me a machorka cigarette and I lighted it on the stove. I hated smoking machorka, but it was the only way to get accepted as a worker among workers. I was a teenager. I wanted to show that I belonged. I remember the horrible taste, the feeling of nausea, the fumes of the foundry, the lice and dirt of the workers — I was dirty too. They accepted me from that day on."

Her initial inexperience in the foundry exposed Rita to certain hazards, especially in working around the molten iron. Once when pouring the iron into the molds she was not careful enough. The metal touched her sackcloth pants and they caught fire. The old Ukrainian who had taught her the work spotted what was happening, though she was far away. He ran over, threw her down, rolled her in the sand, and put out the fire. "That little incident was one of the things that was not reported at home." The apprehensive, then relieved, words and looks in the eyes of the workers told Rita that she had become one of them. She no longer needed to prove she belonged by smoking machorka. Eventually she became a skilled factory worker and received a sort of master certificate. She was even assigned a Ukrainian apprentice. "The boy's name was Kolja and I remember his respectful treatment of me. I was his boss."

Rita was the first girl to work in the foundry, but others soon followed. Not all had to perform hard labor as she did. Nora, who had dexterous hands with fine fingers, made cigarette lighters and small items out of aluminum. Others did office work.

Rita took part in small efforts of sabotage at the foundry, particularly by the Romanian workers. Jaegendorf had been trained in Düsseldorf, Germany. He was in charge of some of the technical aspects of the construction work at the foundry. Every now and then he would come by and say, "This is not going to be done" or "Slow down." Sometimes "we would destroy a few things." The engineer was selective. For example, the Germans were proud of a large bridge they were rebuilding across the Dniester after the retreating Russians had destroyed the original one. They planned a big dedication ceremony for the completed bridge. A huge plaque was commissioned at the foundry to commemorate the occasion. The plaque, with its inscription to the "Glorious German Army," became an important symbol for the prisoners working at the foundry. Each day Rita and the other laborers worked on it. But at the end of the day one letter was always erased or done wrong so that the plaque was never finished. When the bridge was completed and the dedication ceremony took place, the Germans proceeded without the plaque, which remained faulty and incomplete.

Rita's success in establishing herself as a worker in the foundry strengthened her family's chances of survival. But survival depended on a combination of elements, including a great deal of good fortune. During that first winter of 1941–1942, Rita's other grandfather,

Chaskel Stenzler, died of typhus. Each day people died in the streets of cold, starvation, and disease. Yet through all this her parents conveyed a feeling that the family would survive, was *meant* to survive. Helene strove "fiercely to develop a semblance of normalcy." She fixed meals from "nothing," and even "acted as if it were fun to be huddled together in huge halls with hundreds of people." She told her daughters constantly that "we will survive and we girls will have beautiful lives, including beautiful clothes." A deepening sense of closeness and "the shelter of togetherness" grew within the family. Even in Mogilev Rita felt a "protectiveness" around her. "My mother attempted to preserve for us whatever she could of the niceties of life. Mogilev catapulted forward her motherliness. She even understood my mixture of fear and excitement when looking at handsome German officers."

Mrs. Stenzler's protectiveness was sometimes direct and forceful. One day an order was issued in the camp that all Jewish girls and women between the ages of thirteen and thirty were to report to German military headquarters for a medical examination. Those who did not go would be shot. "My mother decreed, 'Nora and Rita are not going.' Everybody came to her and said, 'You'll get shot. Rita and Nora will be shot.' She repeated, 'Nora and Rita are not going.'" Rita and Nora did not go, but most of the rest of the young Jewish girls appeared for the examination, which proved to be a form of sexual abuse. Rita and Nora were shielded by their mother from the details of the examination. "What I picked up from the grapevine was that German uniformed men performed the so-called pelvic examinations with other men, probably officers, looking on. I remember outraged women telling my mother, 'You were so right. How did you know?' My mother replied, 'I did not know, but there are some things one does not do, no matter what the order is.'" Mrs. Stenzler conveyed an authority "that had a tremendous impact." As it turned out, Helene's instincts were correct. No one checked up on who had undergone the examination.

"In a way the camp magnified and accentuated all that was in us. First of all we all wanted to live. Then, too, our long-standing identification with Austro-Hungary and Paris had been a defense against being absorbed by the surrounding Slavic nations. In Mogilev, we were more in the East, so we felt superior to all those around us. There was the Ukrainian population whose living standard and style were twenty to thirty years behind ours. Then there were the Ukrainian Jews, who treated us with deference and respect. For them we

were Westerners and they longed for the West. Rădăuţi was transplanted to Mogilev. We, the community, were even more a 'we,'
with our code, our style, our beliefs, our prejudices, and our grandiosity. Somehow in the horror of the deportation my belief that I
was destined for success never disappeared. Indeed it became accentuated."

A very important element in the family's survival was the initiatives of Shaje Stenzler, which in turn grew out of the particular
circumstances of the camp at Mogilev Podolskiy and the special
situation of the Jews of Romania.

The alliance with the Antonescu government led the German
authorities to assign the day-to-day responsibility of the camp to
Romanian officials. Supervision by SS officers of the Jews in Mogilev
Podolskiy, Lucineti, and Sargorod in the Ukraine was less rigid than
in the concentration camps in Germany and Poland. Thus the possibility arose of bribing the Romanian administrators of the camp.
Furthermore, as a result of the fact that Jews in several parts of
Romania had not been deported, Shaje Stenzler had the opportunity
to establish contact with the Jewish community outside the camp,
which could provide backing and support. "We knew that there were
people who hadn't forgotten about us and who were behind us."

As Shaje Stenzler had been the leader of his community in
Rădăuţi, so was he in the camp. Not long after arriving in Mogilev
Podolskiy, he was able to establish contact with relatives in Bucharest.
Uncle Summer Wolf, Helene's first suitor, played a central role in a
secret rescue network that was established a few months after the
Jews of Bukovina had been taken to Mogilev Podolskiy. When a
cousin, Hershale Wohl, who was living in Bucharest, heard that his
parents, brother, grandfather, uncles and aunts, and the entire Jewish
community of Rădăuţi had been taken away, he hastened to inform
Uncle Summer, who was in the synagogue praying as it was a Friday
night. "When he told Uncle Summer what had happened, Uncle
Summer continued to pray and told him, 'We can't interrupt the
Sabbath, but tomorrow evening when the Sabbath is over, we will
see what we can do.' Hershale was furious, but Uncle Summer, true
to his word, never ceased helping us while we were in Mogilev."

Uncle Summer established contact with an Italian general, who
was paid generously with funds Mr. Stenzler held in Swiss and
American banks. "Would a German general have done it? We never
asked ourselves. For us, Italians, fascist regimes or not, were different

from Germans. They were Latins and spoke, behaved, and incorporated fascism through a different ethos than the Germans did.") This general came up the Dniester to an agreed-upon spot each month, from 1941 to 1944, until the Soviets liberated the camp. He brought medicine, including penicillin shortly after its discovery and sulfa drugs, money, food, and other necessities to Mogilev Podolskiy. At the camp the Ukrainian peasants had to be paid — "ten times the value of what was delivered" — so that the chain could be completed and a system for distributing the supplies established. Romanian officials in Bucharest and the Romanian camp administrators must have participated in the proceeds from this bribery, which Rita calls a "flexibility toward survival." The network depended on intricate linkages and exquisite timing. Rita suspects that other such arrangements were established in the camp but never knew of them explicitly. They depended above all on tight community cohesion and the scrupulous keeping of confidences.

Yet the ultimate survival of 300,000 Romanian Jews, both in Romania proper and in the camps and ghettos of Transnistria, may have hinged upon a German misjudgment, the overplaying of their hand with a Romanian administration that, until August 1942, had been all too willing to comply with killing off the Jews. German authorities had planned to remove the rest of the Jews of Romania to death camps beginning in September 1942. Marshal Antonescu had given his consent. But in late August 1942, Radu Lecca, Romanian general commissar for Jewish Questions, was given a snobbish brush-off in Berlin. This insult set in motion a sequence of events that resulted in a complete reversal of Romanian willingness to cooperate with the German extermination policy. As Hilberg writes, "Even a slight incident can be decisive in a situation that is already in delicate balance. By August 1942 the Romanians were no longer at the peak of their enthusiasm. They had just about exhausted their exuberance and were in turn exhausted by it. The Romanian receptivity to German demands for destructive action was at an end."[7]

When the Stenzler family arrived in Mogilev Podolskiy, the Ukrainian Jews shared their small amounts of grain and other food with the Romanians, who were starving. "When things started coming toward us from Bucharest, my father said to the community that everybody had to share with the Ukrainian Jews," who had no outside contacts or any means of receiving additional supplies. He insisted that since "they had been good to us, now that we are better off we must share what we have." Nevertheless, very few of the Ukrainian Jews survived. "Somehow they were always first on the transports. Of course the non-Jewish inhabitants of Mogilev knew their addresses and not ours. The few non-Jewish Ukrainians we dealt with were part of our network."

One Ukrainian Jewish girl, Ella Davidson, became a close friend of Rita's. She had been a medical student in Kiev and her father was a prominent Ukrainian Jew and leader of the Jewish community of Mogilev. She lived with her parents on Poltavska, the main street of the ghetto area. She was a lovely girl with whom each of Rita's male cousins in turn fell in love. "She went through the whole Wohl family." Ella was the Davidsons' only child. "When I met Ella's parents they were elderly and very poor, and her father presided over a frightened, demolished Jewish community."

It was forbidden to speak Russian in the camp, which provoked Rita's adolescent rebelliousness. A habitual student, she arranged for Ella to teach her Russian in exchange for her teaching Ella German. During the three years in the camp Rita secretly studied Russian. "Ella taught me Russian grammar and her love for the Russian language. It was an old-fashioned teaching method. Ella wrote out the words in longhand after I mastered the Russian alphabet. We had no books until I knew enough to read Pushkin. She had a book of Pushkin and I read it from cover to cover and then again. This is why for me Pushkin, Ella, and Russia are eternally interwoven." Rita also discovered in the camp a leftist professor from Bucharest who gave lessons in world history, also without books and at first only to her. "Later we added a strange group of students: professors of math and physics and an engineer, then several other inmates." The mathematics professor offered to teach his subject to Rita, but she was not interested.

As the Ukrainian Jews were always first on the transport list, it was important to find a way to protect Ella. By this time Rita was familiar with the hierarchy at the foundry and gradually worked her in, along with other friends she wanted to protect. After a while these female workers became "like a class of comrades."

Each morning Rita would go by Ella's place and they would walk to the foundry together. One day — there was a seal on the door and a notice saying, CLOSED BY THE OCCUPATION FORCES. Rita asked the non-Jewish Ukrainian children on the street, many of whom she had come to know, what had happened and was told that the remaining Ukrainian Jews had been taken out during the night for transport. She ran to the station and found the train still there. The Romanian and German soldiers guarding the train blocked her way. They said that only people bringing water were allowed through. Rita raced to the foundry and found Kolja, who managed to find a horse-drawn carriage with two huge containers of water, and the two of them returned to the station.

A Romanian guard let them through and they delivered water to the cars, opening each door and searching inside for Ella. "Suddenly there she was with her parents. She said, 'Don't try for my parents. Try just for me.' She sized up the situation. She knew I couldn't get her parents out. At that moment I said to myself, 'I couldn't have done that.' I remember both of her parents nodding their heads at me. So I ran out, dragging Ella at my side. There was a German officer, a guard, standing on the platform with some Romanian guards. He dragged me and Ella to the commanding officer on the platform. I told him, 'You have to let her out. He said, 'You know what will happen. She will become a prostitute.' She was a very beautiful girl. I said, 'No she won't. She will be with us.' Suddenly he said, 'Take her with you.' Ella and I ran out, leaving the water cart and my apprentice. By the time we got back to Poltavska the news had spread and the whole camp knew what had happened." A friend from Czernowitz said to Rita, "This was your real day," and squeezed her hand tightly.

Ella, hidden when the guards came by to check, stayed with the Stenzlers in their small hut until the camp was liberated. After the war Rita and Ella corresponded until 1953, when Rita wrote her from Vienna that she was going to the United States. After this Ella wrote, "This will be the last letter that we will write to each other." Ella married ("We don't know what her name is") and became a physician in Moscow. "She was a kind of sunshine of the whole story."

Rita has never known exactly how it came about, but late in 1942 some of the surviving Jewish families were billeted among a number of primitive huts on muddy lanes and narrow streets near the Dniester. These streets generally led down to the river from Poltavska Street, which ran parallel to it. Mr. Stenzler made "a very special deal" with a Ukrainian couple, Olya and Bronislav, so that the family had a small room in the back of their hut in which they lived for the remainder of their captivity. "Everybody whom I knew before, our

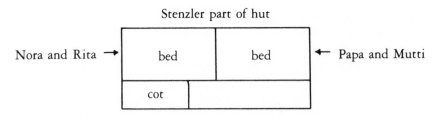

people, were in these houses. It wasn't haphazard. Such a big group could not have suddenly been distributed ¹in little houses and spread out like that in the local population without somebody from the camp administration having been bribed. We weren't ever only four in that room, because there was always somebody coming, somebody who had to be sheltered, somebody like Ella who had to be hidden."

Helene's brother Moishe developed lung cancer and came to stay in their small room. "Whenever the German officers would come to search my mother used to push Uncle Moishe, who was her beloved brother, and the two of us below." Moishe had to be lowered through a trap door into a cellar space. He and the girls were considered particularly vulnerable. The Germans would beat up and sometimes shoot prisoners found to be sickly. At other times, especially when the German armies were retreating, the whole family had to be hidden in the cellar. When they were down there, Olya "would play the dumb one" and say, "There's nobody here." Moishe eventually died in the hut of terrible complications of the lung cancer.

There was barely room for two beds and a cot in the Stenzler part of the hut. Rita and Nora slept in one bed and their parents in the other. When Uncle Moishe was with them, he slept on one of the beds, Nora moved to the cot, and Rita and Ella slept on the floor. The room was lit by a gas lamp and candles. "I don't remember getting on each other's nerves, but then I was out of the house, in the factory or at the Dniester or even in Ukrainian houses — we were not supposed to go to them." There was also a lot of moving around by family members to gather the necessities of life: cutting wood, getting food, and washing at the Dniester River. "The Dniester was for us a connecting link to the other world. It was the border of what was still Romania; it was flowing free; it connected us with other bodies of water."

The river was also the place to wash and do laundry. In the summer everything and everyone was washed in the river. In winter, parts of it froze and people washed in the hut. This was a major enterprise, complicated, sparse, and inefficient. There was an outhouse but no running water. "I remember Papa and Bronislav bringing water from I don't know where. When Nora and I washed ourselves, Mother created privacy for us, with herself and Papa standing outside in the bitter Ukrainian frost. Our first, coldest winter, when we still lived by the railroad houses and shared one room with several families and Zaziu, Mother organized shifts so that Nora and I could wash in privacy. She brought in melted snow in a sort of washbasin — I don't know where she got it. I also remember taking down hard, frozen laundry from outside." Washing oneself and laundry was a matter of survival to prevent typhus. "When I came home from the factory later on, my clothes were inspected and cleaned carefully." The Ukrainian workers were infested with lice during the winter, but they apparently had developed an immunity against *Rickettsia prowazeki*, the typhus organism.

Books were the most precious possession. Some families had apparently slipped out one or two cherished ones, which they circulated. "The professor of world history from Bucharest had brought only books, his most precious possessions. I read incessantly: Romain Roland, Lion Feuchtwanger, and Upton Sinclair, among others. I read better books in Mogilev than in Rădăuţi. In Mogilev, the longing for Rădăuţi was deeply intertwined with the longing for the world out there from which we had been excised like a malignant growth. We had no identity papers, no documents, no residence, no belongings. Our only identification was the yellow star pinned to the left side of our chests." When Helene pinned the star on Rita and Nora, however, it was "with such loving devotion that I never associated wearing it with the ostracism and insult it was meant to evoke."

When we returned to Mogilev in 1981, we learned that Olya and Bronislav had two daughters. Only then did Rita understand "why Olya was so loving to Nora and me. We were her substitute girls. We probably were not told about her daughters because they had retreated with the Soviet army, and this endangered Olya and Bronislav."

Although Mr. Stenzler paid Olya and Bronislav to house and hide his family, the money became a secondary consideration. "We treated them like our family. They were very sweet people," Rita said. Such relationships were, needless to say, exceedingly rare. During our visit Olya said, "These were some of my most wonderful years, when I had you here in my house." To Olya and Bronislav, "we were such big-city people, such a new world for them, from the West. She still did not believe we were from a small city. She kept saying we were from Bucharest. Though they were the owners and took us in, my mother and father spoke with them in a tone they had used at home with servants — definite, kind, but with no question of who was the boss."

Bronislav was a good and gentle man who had lost an arm in a factory accident. He and Shaje Stenzler got along very well. "Bronislav used to appear in the doorway each morning like the people who used to work for my father in Rădăuţi. He would say, 'Mr. Stenzler, what are we going to do today?'" Together they would check on who had been taken away during the night and distribute medicine, food, and other supplies among the inmates. Meanwhile, Helene and Olya did housework, cooked, and baked together. Olya learned how to cook Jewish specialties from Mrs. Stenzler and loved to hear stories about Romania. "My mother and Olya were from different worlds, but they loved each other."

Order, routine, and a regular life gradually were established at Olya and Bronislav's. "People started coming to the crowded hut, which became a gathering place for young people. Olya loved that, especially when mother's specialties were being cooked. She used to say, 'I like the smell. My house smells nicer now.'" Also at Olya's, "birthdays, half birthdays, and memories of birthdays were celebrated." Rita and Nora went to work each day. Also, even though all its inmates were poor, beggars came to Olya's house and Helene fed them what she had. Some of them also carried lice, which created a special dilemma for Rita and Nora. "We knew we had to respect the elderly — the beggars all were — but at the same time we were trembling for Mutticuta's life." Meanwhile the fear was ever present that the Germans, who continued to remove people to the death camps, would take them away.

✳

Rita's reunion with Olya was moving and dramatic. She had been reluctant to return to Mogilev and anxious about the memories that would be revived. Her daughter and my son and I urged her to go. We arrived with our Ukrainian Intourist guide at the outskirts of the town on a drizzly July afternoon. Rita recognized nothing, as she did not know the outer edge of Mogilev Podolskiy. We spotted a peasant woman. Because she looked so old, Rita thought she might remember the camp and asked our guide to stop the car so she could speak with her. The woman said she used to live on Poltavska Street and offered to take us there, but the guide refused, concerned perhaps that allowing a local resident in the car would break a rule.

Rita was terribly frustrated as we drove on. "There was something about the old lady's face which brought back memories. I didn't remember Olya, I must confess. I never talked to my sister about her or to my mother. Not that we talked much about Mogilev or the whole chapter of Mogilev. And then when this woman talked, and when we talked to her, and she said Poltavska, the warmth which emanated from her was the same as Olya's. But still I didn't think of Olya." As we moved on, nothing looked familiar. Then Rita recognized a courtyard and a yellow school where cousins and friends had been housed. We walked around the courtyard, but it still seemed vague to her. After some searching we discovered the foundry, which we learned had been enlarged in 1960.

Somehow we came upon Poltavska Street, unpaved still and muddy as it had been in 1944. We wandered down a lane toward the Dniester, which seemed familiar to Rita. She walked with the guide, Anatol, while Ken, Sheila, and I walked ahead. "I saw the little house that I had lived in for two years." Anatol was afraid to go in. Perhaps there would be a dog, as is likely in peasant cottages, or nobody at home. They rang and a woman in her fifties stepped out. Anatol said, "I have this American tourist who was here during the war." She said, "Yes, yes, my mother always tells me stories about this family." Then she ran back and brought out her mother, who had heard the voices. Olya saw Rita and said, immediately, only, "*Vi Rita ili Nora?*" (Are you Rita or Nora?) Thirty-seven years had not dimmed *her* memory.

Anatol was deeply affected and did not want to leave, but Rita sent him off to fetch the rest of us. We arrived in time to witness some of the emotional reunion. We were all invited in. There was barely room for the seven of us in this tiny hut, warmly decorated with carpet wall hangings. Still not believing her eyes, Olya got up several times during the conversation and embraced Rita lovingly. Rita and Olya talked animatedly. Olya's eyes sparkled with warmth. There was much catching up to do. News of Nora, of families and children, was exchanged. Olya said, "Not a day goes by without my remembering your mama and papa and Nora and you." Yet Rita had not consciously remembered Olya, even as we walked up to the hut, "until the moment she stood in front of my eyes." Bronislav had died several years before. Rita was chided for not having written. The younger woman was one of Olya's daughters. Rita, Olya said, was always on the go and would not sit still. "We never knew what you were up to next," she said. Nora was quiet and nice and "stayed put." Olya asked about a handsome blond boyfriend of Nora's.

It is still somewhat puzzling why Rita had not remembered Olya or Bronislav between 1944 and 1981, inasmuch as the relationship with this kindly Ukrainian couple had been so important to the family's life and survival. The reason most likely lies in the pain of the Mogilev years in general, with which Olya and Bronislav, in spite of their goodness, became associated. More specifically, I suspect that this repression on Rita's part came about as a result of the sad and traumatic events that were still to come.

Among those interned in Mogilev, the situation of the Stenzler family, especially after they went to live at Olya and Bronislav's, was unusual in several respects. Because they were the ones receiving medicine, food, and money from outside, some of their Rădăuţi prestige was reestablished. The loving relationship that grew between the Stenzlers and Olya and Bronislav was also most unusual. The Ukrainians, who were fiercely anti-Soviet, had initially welcomed the German invaders and wished to get on well with them. They were also generally anti-Semitic. Rita was the only teenager in the ghetto to develop meaningful friendships with non-Jewish boys and girls in the Ukrainian community. "The rest of the Jewish community did not have contact with the local people. They had *never* had much contact with non-Jews." Most other Jewish teenagers did not go out of the ghetto as did Rita, and to a lesser extent Nora, after they went to live at Olya and Bronislav's.

Rita and Nora began to supplement their food from other sources. "I stole. Nora did not steal. She remained proper but accepted what I stole." In summer Rita, with her Ukrainian friends, stole peaches and plums and any food they could find. "We helped ourselves very generously to whatever was growing."

Mrs. Stenzler continued to do everything she could to preserve a feeling of normal life in the camp. Rita remembers a time when two Jewish boys were visiting at Olya's hut. "My mother served a tray of something she made look like finger sandwiches. She was trying to preserve the Rădăuţi atmosphere in the misery of Mogilev. It is because of her that Nora and I have carried Rădăuţi with us wherever we went: to Prague, Vienna, Curaçao [where Nora now lives], Albany, Atlanta, and finally to Palos Verdes Estates in California.

"The moment we moved into the hut near Poltavska, my mother insisted we should again have a social life as at home. She encouraged people to come to the hut." Rita became acquainted with the Ukrainian families on the street. She would "slip into" their homes. Rita met Sergei, nicknamed Seryoza, the son of a schoolteacher, and a friend of his, Tolya, while stealing apples from Seryoza's family's orchard. "I remember the first time I went to Seryoza's home. I enjoyed going there tremendously because it was an unbroken household — these people had lived there all their lives. There was a lot of cooking and baking and the smell of food, like at home. I had fun, and I came back and told my mother and she said, 'It's very close by. You could go there every day.' She didn't check out these people or ask, 'What are they going to do to you?' She wanted me to enjoy the life of a normal household, which Seryoza's family had."

Seryoza was very fond of Rita, but she only "tolerated him a little bit." She preferred his friend Tolya Subotenko, who was over six feet tall. "He had black hair, with gorgeous blue eyes and wore a Ukrainian *rubashka* [shirt] and boots, all black like his hair. He walked erect, with pride. He also looked different, alien — not like all my cousins and friends from Rădăuţi." Tolya was from a solid Ukrainian family. His father had been executed by Stalin's hangmen during the purges of the 1930s, and he was very much against the Soviet regime. Rita loved to look at Tolya. "He was gorgeous." Sergei was gentle and shy and stuttered a little. Tolya was a very proper boy and had a special way of knocking when he came by the hut. "His manner was grand, and anybody, at least any teenager, who had read *Anna Karenina* or *War and Peace* could easily transform him into a hero of Czarist Russia."

Rita credits her mother with the idea of swimming in the Dniester, which was "one of the illegal things that the youngsters engaged in. She told us that it must be nice to go to the river." The Dniester was especially beautiful in springtime, when the ice was melting and the countryside glowed green and gold in the sunlight. "We loved that river. In the summer, which was very warm, the river became our life." Rita and Nora started "this river business," and other Jewish teenagers from the ghetto followed. The girls had bathing suits made out of towels and slipped down to the river through the yards of the huts near its banks. Helene got towels from Olya and made the suits for Rita and Nora, who swam and sunned themselves along the riverbank, trying to get tanned. The strong swimmers among the boys in the ghetto would swim across the river to beg, trade small things for, or steal cigarettes from the peasants on the other side.

Rita's most direct contact with her German captors took place at the river, where the German officers and soldiers also came to swim. One day she was there with two or three girls from the camp. "Two Germans in bathing suits — I don't know if they were soldiers or officers — came over to join us. We chatted with them. They were very handsome and they were very nice. Suddenly I looked up and saw my mother standing there." Adults were not permitted to go to the river, but she had apparently followed the girls. "She heard me talk with the German officers — kind of flirtatious talk because I didn't know she was there. She turned around and started to walk back to the street. I ran after her and said, 'Muttika, you are angry?' She said, 'No, you are having such a good time. How can I be angry?' She enjoyed seeing us have a normal time. She probably had a fear of what might happen to us, but when she had been there and saw we were having a pleasant time she would not deprive us." When Rita came home Helene said, "They like you, and you are a teenager and it is nice to be liked. I just had to see them." She did not offer "an ounce of advice."

Another day while Rita was swimming with several friends they saw, on the Ataki side, soldiers with guns, which they thought were aimed at them. The others were scared and dispersed rapidly, ducking under the water and swimming to shore. Rita was in the water close to the bridge. Not a strong swimmer, she had apparently become separated from the other boys and girls and was caught in the swirling current caused by pieces of debris near the bridge. She could not keep her head up; water filled her lungs, and she began to lose consciousness. "My last thoughts were, 'What will they say?' and 'It can't possibly be that this is the end.' I had such optimism for my future and my life."

When Rita next opened her eyes she was on the beach very close to the bridge. A German officer, dripping wet, in full uniform ("I don't know what his rank was"), was standing over her. He had been on guard and, seeing a girl drowning, jumped in. "I had very long hair, pigtails down to my knees. He had pulled me out by the hair, turned me over, and gotten the water out of me. He said to me in German, *'Mein Fräulein, wohin kann ich sie fuhren?'* [Miss, where can I escort you?], and I said, 'To the ghetto.' He quickly disappeared and that was the last I saw of him," Rita slowly regained full consciousness and saw around her not only those from her own street but most of the people from the Poltavska ghetto. One of them took Rita back to the hut. The other teenagers had reached shore safely and gone home on their own.

Rita's family did not know what had happened to her. When she told the story, no one scolded her. Her father said, "I'm going to find that German officer who rescued my daughter." The whole community tried to talk him out of it. People came into the room and said things like "Mr. Stenzler, it's going to be terrible. This man was just fulfilling his duty. He was an officer who stood guard and saw somebody drowning. He was trained to rescue, so he rescued." "My father said, 'Anybody who saved my daughter's life — I'm not going to owe this without giving a reward.'" Mr. Stenzler still had a gold watch that had belonged to his father, his last possession from home. "He inquired and bribed Ukrainians until he found the German officer and gave him the gold watch."

On another occasion Rita's adventurousness, the sense she drew from her parents that she was "entitled to have fun," seriously jeopardized her family and community. Although no one from the ghetto was allowed in the street after dark, one evening in the third year of their internment, Rita decided to go to the movies. "I had by then lots of Ukrainian girlfriends. I hadn't been to the movies since 1941." Without telling her parents, she slipped out of the ghetto with her friends. "I don't remember what film it was." Suddenly there was an interruption. Perhaps the film had broken and had to be rewound. "We went into the hall where music was playing. The boys came over and asked the girls to dance. Then we were asked back again to see the rest of the movie. It was a very exciting thing. It was a beautiful evening. I was euphoric. It was a big event."

On the way back, Rita was walking with nine or ten girls, holding on to one another's hands and arms, "the way one walks in Eastern Europe." A Romanian patrol stopped the group and asked for documents, flashing a light in each of the girl's faces. "Of course,

I had no documents whatsoever." Just before it was Rita's turn, one of the girls put a dark piece of paper in her hand. "So I showed hers. I don't know if I looked like her or not, but they gave it back to me. She said she didn't have one, so they went to her home where she could be identified." When Rita arrived at home the community was out in the street, as they feared something horrible had happened. "My father said, 'You exposed yourself and us, but ten innocent people from our community could have been shot' [the penalty used for the transgression of one Jew]. Everyone moved away silently." Shaje never said, or had to say, anything further, "but I shall never forget his expression when he said 'ten innocent people from our community could have been shot.'"

The Jews in Mogilev had no newspapers or radios and lived by rumor. Rita craved information about the outside world. The inmates heard frightening rumors about the death camps but had little reliable information. There were often rumors that the Jews were going to be repatriated. "We knew that there was a big Jewish community left in Romania who hadn't forgotten about us, who were behind us. In the camp I had the feeling that there were some smart people — I don't know who they were — who started those rumors whenever the community felt despair." Rita refers to such people as "psychological timers" who felt that the community needed something to boost morale. Someone might even claim he or she had seen the order for repatriation on the *commandatura's* desk. There were people "whom we called *postkisteln,* or 'little mail box,' who could be counted on to transmit gossip and rumors through the camp.

"One question we continually asked ourselves was: What is the rest of the world — the decent governments of the world — doing for us?" One day during the winter of 1942–1943, it was learned that the Pope was sending a representative, a nuncio, to inspect the camp. He was coming to the foundry, where each worker was to be given a special meal. "I will never forget. In the morning one could already smell the aroma of the good food. Every worker was given a blanket. We were looking forward to the visit because of the good meal and somebody from the outside world coming. Then the nuncio arrived and we were all put in the courtyard. He started blessing us and making the sign of the cross, which none of us made. (We had grown up to regard the cross as an original source of the Jewish tragedy). We had appointed someone to talk to him, but the nuncio refused. Perhaps the Germans told him not to. Then he left, the blankets were collected before he was out of the gate, and that delicious meal which was supposed to be given to us — I don't know where it went. We got our same old soup. We were furious and more depressed. That was one of the lowest points. We felt that the rest of the world was paying no attention." The period after the nuncio's visit was one of the times when a rumor of imminent repatriation was started.

"The second thing we were depressed about was the Americans. The United States was for us the country where everything was possible. We constantly asked, 'What is the U.S.A. doing for us in Europe?' We were waiting for the Americans to join the war in Europe." Communists in the carpentry shop at the foundry had a radio set of sorts through which they established contact outside the camp. "They kept saying, 'The Americans have not joined the war.' They kept telling us, 'The Americans are just sitting by.' They rubbed it in." The Stenzlers, of course, had a number of relatives in America. It was especially disheartening that this rich and powerful country, with its large, free Jewish community, seemed to be doing nothing for the prisoners in Europe. The Jews of Mogilev felt altogether abandoned by the rest of the world.

By the time the Americans landed at Normandy on June 6, 1944, the Mogilev Podolskiy camp had been liberated by the partisans, Soviet loyalists, including former soldiers, who were left behind the lines as the Russian armies retreated to the east. Dressed in civilian clothes, they formed a kind of underground, scattered about and hidden by the local communities. They were inactive while the Germans were in control, but as the Germans retreated the partisans took charge in some locations, including Mogilev, before the Soviet troops arrived.

One of the partisans was hidden right in the camp. A tall, burly Russian, he was declared to be the "boyfriend" of "Miss" Harnik, a tiny, disfigured elderly spinster from Czernowitz who looked, according to Rita, like a dwarf or gnome. They were a most unlikely couple. "We wondered, 'How come this little creature is with this man?'" Miss Harnik had been a teacher and continued to teach French in the camp without pay. "She almost bribed several of us girls to learn French from her." The girls took the lessons so they could sneak into Miss Harnik's place and see the Russian partisan. "We were told never to mention him to anybody. We loved that. We were spellbound by this man, his deep voice and the mystery about him."

The partisan sent the girls on missions. These were simple at first, but in the winter of 1943 he offered to exchange boots for old shoes and house slippers. This was a difficult assignment, for nobody in the camp had shoes. "It took us naive girls quite a while to figure out that the shoes were needed for partisans, to avoid leaving tracks of boots in the snow, and that Miss Harnik's 'boyfriend' was not a boyfriend at all but one of the partisans who were fighting in the Ukraine against Hitler." The partisan tried to teach the girls Marxism. The "Miss Harnik episode" was Rita's most romantic encounter with communism.

In the winter of 1943–1944, messages began to reach the camp about the success of the Red Army. "One day a foundry worker, a Communist, whispered to us, while standing for roll call, that he had heard that the tide of war had changed for the USSR. This was the first time we heard that Hitler could be stopped. The thrill of this news, which none of us truly believed, was beyond description."

In March 1944, the inmates of the camp began to see German soldiers and officers, and representatives of the other nationalities who had been their collaborators, retreating to the west before the advancing Soviet army. Some passed right along Poltavska Street. "It was like a parade of the nations which composed the Soviet Union. There were Cossacks, led by General Vlasov, a German collaborator, Georgians and Tatars, Ukrainians and Romanians, all fleeing across the Dniester, many in full national costume, trying to cross the one bridge in Mogilev."

In early April of 1944 there came a brief time during the German retreat when the partisans were in control but the Soviet troops had not yet arrived. One evening two very young German officers, perhaps nineteen or twenty, in full uniform, came to the hut and "notified us they were going to spend the night there." They were planning to cross the bridge in the morning. Olya and Helene let them in, of course, "for they were the bosses still." Rita and Nora were sent to the cellar, as they always were when Germans entered the hut. The officers, both from Frankfurt, were happy to discover educated German-speaking people there. "We seemed to them from their world. They felt at home with us. I remember they had a big discussion about literature with my mother, who was happy to talk with them about these things. One of them asked her for a manicure set because he wanted to fix his fingernails. They were retreating officers, coming back from the war, but they were still officers."

In the middle of the night there was a series of explosions. Rita and Nora came up from the cellar to see the Dniester bridge flying into the air, blown up by the partisans who wanted to prevent the Germans from crossing the river before the Soviet troops arrived. "Suddenly these two officers, who had come to us in their German uniforms, and whom we treated respectfully because we were afraid of them, were transformed before our eyes from victors into helpless, frightened boys. Their shoulders became stooped. I remember the tears rolling down the cheeks of one of them." They knew they faced virtually certain capture and death.

Rita's father said, "Bronislav, we need some civilian clothes for these two boys." Bronislav objected. "'Mr. Stenzler, what do you mean? Are we going to help these Germans?' My father said to him, 'Bronislav, it is very simple. Just imagine that you and I are they.'" Bronislav and Shaje found some civilian pants and shirts, and the two officers changed into them. The uniforms were burned and "Bronislav and my father walked down with the two of them through the streets and backyards down to the Dniester, to the narrowest part of the river, where they had the best chance to swim across, the same place where the Italian general used to land to bring us supplies." Bronislav and Shaje had gained a lot of experience with the currents and other characteristics of the river in their meetings with the Italian officer. Rita never learned if the young officers made it across or not, but "they were not let out of our place in uniform to be massacred in the street."

After the destruction of the bridge, the German troops still east of the river had no way to escape to the west. Red Army contingents were on the way. The Ukrainian population was terrified of what the Russians would do to them. They were fiercely nationalistic and right up to the start of the war had opposed the inclusion of their region in the Russian Soviet empire. Stalin's confiscation of Ukrainian land, and the murder of Ukrainian peasants who resisted his collectivization policies, increased the hatred of the Soviet regime in the Ukraine. When Germany invaded in 1941, the Ukrainian troops deserted the Soviet army en masse. The non-Jewish Ukrainian population was largely on the German side during the occupation and collaborated with the invaders. (Olya and Bronislav's situation was unique because of their personal attachment to the Stenzlers.) On the whole, the Germans had not bothered the Ukrainians. Now the Ukrainians feared, with justification, the revenge of the returning Soviet army.

To placate their guilty consciences and persuade the returning Soviets of their intense allegiance, the Ukrainians began to slaughter the Germans trapped in Mogilev and disarmed by the partisans. For three days — until the Soviet troops arrived — the Ukrainian population, overwhelmed with fear, brought out knives and hatchets and massacred the German soldiers and officers who were caught among them. Rita and Nora watched terrible scenes. Not only did the Ukrainians kill German soldiers and officers, but they murdered their horses, cutting their throats. "I remember the slaughtered horses lying in puddles of blood. Mother and Father kept us in the hut, where Olya and Bronislav kept vigil with us. Martin Ruckenstein, Nora's boyfriend, and Bubi Friedman, my so-called boyfriend, were in our hut, I don't know whether for our or their protection. Mother stood by the door of the hut, as if to keep evil out and us in." Yet, "in all this pandemonium, and the exhibitionistic display of hostility, the Jews held back, frightened of what would happen. No Jew in the whole camp attacked the Germans."

The Ukrainians' fear of Soviet vengeance proved well founded. When the Russian troops liberated Mogilev Podolskiy they formed what was called the *Ukrainski Strafni* Battalion, or Ukrainian Punishment Battalion — punishment for the massive desertions from the Soviet army at the beginning of the war. All Ukrainian men between eighteen and fifty were placed — without training, uniforms, or weapons — in the Strafni Battalion and sent ahead to be mowed down in the next encounter with the retreating German army. Rita's friends Tolya and Seryoza were among the young boys who were rounded up as cannon fodder for the Ukrainski Strafni Battalion. "They were children, probably fifteen or sixteen, when the war started" and could not, of course, have deserted. The Russians did not make that distinction.

Ella and Seryoza announced the arrival of the Red Army to the Stenzler family. Ella, who had been raised under the Soviet regime, retained an allegiance to it. Ecstatic that the Russians were returning, she put on the fanciest clothes she could find. She found a large loaf of black bread and a shaker of salt and took them to the outskirts of the city to greet the Russian soldiers with the traditional Ukrainian welcome. "We went nowhere." Seryoza's announcement was different. There was a clock on the wall in the hut. He came in and said, "Mr. Stenzler, you have to turn the clock back one hour" — the time the Germans kept was one hour ahead of the Russians'. "This was his way of notifying us that the Soviets were coming. Then he added, and I'll never forget his expression, 'And that is not the only thing that is going to be put back.'"

The evening before he was to report for duty — he already had his orders — Tolya came to the hut to say good-bye to Rita. He tapped on the door with his special knock. "I remember how he stood there. I walked out to say good-bye to him on the street. The moon was shining and the snow melting. Tolya in his formal, well-behaved way said, 'You know it is a farewell when one knows that one is going to die. One is so young and one still wants to live so very much. I wish I could live, but I won't.' Then I remember that he said the very pretty Russian sentence '*Mozhna vas potselovat?* [May I kiss you on the cheek?] I never kissed you, you know.' When I came back into our room, tears were rolling down my cheeks. Everybody was asleep, I thought. But Mutticuta was sitting there. She knew just what was happening. She kissed the tears on my cheeks and said I would always treasure them. She put her arms around me and her tears mingled with mine. She said, 'Ritterl, this will be remembered as one of the saddest moments, very sad but in a way also very beautiful.' She said that beauty and sadness, extreme happiness and extreme sadness, are closely related."

Of course, Rita never saw Tolya or Seryoza again. When we visited, Olya said that none of the boys and men in the Ukrainski Strafni Battalion ever came back. So Rita received a final confirmation that Tolya and Seryoza were dead, killed with the others when for a time the Germans held the front, east of the Romanian city of Iaşi. It is likely that they never even saw the armed units before which they were helplessly exposed.

On June 6, 1944, the Germans bombed Mogilev Podolskiy. Next to Olya and Bronislav's hut, a field hospital had been set up in tents. The Russian surgeon in charge was a semi-invalid with one leg. When the bombing started, he limped into the hut and escorted its occupants into a shelter alongside the wounded, moaning soldiers from the battlefield. It was not a real shelter, and bees from hives in the neighborhood swarmed in along with the wounded. "To this day when I read about bombing of civilian populations, I hear in my ears the moans of the wounded and feel bees stinging me.

"The Russian surgeon cared for the wounded with tenderness and showed deep warmth for us also. He kept telling me, '*Devushka* [little girl], it will stop soon.' His care and affection was a balm against the sound of bombs falling all around us." At dawn, when the bombing finally stopped and they emerged from the shelter, Rita was greeted by the sight of fires and pieces of what were once people. The smell and the moans of the wounded and dying civilian victims of the bombing mingled with those of the soldiers from the battlefield. A year and a half later, when Rita began to study medicine in Prague, she remembered "my vain attempts to help the invalid surgeon tend his wounded soldiers."

✻

The shattering events of these last weeks in Mogilev imprinted permanently upon Rita the absurdity of characterizing whole peoples in moral terms. The extreme circumstances of international events bring forth the moral complexity and the paradoxes that lie below the surface of human behavior. Human connection and intimacy emerge and endure in unanticipated ways, surviving "all the good and bad regimes, good and bad governments, good and bad wars, and good and bad causes." Having experienced the indifference and cruelty of many different governments, and the simultaneous human kindness of their citizens, Rita harbors no hatred toward the Germans. "I truly did not know hatred when I grew up, so I did not start to hate in Mogilev." Rita's father once observed in the camp that Germany might even be a "fine place to live" after the war, as "the Germans will feel so guilty and they would be very well organized."

After her return to Mogilev, Rita wrote, "Not only don't I like to talk about Mogilev, but I don't like others to talk about their concentration camps. I always felt it was an intrusion." She dislikes the belligerence and arrogance she sees in the concept of "never again" and the rationalization that "one is entitled to everything for survival." As Rabbi Balfour Brickner of the Stephen Wise Free Synagogue has written, "The cry 'never again' has come to mean I can do to you what was done to me."[8]

Rita also avoids regarding herself as a victim in relation to Mogilev and afterward. "I think I learned early that if you don't consider yourself vicitimized, you don't become a victim." In this context, Rita recalled an incident that took place on Poltavska Street when she was walking home from the foundry. "I encountered a Romanian soldier who raised the butt of his gun to hit me and called me a derogatory Jewish name. I am sure that I was frightened, but

I don't remember. I remember only looking him straight in the eyes, and he dropped his gun without hitting me and said, 'I am sorry.'"

When "forced" to talk about Mogilev Rita does not emphasize the horrors of the camp but stresses rather the fruits of the campaign she waged with her mother to preserve some pleasure and joy in life — sneaking to the Dniester to swim, the excitement of becoming a foundry worker, the diverse friendships. "Why? Psychiatrists will say because the other things, the 'real things' that happened are too painful to remember. Perhaps so. But there is another reason. By the time I came to the camp at the age of sixteen, I had received years of affection and therefore had strong, perhaps exaggerated, feelings of self-worth, self-value, and trust that only good things are bound to happen. Even the cattle train to Mogilev did not wipe out that expectation. The harsh experience was continually offset by the radiant spirit of my parents, which shone more than ever under the horrible events of our deportation." Zaziu, especially, showed so much resilience of mind over body, "that my belief in mankind was strengthened rather than shattered." The Chassidic sequence, embodied in Zaziu's attitude and being, that joyfulness will follow sorrow, conveyed to Rita the expectation that a good life is bound to follow hardship.

By the time Rita was sent to Mogilev, she had already experienced the satisfactions of being considered special at home and at school and developed the conviction that this could continue. That is the only way she can explain her initiative in becoming a foundry worker. "I was completely unfit, not dexterous — to this day I can't learn to open a locked door — but I felt good at overcoming challenges."

At the end of our visit, we wound our way up the east bank of the river to a large cemetery on a hill overlooking the city. Here Rita hoped to find the gravesites of her grandfathers and other Jews of Rădăuţi who had died in Mogilev and to transfer Zaziu's remains to Haifa. There were thousands of Jewish graves in the extensive Christian cemetery, but neither the graves of those who died in the camp nor a place of mass burial could be found. "The visit to the cemetery in Mogilev turned out like the visit to the one in Rădăuţi — a terrible disappointment. Again it was horrible to see a cemetery of such Jewish tragedy not in Jewish hands." The guides were drunk and cared little about helping the visitors. But before we left, Rita said to her daughter, "My grandfather will know I have been on the hill."

Rita's experience in Mogilev Podolskiy was, of course, not typical. Her special family situation may account in part for her emergence from the years in the camp less scarred than many survivors, able to continue, and capable of transforming her grim experiences creatively. But at the heart of this ability to continue life is the capacity to feel a sense of belonging, even among alien or hostile people. Essential to this feeling was the fact that her parents survived, in some measure as a result of Rita's initiatives. "During the years 1941–1944, I belonged in Mogilev Podolskiy, for it had been a group experience. I had not gone there, as I came to the United States, by my choice alone. Somehow, because we Jews of Rădăuţi had all been sent together, we had belonged there. Unfortunately, we left many in the deep muck of Mogilev." Rita was able — and enabled by circumstances — to take Rădăuţi to Mogilev, to transplant to the camp the deep sense of community she carried with her from childhood and early adolescence.

But Rita's sense of community in the camp was not restricted to the Jews. Her sense of belonging was extended beyond the usual boundaries of ethnicity, language, religion, or nationality through which human beings restrict their contacts with one another. Rita's ability many years later to apply her insight to the practice of psychiatry and foreign affairs grew out of the experience of the Mogilev period, when she came to know the personal impact of international events. But this impact did not stunt anything in her, as might the twisting experience of a victim. Instead, Rita emerged from the years of internment with a deepened sense of connectedness to others, of belonging, and of determination to survive.

4. A Year in No Man's Land

As Ella went eagerly to the outskirts of the camp to greet the Soviet soldiers, the Romanian Jews waited anxiously, uncertain as to what the future held. When the first Russian soldiers arrived, "they looked exhausted. So did their horses. But they were generous and compassionate. When they saw a child or a dog, they would break off a piece of bread and throw it." For Rita the encounter with the first Russian soldiers was special. She had studied Russian for more than three years and loved the language and literature. But she had never spoken it, except furtively with Sergei, Tolya, and other Ukrainians, for it was forbidden. With Ella she spoke German.

In Mogilev Podolskiy the Germans maintained a pretense that the region was part of Germany or a gift from Germany to Romania. After the camp's liberation, the region once again became part of the western Ukraine in the Soviet Union. The initial joy after the liberation of the camp was followed by new suffering. The troops who came afterward plundered the surviving population, stealing watches and other meager valuables and "went after the women." These were the soldiers who, under orders from their headquarters, sent the Ukrainian boys westward to certain death. The Romanian inmates presented a special bureaucratic dilemma for the Soviet officials. "We told them that we were Jews who had been sent to Mogilev by the

Nazis. In order to repatriate us they would have to have orders from Moscow, and our status was difficult to establish. We kept telling them we were Jews, but in the *Sovietski Soyuz,* they said, all religions are equal. The problem was that the Jewish internees were Romanian citizens and the Romanians were still fighting on the side of Germany against them. We could have understood this, but they never talked about it. We asked for our repatriation. We wanted to go back to Romania, but they didn't permit us to go home. In fact they neither permitted us to stay nor go. They only replied *budet* [it will be]."

The Soviet authorities wanted Rita to stay because she had been such a prominent and effective worker in the foundry. Nora, whose work was less vital, was soon allowed to quit the foundry, but Rita received an official message that she would not be dismissed. "I started telling them that I wanted to go back to school, that I was working there only as a camp inmate. They said, 'You are a foundry worker.'" The impersonation to save her family suddenly "became my destiny, my identity." Having tried to prove to the Germans how *qualified* she was, she then attempted to convince the Russians how *un*qualified she was. It did not work. Foundry workers told the Russians how diligent a worker Rita had been. "'You did good work for the Germans,' they said. 'Now you will work for us.' The Soviets also gave me a kind of master certificate. I remember when I brought it home my father said, 'Yes, the dream of my life has been that my daughter should become a foundry worker for the German and the Soviet governments.'"

Mogilev was liberated by the Red Army in April, but the Stenzlers remained there through the summer of 1944. It was there they heard the news of the Allied invasion of France and of Russian troops moving westward through Romania. On August 23, Russian troops entered Bucharest, and the next day Romania surrendered, but even then the status of the Jewish Romanian inmates of the camp did not change. The Soviet authorities still did not know what to do with them, for the war against Germany continued and Romanians were still considered their allies.

The Stenzlers began to consider how they might leave Mogilev illegally. One day, Nora, who was a fine musician, made contact with several members of a Russian military orchestra that was passing through Mogilev, moving west in a truck. She offered the musicians some money and clothes and persuaded them to take the family along toward Romania. The musicians were also persuaded to take along another family, the Guttmans, who lived on the same street as the Stenzlers in Mogilev, as they had in Rădăuţi. Their daughter, Relly, had been a classmate of Nora's.

Upon liberating Mogilev Podolskiy, Russian engineers immediately built a temporary bridge across the Dniester. The Soviet troops, including the Ukrainian Strafni Battalion, crossed that bridge into Bessarabia, and so did the Russian musicians and their odd passengers. After a few hours, without warning, the seven Jews were suddenly dumped out of the truck near a small Bessarabian village "in the middle of nowhere." The truck took off with the few remaining belongings of the Stenzler party. "We were just standing there in the road. I remember going from peasant home to peasant home. We walked long distances for many days until we found a peasant house where a Bessarabian peasant woman took us in — through bribery."

The wanderers exchanged their clothes for those of the peasant family. Of their brief stay Rita remembers few details. "I helped the woman's son watch the cows and sheep graze. I remember only that the fields were gorgeous and that I did a terrible job as a shepherdess. I almost lost the herd, and for the peasant boy I was more of a hindrance than a help."

None of the seven had any identifying documents. "We hadn't a single piece of paper — nothing! The peasants kept asking us about ourselves and saying we couldn't stay there because we had no permit." Because of their previous experience under Soviet occupation in 1940–1941, the Bessarabian peasants knew that you had to have a piece of paper to be entitled to stay someplace, so the Stenzlers and the Guttmans could stay there for only a few days.

It was now September, and for several weeks of that late summer and early fall of 1944 these two families hitchhiked through Bessarabia and northern Bukovina, toward Czernowitz. These regions, which had been returned to Romania by the Nazis, were again annexed by the Soviet Union after Germany's defeat. Soon the Guttmans eventually went their separate way. It was sometimes necessary for Nora and Rita to separate, but they had an agreement that one of them would always be with their parents. The girls tried to assess the dependability of the drivers they approached for rides. While their parents were hidden in ditches by the roadside they would ask the drivers where they were going rather than tell them where they wanted to go. "Nora and I made ourselves look unattractive, but that was easy. We were without clean clothes or ways to wash." After a vehicle stopped the parents would appear and Rita and Nora made it plain that without them they were not getting into any vehicle. Sometimes, in this way, they were able to persuade a driver to take all four along.

Finally the Stenzlers and Guttmans arrived in Czernowitz. There they once again approached the Soviet authorities who had reoccupied the city for permission to be repatriated to Romania, or at least for a permit to stay in the city. "It was a Catch-22 situation. In the Soviet Union you couldn't stay in a city without a permit. The Soviet authorities said they had no right to give us a permit to stay, and they had no right to repatriate us. We were illegal in Czernowitz, and we had no permit to leave and no permit to stay. That was our status in October 1944."

Jewish families in Czernowitz, especially former friends and acquaintances who had survived the war, took the Stenzler family in, endangering themselves. Some of these people had fled to Bucharest when Czernowitz was given to the USSR and had returned to Czernowitz after it was liberated from the Nazis. Frequently Rita and Nora had to spend nights on roofs or in cellars because the Soviet authorities were rounding up girls, usually at night, for work in the Don River Basin coal mines. The USSR needed mine workers since their able-bodied young people were in the military at the front. The Stenzlers were in particularly great danger because they had no identity papers, no permits to stay, and could be taken for deserters, enemies, spies, vagabonds, or "golans" (Romanian for "hooligans," only gentler).

Soon after the family arrived in Czernowitz, Nora made contact with members of a Czech brigade, a unit of Czech volunteers that was fighting alongside the Soviet forces. In 1939 these Czechs had fled the Nazis and crossed through Poland into the USSR, where they were imprisoned. In jail these prisoners had received notes from General Ludviic Svoboda asking whether they wanted to don a Czech uniform and take part in the liberation of their homeland. In 1941, after Germany attacked Russia, they were released, and Svoboda organized them into the Czech Freedom Brigade.

"Our parents were trembling for us. They were convinced we would all end up in Siberia because we had no permits to stay. Nora was a wonderful accordion player. The Czech soldiers, who were heading westward, suggested that she join the brigade as a musician. Nora did not want to go, but my parents forced her to. I remember the family meeting. My mother and father said, 'Nora, it's your responsibility. Any member of the family who has a chance to be saved has to get out. When there is a possibility for her Rita will get out too, and if there is a possiblity for us, we will get out. It is a responsibility which you have to the family.' Nora and I were also convinced we would end up in Siberia. Our parents said that someone from this family has to get out, has to survive. Through her tears, Nora, imbued with the responsible spirit of being the older, agreed. The brigade put a Czech uniform on her. I saw her being dressed. She did not know a word of Czech, but she played the accordion for the group and they were just delighted. She left Czernowitz with the brigade. On May 9, 1945, Nora was to be with the first Czech troops who liberated Prague, carried on the shoulder of the exultant Czech citizens in St. Wenceslas Square to whom she could say only *ano* [yes] in their native tongue.

"After Nora left there came a terrible period in Czernowitz." Rita was in considerable danger as the Soviets were rounding up girls day and night, collecting them off the street without notifying their families, and sending them off to the mines. "I talked to my parents and we decided that I had to get out of Czernowitz. So I went — I don't know how — to a town called Storozhinets," a small community in northern Bukovina about 15 kilometers southwest of Czernowitz and less than 30 kilometers from the Romanian (southern Bukovina) border. In Storozhinets Rita took some "nincompoop" course in book-keeping — "My talents in mathematics were then as they are now." Nevertheless, she obtained a job as a bookkeeper in a *Zagod Zerno,* a state-run granary for corn and other grains. To explain how a person without a residence permit could obtain a Soviet government job, "one had to know the political and geographic realities of the northern Bukovina in 1944. Storozhinets was fairly close to the border, and the peasants of Romanian Bukovina had gone underground and disappeared into the hills. They also expressed opposition to losing their land by kidnapping and killing Soviet military and government officials. This is why I got the job as a bookkeeper in spite of lack of skill and experience."

The job went badly from the start, but Rita's lack of bookkeeping talent was not the reason. Her boss, the Russian director of the Zagod Zerno, was constantly drunk, and she was terrified of him. In the Soviet bureaucratic system, all vouchers, invoices, and the like had to be countersigned. Rita, therefore, had to countersign all the director's checks and expense statements for equipment, livestock, and repairs. "He would push under my nose checks for buying a cow or a tractor that did not exist; he bought vodka with the money."

This went on for several weeks in the fall of 1944. Rita became increasingly frightened, both of the director and of being caught, as the books became hopelessly muddled. "I lived in the house of a nice Jewish couple, and I am ashamed to say that at night I would slip into the kitchen to eat up whatever had been cooked or baked the day before. I don't remember what they did about it, but they didn't kick me out. Maybe they believed, like everybody in Storozhinets in those days, that the *banderovci* [Romanian bandits — a name given to the peasants who were hiding in the hills] were stealing their cooking."

Rita had friends in Storozhinets, young boys who cleared tables at the restaurant where the Zagod Zerno employees ate, as did Rita and the Russian officials. "One evening a little guy came to me in the restaurant and said, 'Rituchka, I want to tell you there is a big inspector here from Kiev who is inspecting the Zagod Zerno because the bookkeeping is all wrong. I heard them talking and they said they are going to put your director and you in jail.' After he told me that, he disappeared. I tried to talk with him again, but it wasn't safe anymore. I went back to the Jewish couple's house and got into bed. That night, suddenly, someone threw a pebble against my window. I went to the window and there was that little boy. He called to me, 'I think you must leave the town right now.'"

A complaint had evidentally been filed against the director and his bookkeeper. The urgent tone in the boy's voice "and my instinct for survival" persuaded Rita that she must leave quickly. Gathering her few belongings she left the house in Storozhinets "and also my job and career as a bookkeeper" and headed on foot for Czernowitz. She tried to hitchhike but there were no cars. "It was dark, and I was frightened of the banderovci, of the Soviet authorities, and of drunk older men — after all I was nineteen and on a deserted country road. I could not have walked the distance from Storozhinets to Czernowitz." Finally, a peasant and his wife, in a cart drawn by oxen and stacked high with hay, stopped and let her climb up on the hay. "They did not ask any questions, and we arrived at Czernowitz at dawn of the following day."

Meanwhile, Ella Davidson had also made her way to Czernowitz. For Ella, Czernowitz was "the West," and she wanted to be with the Stenzlers because her parents had been deported by the Soviets.

Miraculously, they had survived the earlier deportations by the Nazis and come back to Mogilev. Ella, who had been a medical student before the war, had papers as a Soviet citizen and reapplied for medical school in Moscow. Back in Czernowitz, Rita once again faced the danger of being taken forcibly by the Soviet authorities to work in the mines and went briefly into hiding.

Ella considered Rita's problem and said that the one way to be safe was to become a music student. Music students and athletes, she said, were especially valued and protected from military service or from deportation to the mines. "'There is no other possibility,' Ella said. I knew she was right, because whenever we saw an able-bodied young man or woman not in uniform on the street he or she was invariably an athlete or a music student. The Soviets and Russian people cherish these and want to preserve them for the nation. There was no question then and now that my athletic talents were nil." Rita worried that she had no musical talent, either. "My sister was very talented. I just practiced. Ella said, 'You'll pass.'" Although Rita was not a particularly gifted musician, she had taken piano lessons for ten years. Ella got Rita application forms for the conservatory and arranged for an audition. Rita prepared for the entrance exam and practiced with diligence. She played Mozart's "Turkish March" and passed the test.

But, to enter the conservatory, it was necessary to take another test, on the history of the Communist Party, "which I knew nothing about." Rita learned that this quiz consisted of repeating what Stalin had said in each of his speeches given at celebrations held in November, commemorating the October Bolshevik Revolution. She began memorizing those speeches hour after hour, day and night. On the day before the exam, Bubi Friedman's mother interrupted Rita's studying to ask her to come see her son, who was about to be smuggled across the border into Romania. "'*Der Bubi will nicht gehen ohne sie noch einmal zu sehen* [Bubi does not want to go without seeing you once more],' she said. I remember thinking for a minute what to do and then telling her I could not go with her. I had to study. I remember my guilt pangs when she slammed the door without saying good-bye. These guilt pangs increased when in the summer of 1945 in Iaşi I heard that Bubi had been killed on Soseaua Kisselev in Bucharest. He had been smuggled across the border in the uniform of a Russian officer. In Bucharest he lived, wined, and dined in the old style that he had been used to before the war. One evening he was stopped on the street and asked to give his fancy watch to Soviet soldiers, which was very common in those days. He refused and was shot, after which they removed his watch and other valuables." Rita wonders whether her feelings of discomfort whenever she is in Bucharest are related to not having gone with Mrs. Friedman to say good-bye to Bubi.

Rita passed the exam, entered the conservatory, and got a job in Czernowitz as a secretary at a music school for children. "I became a conservatory student. I had a piece of paper which *said* I was a conservatory student. When a policeman, or one of the people who would take you to the Don to do mine work, saw you had a piece of paper showing that you were a music student, you were holy; you were safe." Rita does not recall ever having been detained. However, she spent most evenings at the conservatory out of fear of being stopped by Russian officials making street checks or by drunken soldiers, some of whom were carrying weapons.

Rita entered the conservatory in Czernowitz as Nora Stenzler. She was afraid that someone from Storozhinets might connect her with the "Rita Stenzler" who had escaped arrest at the Zagod Zerno. Nora herself was safely away in the Czech army. Once on the street in Czernowitz Rita did see an official from Storozhinets and ducked into an alley to avoid him. Through the grapevine she learned that "my drunk director" from the Zagod Zerno had been taken to prison. The danger that the authorities would spend time looking for the codelinquent, Rita Stenzler, was diminished by the fact that in those days the rebellious peasants, the banderovci, were hostile to the Soviets and could easily have kidnapped and done away with a "collaborator" like Rita Stenzler at night with little fanfare. To reduce further the likelihood that Rita would be tracked down, Ella filed an official paper that "Rita Stenzler" had disappeared with the banderovci.

Rita's experiences in the conservatory, where she remained for six months until she and her parents were repatriated in May, were happy ones. "I loved the conservatory students. This was my first contact with young Russians. I was treated nicely and ate well." Rita was also fond of the Russian children at the music school. She could not get over how pampered and loved they were. Invariably their mothers, who most often were wives of officials, tried to convince the teachers at the conservatory that their youngsters were gifted musicians, even when they were without a shred of talent. "For me, who had no taste for equality, with an immense appetite and experience of being pampered and spoiled, this was perfectly acceptable."

Rita also became fond of the Ukrainian director, Vasily Vasilevitch, a veteran who had lost an arm and a leg in the war. He treated teachers, students, and secretaries like one family. "I shall never forget that New Year's Eve, which we celebrated at the music school in Soviet fashion — Christmas wrapped into New Year's. I was chosen by the director to be *Dedushka Moroz* [Grandfather Frost], who brought gifts [little poems or expressions of affection and attention] to all the staff and children. Vasily Vasilevitch told me, 'I knew you would be able to give gifts to each and every one of us,' and he gave me a photograph of his with a nice long inscription. Even though I was called Dedushka Moroz, I knew that I was as close as I would ever get to being Santa Claus. It was a long way from when maids had 'smuggled' into our nursery, with my parents' approval, Christmas trees, money, and gifts."

While she was a music student Rita lived at the conservatory, even though she had no official residence permit, as her parents' situation remained difficult. They still had no permit of any kind and had to stay with former friends who were also acting illegally in harboring them. Helene and Shaje changed residence every two or three weeks during these months. Like them, the other survivors of Rădăuți were spread all over Bessarabia and northern Bukovina between Mogilev and Czernowitz, permitted neither to go home nor to stay. Rita and her parents developed a "little underground message system" so that she could learn their whereabouts and visit them at the different houses where they were staying.

Rumors and gossip circulated continually. The same people who in the camp had spread ominous rumors about the impending extermination of the Jews now spread them about their imminent deportation to Siberia. Those who had spread information that they had "seen" a repatriation order in German hands how had "seen" a repatriation order in Soviet hands. The two groups also gave different reports about missing friends. The "optimists" said they were already in Rădăuți; the others informed the Jewish families that they were already in transports on their way to Siberia.

"My musical career continued until we were finally repatriated, all that were left of us, in May 1945." The same authorities who would not issue permits for them to stay in Czernowitz and, presumably, did not know that the surviving Romanian Jewish families even existed, suddenly repatriated them when the war ended. Although the Stenzlers had kept changing residences, they, too, received notification of repatriation on May 9, the day after Germany's unconditional surrender was signed in Berlin. They in turn sent Ella to notify Rita, who had not heard. "I don't think the Soviet authorities wanted to smear the beloved institution of a Russian conservatory with such a grimy business as repatriation to Romania."

On May 9, Jews from southern Bukovina were to appear at a particular office to receive a repatriation *propuska*, or permit. "The way they handled that I'll never forget. It was a circus. No lines. No order. Somebody stood on a balcony and threw down pieces of paper." The permits fluttered down to the jostling crowd, and the people of Rădăuţi and other southern Bukovinian communities fought "like a pack of hungry dogs" to catch one.

The papers had no names on them, but it was essential to catch one in order to be allowed to return to Romania. "My father saw the situation and gave up." Somebody who had worked for him in Rădăuţi ran to the temporary residence to which Mr. Stenzler had returned. He said, "Mr. Stenzler, you and your family are going." Shaje said, "Do you have a paper?" The man said, "I'll catch you one and you'll go with us." And he did. Each family was notified by name at the specific illegal address at which they were residing and were told to appear at 10:00 A.M. at a specified address.

At midday on May 9, the Stenzlers began the journey toward the Romanian border, 40 kilometers to the south. "We were a real caravan — all of the Jews who came back from the camp. The Russians brought us in carts drawn by horses." They traveled the remainder of the day and evening, arriving at the border during the middle of the night at a point opposite the Romanian village of Siret, through which their cattle cars had passed four years earlier. Upon arrival near the border on the Soviet side, the Jews were gathered in one place. "The weak, sick, and elderly were no longer with us. They had died mostly in the winters of 1941–1942 and 1942–1943. The returnees were physical and, I suspect, mental survivors. Getting from Mogilev to Czernowitz and not getting caught by the authorities had taken special skill, help from the community, and a huge dose of luck, probably the most important ingredient.

"We had almost no belongings. I had an edition of Pushkin's works, a hundredth anniversary edition, which I received from Tolya and which Ella and I had read together. They took this away from me. They went through our belongings as if we had been accumulating God knows what. We had nothing. And then we had to walk, in mud, through a no man's land to the Romanian border." The returning Jews crossed the border at Siret on foot around 2:00 or 3:00 in the morning of May 10.

At the border a Romanian lieutenant approached the group and said, "Who speaks Russian?" Rita was the only person who did. "We were all anxious to tell how we had suffered under the Russians during the past year. We knew nothing about what was going on in Romania. The lieutenant said that I was to make an official thank-you speech to the Russian commanding officer at the border for the magnificent treatment we had received and how expeditiously we had been repatriated to Romania — which took a whole year. 'But that is not how it was,' I told him in Romanian. And he said, 'Then you do not know to what country you are coming back because that is how it is here now.' This was our notice of what we were coming back to."

On the Romanian side, horse-drawn carts were waiting to take the repatriated Jewish survivors home. "The people from Rădăuţi were very sweet. Someone said, 'Mr. Stenzler, we want you to be the first one to come back to our town.' I remember how we approached Rădăuţi, sitting in the cart, all three of us holding hands, silent, overcome by emotion, remembering those who had not come back with us and wondering what we would find, whether our house still stood, and what it was like." Rita remembered her grandfathers, aunts, uncles, and cousins and the other Jews who were not returning. "There were very few of us. There were no men between eighteen and forty-five. The Soviets had taken all who remained to labor camps or into the army. Orphans had been taken by the Zionists from Mogilev to Palestine. Of the rest, the majority had been decimated by the typhus epidemics, by typhoid and other diseases, or murdered by the Germans."[1]

"In Rădăuţi my father talked to my mother, preparing her, saying, 'You know the house might not stand, this might not be, and that might not be.' And she said, 'I don't have a worry. Rita is with us and Nora [who had kept sending us messages] is safe in the West and we are fine.' So this is how we came back, my father, my mother, and myself. We left on October 13, 1941, and returned on May 10, 1945."

5. Prague: A Taste of Freedom

During the years that the Stenzler family was interned at Mogilev Podolskiy, their house was occupied by a judge and his family. "They had kept it in good condition and had the decency to move out the day before we arrived, so that we should find our home without strangers occupying it." The Stenzlers started reestablishing themselves, "and my mother started immediately conducting as normal a life as she could. She fixed things up in the house." Returning Jewish survivors gradually trickled into Rădăuți as did new arrivals from the northern Bukovina who slipped over the border to escape the Soviet occupation.

But for Rita the return felt temporary from the start. She stayed only long enough to prepare for the university. Returning students were given an opportunity to make up for the high school classes they had missed by taking the Romanian *matura*, a series of examinations modeled after the French baccalaureate. Without passing these one cannot enter the university. Rita passed the matura at the end of May and in July registered at Iași, the leading university in Romania.

Iași, now a modern city of over 200,000, is in eastern Romania, 100 miles southeast of Rădăuți, close to the border of the Moldavian Socialist Republic of the USSR. A cultural center from the time of the Renaissance, Iași became the Moldavian capital in the sixteenth century and remained the headquarters of the Romanian government until the capital was moved to Bucharest in 1861. The first Romanian-language book was printed there in 1643.

"I was so overcome by the opportunity to enroll at any university that I registered with four different departments in one day." Rita signed up for philosophy, languages, law, and agriculture, "strange choices for which, except for languages, I had neither aptitude nor background. It was like an intoxication, a completely illogical thing, like somebody who has been starved and suddenly sees a huge buffet and can pick and choose anything they want." For a few weeks Rita had a marvelous time in the Department of Linguistics, studying German and French as main subjects and English and Italian as secondary languages.

The French courses were particularly exhilarating and brought back memories of lessons in Rădăuţi and new dreams of Paris. Rita read a passage from Voltaire to the class, and the professor remarked on the pathos of the reading and her evident love of the French language. This and other experiences brought back warm memories of Rita's professor of French in the Liceul Elisabeta Doamna.

Rita's stay at the university, however, was to last just over a month. Even before she came to Iaşi, university students were being recruited to join the student Communist organization. One evening a student leader, wearing Romanian national costume, had called her to a meeting in Rădăuţi. It was "blatant unadulterated propaganda," and she hated it. Attempts were made to work on "our ideals" and to indoctrinate and manipulate Rita and other students "toward building a Communist Romania." She found especially revolting the discrepancy between the use of the national costume and "the cause, method, and regime that was advocated." She also objected to the polarizing nature of the propaganda, depicting one side as all good and right and the other as all bad and wrong. "To this day I have a profound disgust for political propaganda, right, left, or otherwise." Rita sized up what was happening and soon realized she could not stay in Romania. The recruiting attempts were the deciding factor. She made up her mind to escape to the West.

In the meantime, Nora had continued to send messages from Prague by one means or another, sometimes through Czech officers or through "the Bukovinian grapevine." Out of concern for her parents' peace of mind, she sought and received one of the first passports to visit Romania, suddenly appearing in Rădăuţi dressed in a Czech military uniform. After a short visit, she had to return to her unit in Prague.

Rita determined that she would go to Prague too, reverting to her characteristic trait of allowing Nora to choose first and then choosing the same thing. During Nora's visit, Rita learned of the United Nations Relief and Rehabilitation Agency. UNRRA trains bound for Prague and Bratislava picked up relief supplies from the United States, which had arrived by ship at the Romanian Black Sea port of Constanța, and Nora was planning to return to her unit on one of those trains.

One evening in August, without notifying her parents, Rita boarded a train in Iaşi and went to Bucharest. Nora was still there, and Rita announced that she, too, was going to Prague. Rita had more difficulty persuading her uncle Summer Wolf, at whose home in Bucharest she was staying, of the wisdom of going to Prague. "'After all, who will know in Prague that you are Shaje Stenzler's daughter?' Poor Uncle Summer was in deep turmoil over my departure. But he did not tell my parents about it because he had promised me, before I told him what I was about to do, that he would not tell, and as a pious Jew he never broke his promise."

From Bucharest, Rita took a train to Constanța, where she got in touch with the Czech military officers who were to accompany the next UNRRA transport train bound for Prague. Somehow, without knowing a word of Czech, except, like her sister, *ano* — yes, and lacking a passport or official papers that would entitle her to travel from Romania through Hungary to Czechoslovakia, Rita was able to persuade the Czech officers to take her along. ("I notified them that they would let me travel along with them to Prague.") They gave her a Czech uniform and cap to wear.

"The train went through Transylvania. The Carpathian mountains and the lovely countryside blended with the lakes, the moon, and the stars. Never again will I hear a train whistle without the image of the Carpathian mountains appearing in my soul." As she traveled slowly through Transylvania westward, Rita sensed that this was her real good-bye to her native land and the way of life of Bukovina. She remembers standing by the window of the train, wearing the uniform of a country she did not know, and thinking with longing of all that she had loved at home and was leaving behind — the Romanian folk songs, the dances, the poems of Eminescu, "the romanticism and zestfulness of Eastern Europe," and, above all, her parents and the rich memories and feelings associated with them.

The ride was long, and the train was often sidetracked in order to let the huge transports carrying homecoming Soviet troops and material pass through. The train was stranded in a small town in Hungary for several days. One of the Czech officers decided that Rita should go along with several of them to try to convince the Russian commandant at the station — the Soviets still occupied Hungary, which had been officially allied with the Nazis during the war — to permit the train to continue on to Prague. The argument went, "You talked us into taking you against our wishes and our better judgment; you'll talk him into letting our train go by."

"Without thinking, I went. A catastrophe developed. When I started talking to the Russian officer as a so-called translator, he realized that this girl in a Czech army coat and cap didn't know any Czech. He became suspicious. He was very pleased with my Russian, but he thought there was something strange. So he asked me for my documents. The Czech officers whisked me out of there in no time. I barely escaped the wrath of the commandant. I still don't know how we got out of there." Rita's unsuccessful intervention may have cost her and her traveling companions a few extra days, during which she had to remain hidden among the crates on the train. There was plenty to eat, as the supplies included sardines and other food. "I think only the chaos which existed at that station, with trains full of returning Soviet soldiers, German prisoners of war, and displaced people milling around, saved my skin." Rita arrived in Prague in the late summer of 1945. She was just twenty. Except for short periods, she would never again live under Communist rule.

Shaje and Helene's insistence that Nora join General Svoboda's Czech Freedom Brigade was to have important consequences for Rita as well. Nora did not take enthusiastically to soldiering. She was given a small revolver, but it frightened her and she would leave it outside her tent at night while she slept. In the brigade, however, Nora met Bertold ("Tussi") Weiss and his wife, Else, Romanian Jews from Czernowitz. Tussi had been a medical student in Prague before World War II, and Else had lived with him there. After the war began, he returned to Czernowitz. When the Germans captured northern Bukovina from the Soviets, Tussi Weiss was sent to Mogilev Podolskiy by the Nazis because of his leftist leanings. The other members of his family escaped to Bucharest. The Stenzlers had not

met Tussi during the time they were all in Mogilev. Like the Stenzlers, Tussi made his way to Czernowitz some time after the Soviets
liberated Mogilev. He and Else, who was trained as a nurse, also
joined a Czech brigade in Czernowitz, as members of the medical
corps. Nora, Tussi, and Else became friends and were together when
the Czech Freedom Brigade, attached to Soviet Marshal Ivan S.
Konev's forces, entered Prague on May 9, 1945.

Tussi's cousin, Herbert Aleš, a lawyer, was a high-ranking officer
in the Czech army. His position was so exalted that he was assigned
to Paris to negotiate with the Allies the relief for Czechslovakia that
was to come through UNNRA. Herbert's rank entitled him to an
apartment in Prague in which he installed his widowed mother,
Gusta. Tussi arranged for Else and Nora to live in Herbert's apartment, though he continued to be billeted with the army. It was there
at 2283 Na Kleovce Street, in spacious rooms on the ground floor
overlooking a nice yard, that Rita went to live after she arrived in
Prague. The apartment was located in a comfortable neighborhood
on the right bank of the Vltava River — Smetana's Moldau — not
far from Karlova (Charles) University Medical School.

✳

Architecturally, Prague is the greatest treasure of Central Europe.
Although most of its prominent buildings date from the seventeenth
century, the city's feeling is as much medieval and Renaissance as
baroque. Hundreds of delicate church towers on the Vltava's right
bank contrast with the massive Hradcany Castle rising on the bluffs
to the south. Every building seems lovingly embellished. Although
there had been German air attacks and artillery bombardment in the
last days of the war, the city's magnificent structures were largely
spared.

Prague is a city of poetry and poets, of music and musicians. It
is also a city of German, Czech, and Jewish cultures, largely segre-
gated one from another. Prague was the home of Rilke and Kafka, a
city in which Mozart was happy. But in the memory of the city,
profound suffering has been woven with sophistication and joy. German and Czech nationalists have fought there for centuries.

Under six years of Nazi occupation, Prague was plundered of its
wealth, and thousands of its citizens were executed. Of 315,000 Jews
who had lived in Czechoslovakia, most of them in Prague, only 44,000
survived the war. When Rita arrived, the city was still rejoicing in

its newfound freedom, although the seeds for the Communist takeover had already been planted.

＊

"Prague was my first real city. I was finally in the world of my dreams. From 1945 to 1948 the city looked, sounded, smelled, and behaved just like the Prague I had always dreamed of and read about. It was exquisite, clean, and welcoming. Prague breathed freedom after the German occupation and so did I after my Mogilev years. The mood was jovial and people danced in the streets. Prague was not destroyed by the war and neither were my dreams nor my soul. I loved Prague and also fell in love in Prague." Rita's Prague years were a special time, joyous and idealized, full of promise, a time to be remembered and recreated whenever possible.

The household Rita joined consisted of Nora, Else, Herbert Aleš's mother, Gusta, Herbert himself when he visited from Paris, and Tussi's sister, Herta. Herta, who was to become Rita's closest friend, was the youngest of three children and the only girl. Their father had been a successful judge and landowner in Czernowitz, and the family, except for Tussi, had managed to avoid deportation by the Nazis. When Stalin had first occupied northern Bukovina in 1940–1941, the Weiss family suffered hardships under the Soviets. Because it seemed likely that Herta's father would be in danger when the Soviet armies reoccupied northern Bukovina the Weisses left Czernowitz at the end of 1943 for Bucharest, where they spent the remainder of the war.

In Bucharest Herta was courted by Bubi Korn, a young engineer from the Bukovina, who was pressing her to marry him. Needing time to decide, Herta elected to travel to Prague in August 1945 for a last fling before getting married, a trip that was supposed to last three weeks. But Prague with her relatives and the Stenzler sisters proved to be so delightful that the three weeks became three months, then nearly three years. Letters and ultimatums from Bubi arrived regularly, but Herta did not return to Bucharest until 1948, and they did not marry until 1950, when they were in Vienna.

Herta, who is five years older than Rita, was lively, adventurous, and full of enterprising energy. During the Mogilev years Rita had heard of a woman who had sneaked into the camp to visit certain inmates, and Herta was that woman. She had gone to Mogilev because her brother was interned there. Learning in Czernowitz that Antonescu was traveling to the Ukraine to visit the troops, she ascertained his route and itinerary and boarded the same train. She bribed the conductor to let her board the train and hid in the broom closet all the way to Mogilev Podolskiy, where she managed to get into the camp. Using the same tactics of bribery and winning words and smiles, Herta was able to get out of the camp and return by train to Bucharest.

"When I arrived at Na Kleovce 2283 Herta answered the door in hair curlers. She was extremely hospitable and welcomed me. Herta and I became friends from the moment we set eyes on each other. We both inhaled Prague. We practically swallowed it whole. We went out every night. Herta and I danced in every single nightclub in Prague and attended every concert, as if to make up for the war years. No adventure was too dangerous for us." In Herta's more sober words, "We were free girls. During the war it was terrible. In Prague we were young and our sorrows were small." Gusta was perhaps the liveliest and most enterprising member of the household. "She was in her eighties and very elegant. She adored life. When the sun started to set she always asked, 'Where are we going, girls?'" Rita, who had little money of her own, benefited from Gusta's generosity as well as from the salaries of Herbert, Nora, and Tussi. Herta also received money from her parents.

During the war the house on Na Kleovce had been occupied by a German professor. It was assumed that he was a Nazi, as all Germans in Prague during the Hitler period were so labeled. His whereabouts were unknown. He may have been killed by the Czechs when the Germans were driven out or left for Germany when defeat became certain. But the new residents of the house discovered that his wife, Marie, was still in Czechoslovakia, interned in a camp for Germans. Herbert Aleš had a Czech document authorizing him to engage an escort or housekeeper for his elderly mother. "So we decided that the appropriate person for the position was the previous lady of the house." They discovered where she was being held, and on one of his visits from Paris, Herbert went to the camp and had her released under the pretext that she would be his mother's attendant and the maid in the home.

Marie, a beautiful woman, was, of course, delighted to join the growing household. It soon became obvious that she was not a maid, especially when she put on her black finery and walked about the streets of Prague. The group on Na Kleovce became "really a household." Its members sometimes discovered unexpected treasures accumulated by the Germans, such as powdered chocolate hidden in a suitcase underneath a couch.

✳

When Rita, Sheila, Kenneth, and I went to Prague in July 1981, we walked from Vaclavske Namesti (St. Wenceslaus Square), past the National Museum at its southeastern end, and continued in the same direction toward Na Kleovce Street. As we neared our destination, Rita asked directions of a passerby, a woman who, it turned out, had also lived at number 2283 in the fall of 1945. Soon Rita and this woman were absorbed in conversation, recalling the parties and the transformation of the ordinarily quiet atmosphere on Na Kleovce when "the Romanian girls" came there to live. Everyone in the house believed that "the Romanian girls" must have come from Bucharest, as their lifestyle was so "high and lively." "We did change the flavor of the house. The professor who had lived there had been so quiet, and now we had this Romanian bunch who spoke no Czech."

But there had been problems. Czech hostility toward the Germans was intense, and speaking German in Prague was forbidden, even in the home. Several times Rita was stopped in the street when she was overheard speaking that language. For a while it was not permitted even to play Beethoven's music. Neighbors on Na Kleovce Street complained because there was always a party going on, and on occasion the police were called to quiet things down. "You can imagine the scene when the police came. Here was this German woman, Nora, Herbert, and I, and the others all talking German. Yet two of us, Nora and Herbert, were wearing Czech uniforms. It must have been quite puzzling." During our visit we caught a glimpse of an old man who turned out to be the janitor who had tended the building since 1945. It was he who called the police when he heard German being spoken. This "horrible man" also informed on the residents of the house when the Communists took over in 1948. Before she left Prague in 1948, Rita was told that this same man was responsible for several people being sent to jail, a statement confirmed by the woman we met on Na Kleovce Street.

✳

Soon after she arrived in Prague, Rita decided to study medicine. "It wasn't a deliberately figured out plan. I think my reason for going into it was really that it was the hardest thing to get into, or something like that." And the memory of her cousin Buschku's ministrations in Mogilev Podolskiy, as well as those of the invalid Russian surgeon there, undoubtedly contributed to her decision. Whatever the motivation, in September 1945, she registered for study at Charles University Medical School.

Rita immediately made two alarming discoveries. First, the class that had been admitted was huge. Charles University had been closed for six years during the Nazi occupation and hundreds of students were waiting to enroll. (A docent in anatomy, who had entered the medical school in 1946 and was still there in 1981, told us that the first postwar classes had about three thousand students.) Second, she discovered that classes were taught only in Czech. Until the Nazi occupation there had been both a Czech and a German university, and Tussi and other foreign students had attended the latter. During the occupation, classes were held only in German, but after the war ended, the German professors were persecuted and diplomas from the German school were not recognized.

At first Rita did not understand the lectures or any of the instructions. "I didn't even know what subject was being taught." The preclinical lectures were given in Lucerna Hall, a nightclub near the Vaclavske Namesti, as the lecture hall had been bombed out in the closing days of the war. A student sitting next to Rita observed that she was not following the lecture, and when he spoke to her realized that she did not speak Czech. He brought her situation to the attention of the student organization. They were pleased to have a foreign student from Eastern Europe and arranged for her to study Czech with "a very nice, handsome teacher." But "as I was the first non-German foreign student" in Prague "everybody helped me learn Czech." It was not easy, but after a few months her industriousness and gift for languages paid off and she was able to study in earnest. According to Herta, "Nora and I — we *could* study. But we thought only to dance and flirt. Rita was the only one who started to study from the beginning of her time in Prague." Rita reported that "on Na Kleovce Street, everything was against my studying. I had to sneak out to go to lectures. Gusta was the worst of all. She wanted to go out only to good music, dinner, and dancing."

Rita studied the preclinical or basic science subjects, biology, chemistry, physics, anatomy, histology, and physiology, which comprised the first *rigorosum* [one of three groups of exams]. She did her laboratory work in the dingy, gray buildings of the centuries-old Charles Medical School. One building was named after Johannes Purkinje, the great Bohemian neurophysiologist. The anatomy building had huge rooms with enamel-topped oval dissecting tables. (When Rita visited the medical school in 1981, she stood in this old institute and noticed "the same smell as during my real beginning in medicine." There she met a lecturer whose "tattered briefcase looked as old as Charles University, the oldest university in Middle Europe.")

Anya Kosteckova, the daughter of the dean of the medical school, lived close to 2283 Na Kleovce. She, too, was a medical student, loved parties, and sought out foreigners. Anya and Rita met in the dissecting room. "She spotted me as a foreigner, handed me an open bottle of cognac, and said, 'Take a sip. You will need it here.'" The two became close friends. With Anya's younger sister, Yitka, also a medical student, they studied on the balcony of the Kostecka apartment, from which there was a handsome view of the city. A fondness also developed between Rita and the dean, Frantishek Kostecka. The family had a country house near the town of Mojdanek, to which Rita accompanied them on weekends. She was never so homesick for her parents as on those visits, which reminded her of Rădăuţi before the war. "There were dogs and servants and the smell of good food and the joy of life. We made ice cream. The family cherished their two girls as my parents had cherished and treated Nora and me."

In Prague, as everywhere she has lived or visited, Rita was drawn to people who were firm in their national and personal identities — "not wishy-washy." Her favorite friends in Prague where those who were most "clearly Czech." In Prague she fell in love with a Czech medical student, Kristian, who was the captain of the national ice hockey team that won the gold medal at the winter Olympics in Davos in 1948. Kristian was the son and grandson of Czech nationalist leaders and famous athletes. Later, when Rita went to Vienna, she did not want Kristian to follow her. "I could not bear the thought of his becoming a displaced person. He belonged to Prague and Prague to him." (In 1966, Kristian traveled to Yugoslavia and walked across the mountains to the West.) Although she was much involved with the hockey team, Rita never really learned what the game was about. "First of all, I looked only at Kristian when he played, and secondly, out of vanity, I never wore glasses at the game and could not see the puck. I would embarrass Kristian and his team by cheering or clapping at the wrong time." Those days in Prague are among

Rita's happiest memories. "The Petrin Park on the brink of the Vltava River was full of happy people who felt that their golden city blended with the golden leaves at their feet, and I was twenty years old."

After returning to Prague in 1981, Rita described her feelings during her first year there. "Both the city and I rejoiced in freedom. Prague had gotten rid of the German yoke, and I was out of the camp in a beautiful, civilized, undestroyed Western, in my eyes, city. The Vltava glistened, and so did the towers of *zlata Praha* [golden Prague], and there were good concerts in lovely settings, full shops, and lively, cheerful people — everything I had so missed during the Mogilev years. And I could do all the things I could not do before."

Prague also provided Rita with her first official activity in the practice of international relations. Between 1945 and 1948, the city was a mecca for students from all over the world. It became the headquarters for international student organizations because of the heroic stand Czech students had taken on behalf of their Jewish colleagues. "There was congress after congress. My knowledge of foreign languages helped me take part. Finally, contact with the people of the world became a reality and no longer just a dream. It was thrilling to inhale the buoyancy of Prague with students from countries just liberated from the colonial yoke — Egyptians, Moroccans, Malaysians, and many others — as well as from Nazism."

The first world youth festival, the Jan Opletal Student Congress, was held at the beginning of November to honor the heroic Czech medical student who was murdered by the Nazis in 1939. Opletal was not Jewish, but he marched on the Vaclavske Namesti with Jewish and non-Jewish colleagues to demonstrate, in the tradition of European students, against the Nazi occupation and the explusion of Jews from Czech universities. Opletal and nine other medical students were shot by the Germans. After that, Czech universities were closed to all except to collaborators. Between 1939 to 1945, no decent Czech attended a university.

The congress celebrated the first reunion of students since the capitulation of the Nazi regime. "I remember especially the enthusiatic speeches about friendship, togetherness, and freedom." Participants came from all over the world. Rita recalls Malaysian and Indonesian students walking and parading hand in hand with Dutch students, Algerian students hand in hand with French students. The few American students seemed to Rita very casual and somewhat disorganized. "I was not very impressed by them." The Russian delegation was well organized. They were good-looking, much taller than the Russian young people Rita had met before, and very elegant. "At the reception given by Hana, the wife of President Edvard Beneš, the Russian girls wore long gowns, smoked, and distributed long cigarettes. In 1945 we students — five or six of us — used to smoke one cigarette and pass it around, so it was very impressive to see them give out cigarettes."

Rita and Herta had heard that there was to be a Romanian student delegation and went in search of it. Before they knew what was going on, they were surrounded by the organizers of the congress, who handed them Romanian flags and told them that *they* were to be the representatives. "We said no, they said yes, and we became the Romanian delegation." Later Rita and Herta pieced together what had happened. In October of 1945 Romania was still officially a monarchy with Michael still king. The Romanian students in Bucharest who had been chosen to attend the Opletal congress organized a parade to celebrate King Michael's birthday. The internal ministry, however, was already controlled by Communists and had canceled the birthday celebration, notifying the students that a celebration would take place instead on November 7, the date the Russian October Revolution was commemorated. The students decided that this was not an appropriate way to celebrate a king's birthday and chose to defy the ministry by announcing that they would march in the street on November 8. Instead of traveling to Prague they were thrown in jail. Rita and Herta, who was not even a student, as the only young Romanians available in Prague, became the delegates to the student congress.

The festivities continued for a week. "We were wined and dined, danced on Vaclavske Namesti with students from the entire world, traveled as good-will ambassadors from Romania around the entire Czecho Slovenska Republica (CSR), had a marvelous time, and became friends for life." Herta told me, "It was a time of youth. We said we were from the Romanian delegation and all doors opened to us." In addition to being asked to Mrs. Beneš's party, the two young women were invited by Jan Masaryk, the popular foreign minister and son of the founder of the Czech republic, to a reception at Hradcany Castle. There was even a special breakfast for Jewish students. Her first taste of international affairs was very exciting to Rita. "The congress was extremely important to me. The thrill of seeing and being with people from other lands — the first time I got the full flavor of it — is something which has remained for a lifetime."

Each day at the congress it was rumored that the Romanian students were going to show up, but they were still in jail. "The student organizers didn't want that to be known, so every morning we would arrive and they would say, 'Well, remain delegates until the Romanian delegation arrives.' So every morning we appeared. After a while it became clear that even if the Romanian delegation arrived, we would still be the delegates."

On the final day there was a parade in the stadium. The national groups marched in alphabetical order. "They waved tiny flags, like children's flags. The Soviet student group was toward the end. They were wearing white trousers or skirts and red *rubashkas* [shirts]. Each carried a tall Soviet banner, with the sickle and hammer, so that from the viewing stand you saw a red sea of flags towering over all the other groups with their little flags. I remember feeling that all the students from other countries were unorganized and that the Russians 'knew what they were doing.' I also remember conversations at Mrs. Beneš's party with one Russian student who seemed older than the others. He was well informed, and we discussed colonialism about which he voiced some definite ideas."

Toward the end of 1945 and in the early weeks of 1946, people arriving in Czechoslovakia from Romania began telling of political changes there. Meanwhile, Rita, as a foreign student, was frequently asked to show her passport, particularly when she spoke German in the Prague streets. Her situation became increasingly restrictive, especially as she could not travel. For example, she needed a Romanian passport to be able to go home to visit her parents and return to the CSR. So early in 1946 she went to the Romanian embassy to try to get one.

In the closing months of the war, the Red Army had occupied all of Romania. Despite the opposition of the king and the majority of the population, and the temporary revival of democratic parties, Stalin and the Soviet regime put increasing political pressure on the Romanian government, which gradually slipped into the Soviet orbit. Aside from uttering high-sounding phrases about self-determination, democratic and representative government, and free elections, the Western powers did virtually nothing to protect Romania from exploitation by the Soviet Union.

Petru Groza became premier in March 1945 after two short-lived governments that tried to oppose the Communists had collapsed under Soviet pressure. Eventually he presided over a Communist-dominated coalition government. Despite his denunciation of Ana Pauker[1] and Vasile Luca, Moscow's most trusted representatives, Groza was little more than a Stalinist puppet. The Western governments refused to recognize the Groza regime, so American and British ambassadors were invited to Moscow to discuss the broadening of the "democratic basis" of the Romanian government. The so-called Moscow Agreement recommended cosmetic changes in the composition of the Groza government but left a Communist-dominated regime. Andrei Vishinsky, W. Averell Harriman, and Sir Archibald Clark-Kerr then went to Bucharest on December 31 to implement these changes. The formal recognition of this government by Britain and the United States on February 4, 1946, assured the permanence of communism in Romania.

This was the political climate when Rita went to her country's embassy. "They marched me from one person to another, because it was strange for a Romanian citizen to have arrived in Czechslovakia without a passport. I said that I had never had one in my life." Rita ended up with the ambassador, a kindly career diplomat, who asked how she had come to Czechoslovakia. When she told him, he asked, "Why didn't you request a passport from Romania?" "Because I wouldn't have gotten one," she replied. He said, "*Ţara spune ba, atuncia eu spun da.*" [The country says no; that's why I'm saying yes.] So Rita Stenzler received her first passport, a proper Romanian one, but strange in its being issued in Prague by a sympathetic man of the ancien regime when the new rulers of her native country would never have permitted it. She has it to this day.

After they had talked for a while the ambassador said to Rita, "I think you should come to work for the embassy." The embassy had many difficulties dealing with Romanians who had come to the CSR. By this time Rita spoke some Czech and he made her a good offer to work as an interpreter. Her knowledge of French, English, German, and Russian was also useful in this work. The flexible hours dovetailed well with her work at the medical school. "It was a pleasant job. I was paid in hard currency and I had a diplomatic ration card (after the war there were problems in Prague with ration cards). My job of translating consisted of going with [the ambassador] to receptions and conferences. I went from one party to another, one reception to another, with the Romanian embassy car driving me and my friends all over the city. I met the whole diplomatic corps of Prague. It was a good life."

Through her embassy work and participation in student congresses, Rita picked up a new language, Italian. In 1946 she was supposed to be the French-Czech interpreter for a group of Italian students who had registered as being fluent in French. When she picked them up at the airport she discovered to her dismay that they spoke only Italian but had listed French because all participants had to know one foreign language. "They suggested that I not inform the organizing congress committee and that instead they would teach me Italian. It was easy for me to understand them because of the similarity of Italian to Romanian. That superficial way of learning forever bastardized my ability to speak Italian."

This smattering of Italian nevertheless stood Rita in good stead in a thornier situation she inherited at the embassy. As a result of retaliatory expulsion of Sudetan Germans from Czechslovakia at the end of the war, there was a shortage of farm help. The Ministry of Agriculture, therefore, signed a contract with the Romanian and Italian governments to bring five thousand Romanian peasants and a smaller number of Italians to Czechoslovak farms. Following a drought in Romania that year, this work was welcome. "The Romanian peasants got along famously with the Italians. They did not know how to sign their names, but they knew and could understand Italian, and the Italians could understand the Romanians — without ever having learned each other's language." In addition to the similarity of the two tongues there was a "closeness of mentality." Rita could work with both.

The peasants had to sign a contract in the Czech Ministry of Agriculture when they arrived. As she helped in this procedure, Rita placed a large blotter in front of her to block the view of the Czech representative in an effort to hide her countrymen's illiteracy. The peasants seemed to know that Rita was protecting their reputation, and as they marked their crosses in lieu of signatures, "they twinkled in conspiracy with me."

There were immense problems from the beginning of the arrangement. The Romanian peasants were transplanted from their native land without preparation and did not fit into life in Czechoslovakia. "While Romanian and Italian farmers bridged their language and cultural differences with ease and shared a common hostility toward the more civilized Czech farmers, open sociocultural warfare broke out between Czech and Romanian farmers."

The days of the industrialized Czech farmers were regulated by electricity and alarm clocks. The Czechs wanted the Romanians to work in the evening after sundown. The Romanians were used to getting up when the rooster crowed and going to bed when the sun went down, and "this did not go over at all." The Romanians were dispersed on the farms and became very lonesome, especially as they could not speak with the Czech farmers. In Romania, before the war and the Communist takeover, the peasants had been accustomed to hopping on trains and traveling around to visit their families and friends in different villages. If they were caught they would bribe the train conductors, who, like many civil employees in Romania, could not survive on their meager salaries alone. *Baksheesh*, a Turkish word for bribe, was an established fact of life in Romania, and, we discovered, apparently still is. When the Romanians tried to hop trains in Czechoslovakia without paying, they were always caught. When they tried to bribe the Czech conductors they made things worse. They were also "too nice" to the Czech farmers' daughters, trying to slip into bed with them whether or not they were invited. For these and other infractions the Romanians were frequently thrown in jail.

"We had to rescue them all the time. We at the Romanian embassy received daily complaints from the Czech authorities, and we always sided with the Romanians. Every day we got reports on how many Romanian peasants they had in jail, and we used to travel from the embassy to get them out. The whole arrangement was a catastrophe."

In the meantime Rita longed to visit her parents in Rădăuți. Although she had a passport, she was unable to get a visa. In order for a Romanian citizen to reenter Romania in the postwar period, it was necessary to apply through the Soviet embassy. "I remember a long visit to the USSR embassy in Prague, a charming visit with their cultural attaché after sitting without information for three hours in a deserted waiting room, and a promise of a visa that never arrived."

But an opportunity came from an unexpected direction in July 1947. A Communist-sponsored youth festival, to which Romanian students were "escorted" on their own train, was held in Prague.

Rita, who was the students' translator, traveled back to Romania with them, without a visa. "The students simply took me along in their train and hid me when we crossed the border from Hungary into Romania." From Bucharest Rita continued by train to Rădăuţi. "The whole town was there to meet me and my mother was out front. To hide her emotions about having me back home finally after two years, her first sentence to me criticized my hair style. Her eyes were moist with tears, her face quivery. She did not want to show that she had missed me because she knew that I had to go back, and she wanted me to go back. She put her arm around my shoulder and patted me all the way from the train station through town until we reached our house on Pictor Grigorescu. My cousins and friends followed, and when we arrived there were trays of nicely decorated finger sandwiches which they and I gobbled up just as we used to do in our childhood."

But the Romania to which Rita returned was very different from the country she had left two years earlier. British and American recognition of the Groza government had been based on assurances of free elections, which were duly held in November 1946. However, not only were they rigged, but political meetings of the opposition were invaded by thugs sent by the Soviet-dominated Groza government, and those who attended were beaten up and arrested. Protests by the Western powers were ignored. In spite of all this, the Communist electoral slate was decisively defeated, whereupon falsified results, giving the Communist-led bloc of "Democratic parties" an "overwhelming majority," were published.[2] The Romanian people greeted this outcome with bitterness, anxiety, and rage but were helpless to affect the results. King Michael refused to open Parliament, but the Communists began a reign of terror in which tens of thousands of political undesirables were murdered or "disappeared." Among the families that escaped from Bucharest during this period were Herta's parents, who fled to Austria.

In February 1947, a peace treaty signed in Paris made official the theft of Bessarabia and northern Bukovina by the Soviet Union, despite the pleas of Jan Masaryk, who recalled the sacrifices Romania had made — 170,000 of the 360,000 Romanian soldiers who fought alongside the Russians in the last months of the war were killed. After this, the denationalization of the Romanian Communist movement was accelerated and the Romanian Communists were replaced by Stalinists. At about the time Rita arrived in Romania, the country announced its refusal to attend a Marshall Plan meeting in Paris. Stalin thought participation in the plan would lead to Western "interference" in Romanian affairs. All opposition political parties were dissolved and their leaders subsequently arrested or murdered. When we were in Rădăuţi we received firsthand accounts of the reign of terror in the postwar years from surviving children of relatively well-to-do families. Many of their friends and relatives who were not killed outright died in prison. Some of the children of the more prominent citizens have sought oblivion in the greater anonymity of Bucharest. Rita's childhood friend Lucica Dumitriuc was among those who never again returned to Rădăuţi.

For reasons that are still unclear to Rita, one member of her family, Hershale Wohl, became an active Communist. He was her oldest cousin, the son of her mother's older brother Bendits. Hershale was an intellectual who was exposed to "progressive ideas" in the early 1930s. He was bright, sarcastic, and read voraciously. Hershale went to Bucharest when Rita was a child, so she did not know him very well. In Bucharest he worked as the right-hand man of Ana Pauker, a leading member of the "Jewish" or Stalinist — non-Romanian — faction of the Romanian Communist Party, which brought about the Communist assumption of power between 1945 and 1947.

In Bucharest, Hershale changed his name to Visan. He became an integrated member of the Romanian Communist Party and remained there until his death of a heart attack in 1982 at age sixty-one. In 1966, when Rita and her husband were in Bucharest, they visited Avrumabe Wohl, Hershale's younger brother. She talked with Hershale on the telephone from Avrumabe's apartment. Hershale asked about Nora and wanted very much to visit Rita and her husband, but Avrumabe sternly discouraged their visiting him.

Rita still ponders what might have led this one of Shaje Wohl's many grandchildren to deny the values of his background and his Jewish identity to become a dedicated Communist, alienated from other members of his family. Hershale was the only cousin who was not in Rădăuţi when the family was deported to Mogilev. In this hour of sorrow, with so much of the family deported, he and Uncle Summer Wolf were in Bucharest and escaped the fate of so many others. Summer and Hershale, being of different generations, turned in different directions. Summer appears to have turned more to his religion, while Hershale, still a teenager and cut off from his parents and community, moved away from it, perhaps toward a different sort of faith.

Before Rita left Rădăuţi another event that took place in Romania dramatically affected her stay. The state terror was accompanied by increasing economic chaos, unprecedented in Romanian history. Famine was threatening, and the country, increasingly dependent on outside food shipments, was approaching bankruptcy. Inflation reached the point where the Romanian leu, in the summer of 1947, had less than one three-hundredth its buying power of 1945 when matched against the British pound sterling. There were multiple causes for this, including the aftermath of the war itself, the deliberate disorganization of production by the Communists, and two consecutive droughts in 1946 and 1947. But the most important cause was the plundering of the Romanian economy by the Soviet Union. On August 15, the Groza government announced the currency reform it had long been preparing in secret. Except for certain farmers and workers, who obtained a privileged exchange rate, the Romanian populace received new lei to replace old ones at the ratio of 1 to 20,000. "For all of us it was a disaster. We woke up one morning with the news. I remember my father telling me, 'Rita, you have to get back to Prague.'" Rita has often speculated that had her parents been more selfish, less quick to place the interests of their children first, they might not have had to spend so many lonesome years away from them.

"Under the impact of these events I had to finagle my return to Prague, for which I needed a visa and a ticket. After several weeks and circuitous, byzantine manipulations, I obtained both and returned to Prague." Her Romanian passport had made it possible for her to obtain a visa from the Czech authorities, especially as she was a medical student registered in Prague. Uncle Summer, who still lived in Bucharest, helped her obtain the train ticket.

After Rita returned to Czechoslovakia at the end of August, events moved rapidly in Romania, with disastrous results for the embassy in Prague. In October and November, Iuliu Maniu and other leaders of the National Peasant Party were tried and condemned to hard labor for life, while all remaining non-Communists were dismissed from the Groza cabinet. With the appointment on November 7 of Ana Pauker as minister of foreign affairs and Vasile Luca as minister of finance, Romania became, in effect, a Soviet colony.

On November 12, King Michael, who was powerless to prevent any of these changes, went to London to attend the marriage of Princess Elizabeth, and while abroad he became engaged to Princess Anne de Bourbon Parma. Determined to stay on the throne, he returned to Romania on December 21. Nine days later, he and the

Queen Mother were summoned by Groza and Gheorghe Georghiu-Dej, who had emerged as the chief instrument of Stalin's exploitive colonization policies, from their country retreat in Sinaia to the royal palace in Bucharest. They were presented with an abdication document for immediate execution. Michael twice refused to sign, but the telephone lines were cut and the palace surrounded by Communist troops. When Groza threatened great bloodshed, perhaps civil war, the king finally signed. On the same day — December 30, 1947 — the Romanian Peoples Republic was established and a new constitution drafted. Thus ended the Romanian monarchy and the seventy-year period of Romanian national sovereignty.

As soon as the Romanian ambassador in Prague learned that the king had abdicated, he and his entire staff attempted to escape by plane during the night. The plane crashed and all its passengers were killed. A considerable amount of gold, found in the wreckage, was, according to the Czech papers and the talk at the embassy, Romanian treasure held abroad. These allegations were never substantiated.

When Rita arrived for work at the embassy the next day, she found only the janitor. Thinking this was the end of her diplomatic experience, she turned around and went home. But the new ambassador who soon arrived knew no French, the diplomatic language, and spoke Romanian with a Russian accent, reflecting years spent in the Soviet Union. "He immediately sent for me. He said that he needed me and he actually did need me more than the previous ambassador, who spoke French fluently. I told him I was busy studying medicine. It was the exact same story as it had been in Mogilev and the foundry. He said, 'Ah, for the Royalist regime you could work, and for us, not.' For me it was horrible, because I didn't like him. The whole atmosphere was different."

One day the new ambassador gathered a large group of Romanians, including some of the peasants who had come to work on contract, into the courtyard of the embassy to tell them that the king had left the country. The ambassador spoke to the assembled group, telling them "how the king had sucked the blood of the Romanian people and so on. I was supposed to stand there and translate it into Czech because there were also Czech officials present. I didn't want to do it because I didn't like what he said about the king. That was one of our first controversies, as he recognized in the inflection of my voice that I was not rendering his words accurately."

The Romanian peasants also did not like hearing what the

ambassador had told them, "and then, in old Romanian style, they said, 'We want to answer' and 'The oldest among us will reply.' It was a very old peasant. We could not even understand how he had happened to come. He took off his *caciula,* his fur hat, and said, 'Mr. Ambassador, we heard what you told us, but we have one Lord in heaven and one king on earth, and whom do we have now?'"

Once the Communists gained control of the Romanian foreign ministry they no longer wanted to have their workers in Czechoslovakia and decided to pull them home. The difficulties between the Romanian and Czech farmers became a pretext for the cancellation by the Romanian embassy of the contract with the Czech Ministry of Agriculture. The Romanian embassy gathered the Romanian farm workers from all around the country at a railroad station close to the Slovak border. The Romanian workers were confined to a roped-off area there until they were sent home by train. The embassy placed a Romanian flag within this confine. "One day the embassy received a call saying that all the bicycles in the village where the farmers were collected had disappeared. Everybody knew where they had gone." The Czechs could not go into the area because it was considered Romanian territory. Inside the enclosure, which was about the size of a large football field, the Romanians were riding around on the bicycles, which they were planning to take home with them on the train as bounty. Expecting to take or send home a certain amount of money, they had felt cheated when the contract was broken.

Rita and the cultural attaché went to urge the Romanians to return the bicycles. "We were scared, thinking the Czechs would take it out on us because we were coming from the Romanian embassy. When we arrived angry Czech villagers stood in a circle around the territory, shouting at the Romanians. The Romanians were laughing and riding around on their bicycles." Most of the Romanians recognized Rita. The Czech authorities from the Ministry of Agriculture insisted that Rita and the Romanian cultural attaché cajole the Romanian farmers into returning the bicycles, which they did reluctantly.

Not long after the final Communist takeover in Romania, and the replacement of the embassy personnel, changes took place in Prague that signaled the end of Czechoslovakia's brief taste of freedom. Although the official Communist takeover did not occur until early in 1948, the ground had been prepared in the closing months of the war.

Having been betrayed by the West in 1938, the Czech leaders Jan Masaryk and Edvard Beneš did not feel they could rely on the Western democracies to protect their country from Stalinist Russia in the postwar period. Beneš, therefore, maintained fairly constant contact with the Soviet leadership. In March 1945, as Red Army soldiers advanced across the borders of Slovakia, he was in Moscow preparing for his return from exile in London to the Czech homeland. In April, a temporary Czech government was established in the Slovak industrial city of Košice. The cabinet included several prominent Czech Communists who were plotting to transform the country into a Marxist-Leninist state.

Winston Churchill, Franklin D. Roosevelt, and Joseph Stalin decided at the Yalta Conference in February 1945 that Berlin, Prague, and Vienna could be taken by whomever got there first. In mid-April the left flank of General George Patton's Third Army crossed the Czech border from the west, while the right flank to the south swept through Linz in Austria on the way to Vienna. After Roosevelt's death on April 12, Churchill and Anthony Eden urged President Harry Truman to press ahead and liberate Prague and as much Czechoslovakian territory as possible to strengthen the hand of the Western powers in postwar dealings with Stalin. Patton's armies continued their rapid advance to the east. But alluding to agreements made with the Russians that Czechoslovakia was to be in the orbit of Soviet control, Truman, through General Dwight D. Eisenhower, instructed Patton on May 6 to halt his advance into Czechoslovakia, although the Russians were still many miles to the east of the Vltava. Despite these instructions, Patton, acting secretly, and characteristically, on his own, sent emissaries to Prague, proposing that the city be liberated by the Americans the next day if the newly organized Czech National Committee so wished. But the emissaries were greeted by a leading Communist, Joseph Smrkovsky, who told them that the citizens of Prague preferred to be liberated by the Russians, though they were still a good day's march away. Patton felt he had to accept Smrkovsky's decision and held his units back. On the morning of May 9, Soviet Marshal Konev's forces entered Prague, assuring the eventual Soviet domination of Czechoslovakia. By the end of 1945, all American troops had withdrawn from Czechoslovakian soil. As we discovered during our visit in 1981, this second betrayal by the West remains a source of bitterness for the Czech people. "Why did [the Americans] abandon us when they had already liberated most of Moravia?" a taxi driver asked Rita. The formal Communist takeover in February 1948 was just the last scene of a drama, the script for which had been virtually completed in May 1945.

The coalition government Beneš established in Prague in the late spring of 1945 was a kind of Trojan horse, with several crucial ministries already under Communist control. The Communists had initially sought to gain power through the cover of a parliamentary process, but the high-handed political tactics of the Soviet-controlled Czech Communists became increasingly unpopular. As their chance of seizing power by parliamentary means ebbed away, Klement Gottwald and the other Communist leaders determined to seize power by any means. The Communist-controlled trade unions and police formed revolutionary "action committees" to agitate workers and farmers in towns and villages against the government, while the democratic leaders were intimidated by a systematic campaign of Gestapo-like brutality, threats, slander, and fabrication of alleged plots by the United States.

On February 19, 1948, Soviet Deputy Foreign Minister Valerian A. Zorin arrived in Prague. The transfer of power to a government headed by Gottwald, with a list of ministers approved by Zorin, was accelerated. Beneš was forced to submit to Gottwald, bringing to an end the brief revival of Czechoslovak democracy. Two days later, Beneš left Prague for his country home in Sezimovo Usti, south of Prague, where he remained president technically but without power until his resignation in June. He died on September 3 after several months' illness.

Following the February coup, the Communists moved quickly to consolidate power. On March 10, Masaryk's broken body was found in the courtyard of his residence at Czernin palace. The suspicion that he was murdered by the Communists has never evaporated, especially as other convenient "suicides" took place in Czechoslovakia in the months and years that followed. Many Czech professionals rushed to join the Communist Party, which has raised questions about the "political opportunism" of the Czechs. At its peak in November 1948, which was the month that Rita Stenzler was to escape from the country, party membership reached 2.5 million, 18 percent of the population, or one of every three Czech adults. No other Eastern European country has such a high membership in the party, including the Soviet Union itself, in which less than 6 percent of the population were Communist Party members in the early 1970s.[3]

Late in the spring of 1947, shortly before Rita's visit to Romania, the household at 2283 Na Kleovce had broken up. Herbert Aleš married a Belgian woman and moved into his apartment with her. Eventually he and his wife returned to Paris, taking his mother with them. But Gusta got along poorly with her daughter-in-law and Herbert put her in a home for the aged, from which Gusta, by then ninety, sent Rita long letters in extravagant Gothic handwriting. She complained of the dull old people in the house and told sadly of how she missed her young friends on Na Kleovce Street. Tussi and Else moved out and bought an apartment in Prague. Herta returned briefly to Bucharest before moving with her parents to Vienna in 1948. The German professor's widow, Marie, was repatriated to Germany.

Rita and Nora rented an apartment at 29 Veletrzni, on the left bank of the Vltava, not far from the Romanian embassy, from a young couple, the Mautners. The husband, Victor, was a Jew who had been hidden by a young Czech girl in the country during the war. After the war the two were married and bought the building on Veletrzni Street. The Mautners were fun to be with and the apartment was pleasant and comfortable.

Life on Veletrzni Street was different from that on Na Kleovce. Nora was out of the army and had a job making leather handbags. Evenings and mornings before work she cooked meals for Rita to have when she came home between or after classes. "She was like a mother to me. With shame I must acknowledge that not only did I and my friends eat her deliciously prepared Rădăuți-style meals, but I also wore her clothes, which were always immaculate while mine were in disarray." Rita, in Nora's clothes, would sneak home before it was time for Nora to return, change into her own clothes, and hang Nora's back in her closet. Nora invariably could tell, just by the way the clothes were hanging, that Rita had worn them and was furious with her.

Rita studied more in Veletrzni than had been possible at Na Kleovce, with so many parties. Chemistry, physics, and histology were particularly difficult for her. "They were too precise for my unprecise brain, and studying in Czech made it more difficult for my technically untalented mind." Her excellent memory and perseverance helped.

The short-lived free Czech republic of 1945–1948 was in many ways a traditional democracy. Students could come to Hradcany Castle, the historical center of authority in Prague, where Beneš resided. A gentle man, he would come out and talk with students and others strolling in the castle area. After the coup in February 1948, Rita stood with the students outside the castle as they shouted to Beneš, "Don't sell us out. Don't let us become a police state." But it was, of course, to no avail, as Beneš was soon to retire to his summer home.

Rita remembers the rumors of murder after Jan Masaryk's body was found. "Specifically, they said that Jan Masaryk had been shot and pushed out the window because of his strong opposition to the Communist takeover and the strong emotional tie the Czech people felt toward the son of their first president. He was democratic, charismatic, and lovable." At Masaryk's state funeral, Rita heard the weeping Czech women on the sidewalks of Vaclavske Namesti say that the violets they had seen when viewing the open casket of Masaryk "were at his temple to camouflage the gunshot wound there." There was mutual affection between the students and this charming man, who had gained a reputation as a playboy in the West. Once when the violinist David Oistrakh was to play at a concert in Prague, Rita could not get a ticket. Masaryk spotted her at the entrance to the theater. Recognizing her as one of the students he had entertained at the Jan Opletal student congress in 1945, he smuggled her into his box. Rita, needless to say, enjoyed herself immensely in his splendid, prestigious seat.

In May 1948, there was a *sokol* in Prague, an Olympic-like sports meet held every four years in Czechoslovakia. No sokol had been held during the German occupation. The Communists did not cancel the event. Gymnasts, equestrians, and other athletes came to Prague from all over the country. Rita stood in front of the Ambassador Hotel in Vaclavske Namesti and watched the mounted athletes on their horses as they shouted in unison, *"Praha se nam libi ale nas President nam zde chybi"* [We like Prague, but we miss our president].

When Beneš died in exile in September, his people said good-bye to him at Hradcany Castle. "They cried for days. I never saw such an outpouring. It was not just Beneš's death. Their freedom died too." The students invited Rita to go to the castle with them, but she did not. Though she had gone there before, she did not feel entitled to now. "This man cannot mean to me what he does to you," she explained.

When we visited Prague in the summer of 1981, we saw at the Vaclavske (National) Museum life-sized statues of Smetana, Dvořák, and Tomáš Masaryk, the first president of the Czech republic. There was no sign of Beneš. It was as if he had never existed. Rita asked a clerk at the museum check-in counter for the Beneš and Opletal monuments (Opletal had been murdered on the steps of the museum). The woman said the only thing she could say — that they did not exist. But her eyes said much more. They told of the pain of a people whose history had been rewritten to fit a political ideology and purpose.

✳

Rita's emotional involvement with the Middle East conflict began at about this time. The British mandate in Palestine ended on May 14, 1948, and on the same day the State of Israel was recognized by the United States and the Soviet Union. The Arab-Israeli War of Independence broke out almost immediately. "I was in Prague at Veletrzni 29 and remember hearing on the radio that Jerusalem was besieged and had its water supply cut off. The religious Jews in Jerusalem would not permit the first caravan of water to desecrate the Sabbath. They insisted, the report said, that the water for the thirsty city wait until sunset and the appearance of the first star. The moment I heard this announcement, Zaziu emerged in my memory. Whenever I arrive at the outskirts of Jerusalem and see the terraced land, my heart remembers this first fantasy encounter with Jerusalem and my grandfather who inspired my relationship to the Middle East conflict." For Rita the word *Jerusalem* has always been connected with her grandfather, for every year at the Passover Seder he would say, *Hashanah habaah be Jerushalaim* (Next year in Jerusalem).

Rita has always found it easy to understand the passion that Jerusalem evokes for both Jews and Arabs. "When I hear a Muslim say, 'I am from Jerusalem,' I can see in his eyes the memory of the colors, the light, the smells, the sounds, and the hustle and bustle of Jerusalem. When I stand at the Western Wall and watch the Chassidim dance on Friday night at sunset, then I remember all the stories Zaziu told me from the Talmud." For Zaziu, and thus for Rita, too, Jerusalem was a spiritual experience, associated with feelings more than politics.

✳

Before long, the efforts to recruit Rita to the Communist cause began in Prague as they had in Romania. "One day I was in our apartment, reading *I Chose Freedom* by a Soviet defector who had fled to Canada. I had reached the part where he broke emotionally with communism and as a secret act of vengeance used Stalin's picture as toilet paper. I was just reading that passage when the doorbell rang and two students came into my room, asking me to join the Communist Party. I quickly sat down on the couch on top of the open book, which was forbidden literature after the Communist takeover. I remember feeling the inner comedy of that encounter." This and similar episodes made Rita wonder if she would not soon have to leave Prague.

"As the political events in Prague in the spring and summer of 1948 impinged on us — janitors, for instance, forcing us to march in the May Day parade — student friends from western European countries contacted me and attempted to help me get out." The French and Dutch student associations particularly reached out to her through their representatives, who had met her in Prague. "It was heartwarming to feel the care and concern of foreign students whom I had met under heavenly circumstances and who, now times had changed, concerned themselves, on their own initiative, with my fate."

In the fall of 1948 Rita took her remaining examinations for the first rigorosum. The second rigorosum, consisting of pharmacology, pathology, internal medicine, pediatrics, and psychiatry/neurology, and the third, which included hygiene, forensic medicine, obstetrics and gynecology, ophthalmology, dermatology, and surgery, still lay ahead. In spite of the encroachments on her time and freedom of the increasingly oppressive Communist regime, Rita wished to continue her medical studies. But the atmosphere of joyful freedom in Prague was gone. The people in the streets, streetcars, and shops were sullen and angry. "The students and my friends were fiercely angry." Rita was increasingly harassed about joining the Communist student organization. Fear and secrecy grew at the Romanian embassy, and Rita's contacts with Western embassy personnel were frowned upon, especially her sneaking into the Italian embassy across the street.

Rita's passport was to expire on November 9, 1948. As this date approached, Rita decided to attempt to extend it. When she asked the consul general to grant it, he referred her to the ambassador. The ambassador called her into his office and said, "I am your father here because I am the father of all the Romanians and you are the only Romanian student here in Czechoslovakia, so I am going to advise you like a father that you should take your passport and go home to have it extended." "I said, 'When should I go?' He said, 'I will have a seat on a plane for you tomorrow morning.'"

Rita believes firmly that if she had indeed gone home the Romanian regime would have arrested her and sent her to prison, for it was well known that she did not subscribe to the party line. The ambassador had made three or four attempts to convince Rita to join the diplomatic corps, which meant first joining the Communist Party. ("He knew me and I knew him, and we had quite a few ideas that were different.") Furthermore, she was carrying a passport, given to her by an ambassador from the previous Royalist government, "which had no rhyme or reason ever to have been issued at all."

The ambassador was telling Rita what, in his official capacity, he was supposed to say. From his point of view, it was the only way he could act. "He had to make my situation fit into the regime. I told him I thought that it was a very good idea for me to go home, but I didn't even go back to the apartment. I still had my passport, which was good for two more days. I went straight to the Austrian embassy." Rita went to the consular office and said she wanted a transit visa for Vienna so she could stop there on the way to Bucharest. A young woman asked, "Why would you want to go from Prague to Bucharest via Vienna?" "I said, 'Well, I want to buy anatomical atlases in Vienna.' That was a story. The woman went to see the consul. She reappeared and said the consul insisted on seeing me personally. I knew a lot of ambassadors and consuls, but when I went in I realized he was somebody I didn't know. He regarded me suspiciously because at that time Prague was full of spies and a lot of students were spies. He said, 'You explain to me why you need to go to Vienna when you are on your way to Bucharest.' I decided that this was a moment when the truth was the best lie, and I looked him straight in the eye and said, 'Because I want to get off in Vienna.' He said, 'That's a very good idea.' Then he looked at his watch and said, 'Don't go anywhere. Go straight from here to the train station.' He told me there was a train leaving at such and such a time. I did exactly as he said. I did not go home to see Nora. (I had never involved her with my visa or passport issues.) I had a little bit of money — just enough to buy a ticket to Vienna."

Rita had several close friends in Prague, but she did not tell anyone, even Kristian, that she was leaving for fear that they would have been considered accomplices and suffered the consequences if they knew. The train was quite deserted. There was one compartment in which there were several Romanian officials. "They were truly going to Bucharest via Vienna and Budapest as I was only pretending to go. I went to the opposite end of the train. But lo and behold, they spotted me, and the whole group came to join me. They sat with me, and they talked about going to Bucharest, and I talked about going to Bucharest. The moment the train pulled into Vienna and stopped, I saw that they were selling corn on the cob at the station. I said, 'I'm going to get some corn on the cob for all of us.' I hopped off the train, and that was my departure from Czechoslovakia."

Rita entered the depot and told a stationmaster, "I'm a refugee from Eastern Europe." Because of the political atmosphere, people were converging on Vienna from all over Eastern Europe. When Rita declared herself a refugee, the Viennese authorities who had jurisdiction for displaced persons immediately helped her. "They gave me a piece of paper that said that I was a displaced person, that I have no land of my own and cannot claim help from any country. Then they put me on another train bound for the center of the city. That was my arrival in Vienna." She had escaped once again from the communist world, to which she would return only as a visitor.

6. Vienna: Displaced in a Divided City

After a few days in Vienna without papers, Rita obtained an official card at the Rothschild Hospital, establishing her identity as a "displaced person (DP)." The Rothschild Hospital, located in the eighteenth district in the American sector, was the headquarters for DPs in Vienna. To appreciate Rita's strange and precarious situation in November 1948, it is necessary to understand the political circumstances of the divided city to which she had escaped.

Seven years later, in May 1955, the ambassadors of the four occupying powers were to meet in Moscow to sign the state treaty granting independence to a neutral Austria, and in September of that year the last Russian soldiers were withdrawn, leaving the country free to pursue its own political destiny. But in 1948, when Rita Stenzler, age twenty-three, arrived virtually penniless in Vienna, it was by no means certain that this would be the outcome. Starting in the closing weeks of the war, Austria had become a focal point in the East-West struggle.

Vienna was liberated by Russian troops on April 13, 1945, by soldiers of Marshal Fedor I. Tolbukhin's Third Ukrainian Front, after several days of artillery exchange and street fighting that caused considerable damage, especially in the center of the city. During the early months following liberation, the Soviet troops treated the local population brutally, alienating the Austrians from their Communist liberators. The Soviet troops regarded the Austrians as pro-Nazi Germans, and indeed Hitler's army had been greeted with enthusiasm in Vienna when the "Anschluss occurred in 1938. By 1947 over half a million Austrians were registered as former Nazis. As a result of agreements among the four Allied powers, the country was divided into Soviet, U.S., British, and French zones, and Vienna, which, like Berlin, was in the Soviet zone, was divided in turn into four sectors, with the inner city under joint, quadripartite control.

By the end of 1947 the Communist takeover was complete in Hungary, Poland, Romania, and Bulgaria, and in February 1948, as noted, Czechoslovakia had fallen under complete Communist control. The Austrians wondered if they would be next. In July 1948, the Soviets, seeking to thwart the Western economic recovery program for Germany, stopped all rail and road traffic between Berlin and the West. Although the blockade was successfully circumvented by a massive air lift, the Viennese remained anxious that at any moment the Soviets might cut the routes linking the Western sectors of the city with the West. After her experiences since 1944 in Bessarabia, northern Bukovina, Romania, and then Czechoslovakia, Rita took a Communist assumption of control in Austria for granted. "I was determined that if it happened I would take off again."

Other developments, however, made a Soviet takeover of Austria more difficult. In the summer of 1945, still under the Soviet occupation, a provisional government, led by the distinguished Austrian socialist leader and former chancellor Dr. Karl Renner, had established itself with broad powers. This government represented an effective and popular alternative to Communist control. Furthermore, Marshall Tito was demonstrating in Yugoslavia that even within the Communist world successful opposition to Soviet domination was possible. In April 1948, the Austrian coalition government decided, despite strong Soviet pressures, to join the European Recovery Program, or Marshall Plan. The extraordinary economic recovery that resulted from the Marshall Plan began to make a Communist takeover less likely.

Fear of Communist uprisings continued in Austria, however, until October 1950, when a clumsily conducted, Soviet-inspired general worker's strike ended in total failure. Rita recalls the disappointment of her Communist fellow students. "We heckled them." This defeat marked the end of significant Communist strength in Austria apart from the Red Army. Stalin did not order the Red Army to intervene, not only because there were formidable Western military forces arrayed against him, but also because, unlike the situation in Romania, Hungary, and Czechoslovakia, there was no sympathetic internal political structure or continuing economic privation that might give a military attack a reasonable chance of success.

After the collapse of Communist political power in Austria, pressure grew for "liberation from the liberators." Yet treaty negotiations moved slowly. The death of Stalin in 1953 seemed to pave the way for a settlement, but the political impasse was not broken until February 1955, when Soviet Foreign Minister Vyacheslav Molotov made an offer that led to the signing of the Austrian State Treaty on May 15. Three days after the treaty was signed John Foster Dulles, in a televised conversation with President Dwight D. Eisenhower, noted that this occasion "marks the first time that the Red Armies will have turned their face in the other direction and gone back."[1]

Rita's first weeks in Vienna were lonely ones. She still belonged in spirit to the world of Eastern Europe and at first felt no connection with her fellow displaced persons. "Their 'in between' status bothered me. I also felt unconnected with Vienna. It did not correspond to the fin de siècle Vienna my parents had described to me from their youth." Rita had left Czechoslovakia because she knew she would not be able to get out later. "That was the decisive factor. But it was sad, coming to Vienna. I had placed the iron curtain between my parents and myself. They learned about it when I sent them, for their wedding anniversary on November 12, 1948, a congratulatory cable from Vienna."

Vienna was full of displaced persons in 1948. But for Rita the official designation was humiliating. "I felt like an object, a displaced object without rights, with no place to stay, no means, and no permit to work. During the Nazi years, somehow I experienced the yellow star as being singled out, as something special, because that's how Mutticuta conveyed it to me by word and deed." But the DP label was different. "Maybe there was also a feeling of disgust at myself for asking for refuge from Austrian authorities who had so gleefully welcomed Hitler just a few years before. To be a displaced peson was a passive, unpleasant status for me. I didn't like this appendix to my identity. Being in the free world was painful."

Rita's financial situation was further aggravated by the fact that her father, true to his Mogilev habit of helping anybody in Rădăuţi who needed it, wrote her often asking for medication for people who couldn't get it. Since she never wrote her parents about her precarious financial situation — "just the opposite; I always reassured them" — they did not know about it. Rita always sent the medication, even when she had to borrow money to do so.

There was in Vienna a Joint Distribution Committee, an American Jewish organization located at the Rothschild Hospital, which provided minimal financial support and other assistance to Jewish refugee survivors from all over Europe. The committee contacted Rita as soon as she arrived in Vienna and offered her a small stipend, barely enough for subsistence. When members of the Joint Distribution Committee were told that the displaced students could not live on so little money, they explained that the American donors did not understand why students could not take summer jobs, as they did in the United States. Some of the female medical students married or became involved with men who could support them. Others dropped out of medical school, which Rita would not consider. The Joint Distribution Committee maintained a canteen for displaced students and others where she could obtain one free meal a day with her identity card. The canteen, however, was located in the Russian sector, while the University of Vienna Medical School and the places Rita found to stay were in the American sector.

Although a control agreement was supposed to lift restrictions on interzonal traffic, the Jewish Joint Distribution Committee and the Soviet occupation forces had little to do with each other as a result of "profound disagreements." Rita's identity card, therefore, which was good for the U.S., French, and British authorities — who never asked for identification papers — was not valid in the Russian sector. There was a risk of arrest for Czech, Hungarian, and Romanian students should they be stopped by Russian patrols and found to be lacking the appropriate documents. So a group of students without documents would gather each day for the trip to and from the canteen on the principle that there was safety in numbers. During these months Rita somehow managed to avoid being stopped. A number of students disappeared, "but we never knew why or where. Rumor had it that some of them spied for one or several occupation forces."

From her parents Rita had heard of a Vienna filled with music and cakes and other wonderful luxuries. Although she could not afford it, she was unable to resist treating herself once in a while. "I remember I used to go to the Joint Distribution Committee once a month to pick up my stipend and from there straight to a chocolate shop to buy *Negerbrot* [black chocolate with almonds]." The stipend did not provide enough for clothes. "During the five years there I bought only one dress. The Joint Committee would give us what arrived from the United States. I remember during one very cold winter we excitedly rummaged through the boxes, but to our dismay found only bathing suits. The shipment probably represented what New York women had discarded in September."

Rita moved from room to room, selecting each because it was the cheapest obtainable, generally in war-damaged buildings in drab, gloomy neighborhoods. She would stay in each place for about three to five months, then move on when she was unable to pay the rent. Usually the rooms were unheated.

The distance from her parents was especially difficult for Rita. "They knew we belonged to two different worlds which were in profound conflict with each other. They responded in their usual unselfish loving way, expressing their delight that I was in the free world." Separated ("God knows till when") through her own initiative from parents, sister, and close friends, with barely enough money on which to subsist, Rita experienced many sad, isolated days that contrasted painfully with the pleasure of her life in Prague. "My having to wait for handouts for clothes and money did not help my feeling of worthwhileness." In Herta's words, Rita "had days, nights, and evenings when she was depressed. She had reason. She had no money, and it was cold and she had one skirt to wear. And she had so many years to study and didn't know what would happen after . . . I remember once in the middle of the night she called me and said, 'Please come and take me out of the coffeehouse. I have no money to pay for my coffee.'"

When Rita applied to the University of Vienna Medical School, the dean informed her with bitterness that he had lost a son, a medical student, on the Russian front and was not too receptive to this refugee from Eastern Europe. He recommended to Rita, as he had to other displaced students from behind the iron curtain, that she go to a newly opened medical school in Graz or Innsbruck, where she would not have to repeat the first rigorosum exam. "After expressing my condolences about his son, I informed him that I would stay at Vienna medical school and repeat the exams if he would give me credit for the courses I had completed. He said he would if I successfully passed the six exams by Christmastime — within a six-week period." She passed the exams and then had to worry about tuition, which was three times as much for foreign students as for Austrians. By passing additional exams, called "colloquia," with an excellent grade, Rita qualified for the same tuition fees the Austrian students paid and managed to obtain a scholarship to cover her tuition. Once admitted to the medical school, Rita went to the police station every two weeks for the next five years with a letter from the dean saying she had not yet completed her studies.

The University of Vienna Medical School is housed in an austere and commanding building in the center of the city. Along the arcade that borders its huge courtyard are busts of the great figures who studied and taught medicine at the university — Kohler, Werner, von Economo, Kretschmer, Nothnagel, Doppler, Mautner, Freud's teachers Brücke and Meynert — and a poor quality bust of Freud himself.

"I enjoyed the beautiful lectures but knew nothing about how to apply what I heard. I forced myself, but it was dead, like studying Latin." There was little opportunity for practical clinical experience and no small-group teaching. The students sat in huge amphitheaters, "imbued with the glory of the great men of medicine who had lectured there." The professors hardly noticed the students or else treated them arrogantly. They wrote "splendid books," which the students could not afford to buy. Rita enjoyed pathology, a very difficult course, because it required the experience of dissecting many cadavers before the students could present themselves for the exam. "Professor Chiari — we called him the corpses' general — made no compromises and death makes no compromises. Professor Chiari did not like female medical students and denied our existence. When he called on us he addressed us as 'Mr.' So I took my pathology exam as Mr. Stenzler."

The German system of not requiring attendance at classes and presenting oneself for exams whenever one felt ready — a system that still prevails — "was not conducive to accomplishment in my state of lethargy and depression." For the first and only time in her life, Rita found herself making lists of what to do the next day in order to make herself get up, go to the lectures, and study. Everything seemed overwhelming. But there were benefits to studying medicine in Vienna. First, the lectures were in Rita's near-native German, not the difficult Czech language. Then there were other displaced students who had been thrown together from Poland, Bulgaria, Hungary, Romania, and Czechoslovakia by the winds of war and occupation. "Our most common bond was that we were all longing for our homes, our families, and that none of us could, or wanted to, stay in Austria after we finished our studies." Rita was once again able to create a sense of community with the displaced students from the various "people's republics." "They were my buddies in Vienna, much like my cousins had been in Rădăuţi. They were protective of me, and I considered them all like relatives."

As she had in Mogilev and Prague, Rita met and associated with the local people, even though her fellow Jewish displaced students frowned on Austrians. The most dangerous topic of conversation with the Viennese was their whereabouts between 1941 and 1945. Once, over a microscope in histopathology, a classmate told Rita about having served as a guard in a camp in the Ukraine. "He asked me, 'Where were you during the war?' I replied by walking across the laboratory toward another microscope."

Rita found Vienna a center of intrigue. On any given day one could be approached by representatives of several national groups to spy for them. The displaced students were the cheapest and easiest targets. They spoke foreign languages, had little money, and were forbidden by law to work. They belonged to no country, and there was no consulate or embassy to represent or inquire about them. Apparently rootless and without allegiance, they were therefore considered buyable. "On the walks to the canteen I remember a journalism student reporting how one set of recruiters climbed out the window when representatives of an opposing secret service came in through the front door. It was offensive to be found such easy prey. The amazing thing was that in the face of all this chaos and deprivation we studied hard."

Because her living quarters were so terrible, Rita studied in a coffeehouse. Her favorite, close to the Alserstrasse, was the Café Beethoven, which no longer exists. There she could sit all day and study, read newspapers from all over the world, and receive phone calls — she did not have the money to make outgoing calls. One special waiter at the café, an elderly gentleman, would orchestrate her study by directing noisy guests to tables far away from her *stamm tisch* (usual table). He would call her to the phone "with the same respect and discretion as he would call the director of a bank or my Viennese professor of pharmacology." On the day before Rita took her last exam at the medical school, this gentleman, whom she called Herr Oberst (literally, Mr. Superior or Mr. Headwaiter — "whether he really was a headwaiter, I don't know, but Viennese protocol demanded that one address everybody a rank above his actual status"), asked to have his picture taken serving her a cup of coffee, a photograph still in her possession.

Music and theater raised Rita's spirits. "I had no money to buy tickets, but people invited me to concerts, theater, and opera . . . This was the Vienna of my parents' youth, the Vienna they had talked about. Because my lodgings were bleak and cold, and my heart hungry — my stomach also — I savored these concerts with passion. I think one reason people invited me was because they knew I cherished Vienna's music and theater." Rita knew the words of many of the operettas, since her mother had sung them to her during her childhood. "When I sat at the operetta *Die Czardasz Fürstin* [*The Czardas Princess*] by Imre Kálman, I almost felt my mother at my side. Soon after Rita settled in Vienna, letters began to come from Prague. Although it was all censored because it came from Eastern Europe, the mail became "an elixir."

In Vienna, Herta Korn was, and still is, Rita's closest friend. She was then working in the French mission and taking home a small salary. Rita had a second friend, also from Czernowitz, now dead, whose parents invited her to their home on Sundays for a meal. But it was Herta who was her emotional anchor during these troubled years, one of the "sunshines of my life." Herta's parents, who had been Austrian citizens from before World War II, left Romania legally for Austria after the kingdom collapsed in 1947. With Herta, they had settled in Vienna in 1948, before Rita arrived. Herta's father, then in his mid-seventies, successfully passed an examination qualifying him to practice law in Vienna. Herta's fiancé, Bubi, a Romanian citizen, could not get out. He crossed the border on foot twice but was caught each time. He was able to reach Vienna in 1950, when he and Herta were finally married. Then, according to Herta, Bubi began to earn money, and "we all three had more." Bubi would sometimes slip money into Rita's purse.

Herta, Bubi, and their two children, Alexander and Kitty — both physicians — still live in the center of Vienna, next to the church of St. Stephan's. My youngest son, Tony, and I met the Korn family at their home in the summer of 1983. Herta is sensitive, intuitive, and full of vigor, the lively, steadfast friend she has always been. In her sixties, she bicycles with her husband and friends along the Danube River. Herta described her sisterly and "motherlike" feelings toward Rita, who was "very neglected. She didn't keep herself well and I was always after her. I spoke to her like a big sister. It was a really difficult time. She had no money to buy anything. Only a strong person like she is," Herta observed, "could stand so many hours in a coffee shop without money for the next day's breakfast."

According to Rita, "From 1948 to 1953, Herta and I were true, true comrades. I wore her clothes — since I had none and she just a few — I ate her food — she did not have much of that either — but, most important, she trembled with me for each of my exams, for each of my love letters from Prague, and helped me search for a country. When I finally graduated in May 1953, Herta substituted for my parents, my sister, and my hometown. She even gave me a watch I still have — my first watch since being deported from Rădăuți."

For Rita, there is a mystique, an almost magical quality, to the intuitive closeness she feels with Herta. "In 1948, when I got out of Prague and arrived in Vienna, I found Herta there, and I've been finding her there on all my many European trips over the years. I meet her all over Europe and everything between us is still the way it always was. When I came back to Vienna from the United States for the first time in 1963, Herta was at the airport with her adorable two children. They curtsied and handed me little bouquets of violets, and Herta and I continued our conversations from 1953 as if only one day had passed. When I was desperate about the war in Israel in 1973, and I felt that I needed to go there to be with my people and my father, Herta drove me all through Europe until we found a plane willing to take me. In 1971, I was going to Israel and wanted to make a short visit to Morocco on my way there. I cabled Herta to — 'Meet London, Heathrow, flight such and such, for flight to Marrakech. Are you willing?' Her cable reply was *Ein frohes Jawohl* [a happy yes] and we flew to Marrakech, visited Fez, Casablanca, and were delighted to be together. We have had skiing rendezvous in Lech, Saint-Moritz, Gstaad. We have hiked in Kitzbühel, Lucerne, Hamburg, Würzburg, Lübeck, Bremen, and we have dined in the company of our husbands and children in Baden-Baden, Zurich, and on and on.

"But all encounters have been spontaneously arranged. Our rendezvous are incomprehensible for the normal world. We used to meet in cafés in Prague and Vienna two to three hours later than the arranged time, and we would both walk in at that time as if that was the time we were supposed to meet. Herta lives in the heart of Vienna. I live in Palos Verdes Estates in California with frequent hops to Europe and almost always with a stopover in Vienna. We talk half the night in Vienna, we eat from each other's plates in the *konditoreien* as we used to do in Prague, and we don't feel older than we did thirty-seven years ago when we first met. We don't correspond. We call each other in the middle of the night, since this is the only time we're sure of finding each other home, and Herta answers with a delighted 'Ritonzikl' in the same tone of voice that she answered the door at Na Kleovce 2283 in August 1945."

✳

The love letters were from Kristian. In December 1948, his hockey team came to Vienna to play the Russian Olympic team. Rita was at the game with Herta, and they sat in the front row but were careful that the Czech police escorts — who watched the players to prevent their defection — would not know that she was there. The Czech players felt bitterly toward the Soviets because of the Communist takeover, and fights broke out in which they beat the Russians with their hockey sticks, causing a number of bloody injuries. The Austrians cheered for the Czechs, who won the game. One of the organizers of the game handed Kristian, as captain of the winning team, a bouquet of flowers to give to the wife of the Russian ambassador, who was sitting in the front row. But after skating around the rink several times, he handed the bouquet to Rita, whom he had managed to call before the game after eluding his escorts. Photographers descended upon her, and she was whisked out of the arena by her friends.

On New Years's Eve 1950, Rita went with some friends to Semmering, a ski resort in the Russian zone of Austria, where a Jewish student organization had a cabin. They celebrated the New Year by skiing down the slopes with torches. Rita was stopped by a Russian patrol while she was on skis near the students' hut and asked to produce papers allowing her to be there. As a displaced person she had no such documents. She overheard two of the Russians. One said, "Can't you see they're skiing. Let her go." The other said, "They are the biggest spies." While the Russians were discussing the various possibilities, Rita entered the hut. The president of the student organization saw Rita with the two Russians, who had followed her in. Rita said to him in German, "They want my documents." There was a flicker of worry in his eyes. "*Tavarischi,* come in," he said. "It's New Year's Eve. The most important thing is to drink." The Russians came and were offered some vodka.

They then admitted that they resented having patrol duty on New Year's Eve. Pretty soon they were all, Rita included, singing Russian songs. For the students and the homesick Russian soldiers, it was Christmas and New Year's all in one. Then the group got hungry. "Leave it to us," the Russians said. They went down the mountain to Panhans, a famous hotel in Semmering, and came back with a whole pig on a spear. Rita, knowing that "fancy" Romanians and Russians were enjoying a New Year's party at Panhans, later asked one of the Romanians who had been there, "How was the New Year's Eve party?" "Terrible," was the reply. "A Russian patrol came in the middle of the night, speared our pig, and took it away." The Russians, of course, never explained to the revelers in the hut where the delicious pig they were consuming came from. In the middle of the festivities one of the Russians said to another, "Do you remember how she couldn't speak a word of Russian and now she knows the Russian songs?" But by this time they really were tavarischi.

But Rita was still cut off from her family. In July 1950, she had the opportunity to travel to Israel with a group of fourteen students to the first Jewish student congress since the founding of the state. The student delegation had little money and no exit papers. At Rita's request, Pan American Airlines agreed to donate a flight to Munich for the displaced students. From Munich they would go by train to Venice and then "hitchhike" on a ship to Haifa. The students were delighted with Rita's effort and Pan Am's generous gift. Rita, however, withheld from them the information that the plane was scheduled to stop in Prague. Most of the students were from Eastern Europe — some political refugees from Stalinist regimes — and would not have risked getting on the plane had they known. Several had escaped from jails in Czechoslovakia. But Rita wanted to see Kristian and called to give him the flight schedule and he arranged to see her at the Prague airport. This, of course, was not easy for him, for he first had to talk his way into the transit lounge. "We saw each other with a Czech guard standing between us, and while we spoke, Kristian plied the guard with cognac.

"The whole thing was a dirty deal of mine. I still experience the pangs of guilt which I felt when the announcement came over the plane's speaker that we were landing in Prague. My colleagues shuddered and turned white. This was the height of the Stalinist period, and there was much relief when it was announced that in-transit passengers would stay aboard." But the students became seriously alarmed when a Czech airport official summoned Rita Stenzler to get off the plane. They did not know why she had been singled out and worried for her safety, thinking she would be detained or arrested. When she returned to the plane carrying a bouquet of roses and a bottle of cognac, they discovered why they had been placed in jeopardy. Their intense anxiety for Rita vanished. "I'll never forget how they looked at those flowers." None of them spoke to her until they got to Venice, and they never really forgave her.

In Venice, Rita felt she had to "make it up to them by finding a ship willing to take us free of charge to Haifa." "The first captains we approached were appalled by such a request and did not seriously consider taking on fourteen displaced students." The students hung around Venice. Since they had no money for a hotel, "we honored a nunnery with our presence and slept there. The kind nuns passed around a box for contributions, and to our shame I must admit we put in buttons; we saved our change for Cokes. It started to look as if we would not make it to Israel."

One day as Rita was standing in the harbor, she spotted the *Galilah,* a ship flying the Israeli flag. "It was exciting to see the blue and white Star of David waving from the mast. Suddenly, a tall Israeli naval officer on the deck yelled 'Rita Stenzler' and dashed down. It was Kamillo Scharf, a neighborhood friend from Rădăuţi, now first officer of the *Galilah.*" The *Galilah,* a former U.S. Navy transport ship, was in Venice to pick up surviving immigrants to take them to the newly established State of Israel. Kamillo Scharf was the first person Rita had ever seen in an Israeli uniform. "Jewish men in Romania never wore navy uniforms and rarely wore any uniforms at all. Through Kamillo Scharf, Israel and Rădăuţi became linked. For me this linkage will never break."

Kamillo immediately offered Rita passage on the *Galilah.* When she informed him that thirteen others had to go with her, he volunteered, "with typical Rădăuţi largess," to ask the captain to take them all. Offering his cabin to the three girls in the group, he said he would move in with the sailors. The boys could lodge with the *olim,* the immigrants, on the lower deck. Actually they ended up camping on the officers' deck. The captain "was not at all thrilled at the whole idea. He grumbled about our presence for the four days of the passage, but he was the only one who did. We students enjoyed the hospitality of the *Galilah* so much that we arranged to make our return trip on her, which was also free. We were told that the only time the *Galilah* had arrived in Israel depleted of food and drinks was on that passage in the summer of 1950."

Her first arrival in Israel was unforgettable for Rita. As the immigrants first glimpsed the Bay of Haifa, they choked up with tears. They had come to join the other handful of Jews who had escaped Hitler's master plan and were dedicated to building a haven for all Jewish people. "As we approached Haifa, I stood on the bridge with Kamillo and heard for the first time the *Hatikvah,* the Israeli national anthem. The Israeli flag was waving, the Israeli naval officers stood saluting, and the crowd in the harbor welcomed the new arrivals, who instantaneously became citizens of Israel. Each of the immigrants, as they stepped off the ship, kissed the ground of Eretz Israel, the land of Israel. I have since come to Israel perhaps fifty times, and each time I arrive I remember hearing the sound of that first *Hatikvah* and the sight of the Israeli flags welcoming us, the Jewish leftovers of Europe."

Rita took some of the students to Kibbutz Shamir to visit Burschi Schachter, a childhood friend, who, with his parents and baby brother, had been taken into the Stenzler household on Appelgasse 15 as a toddler. Burschi, who was close to Nora in age, was considered her "first suitor"; Mrs. Stenzler had a picture of him in a sailor suit with Nora, aged two, on his arm. In the late 1930s, Burschi had gone to Palestine as a *chalutz,* a pioneer, to build a road and help found the kibbutz Shamir in the northern finger of Israel near the border of Syria and Lebanon. Burschi joined the underground army, the Haganah, and helped to build the State of Israel. Still a leader of Kibbutz Shamir, responsible for its military defense, he chairs the Israeli Northern Council as an elected official.

Their first morning at the kibbutz, Rita and her friends "slept in," not realizing that, in return for room and board, they were responsible for work assignments, which had been posted the night before. The students thought it beneath them to do manual work. Rita, with her poor sense of direction, headed off to where she thought she was meant to go to pick apples. Instead, she managed to cross the Syrian border and was approached by armed Syrian soldiers in white uniforms. Just then Burschi came by in a jeep and extricated her from the situation and took her where she was supposed to be. The next day she was expected to pick apples again, but the group decided to leave. The students were all eager to see the new state and not interested in working. During their four-week stay, they hitch-hiked all through Israel.

At the congress they had come to attend, the Israeli students were critical of the students from Vienna for living and studying elsewhere, so they did not participate for long. Soon they were back aboard the *Galilah*. When the ship arrived back in Venice, the students made their way back to Vienna by train and thumbing rides.

✳

Late in 1949, Nora, a Czech citizen, decided to leave Prague, where she had been working in a leather goods shop. Her train was scheduled to stop in Vienna, and Rita arranged everything, including papers, so her sister could stay. But Nora refused and did not get off the train. She intended to go to Israel and then bring their parents there. "Otherwise," she said, "our parents will have nowhere to come out to." The situation in Rădăuți was deteriorating for Shaje Stenzler, who was always speaking out against the Communist regime. Nora continued on to Israel on a ship from the Italian port of Bari with immigrants bound for Haifa.

Nora stayed in Haifa, where she worked in an atelier devoted to creating leather goods. At first she had to clean the toilets and do other menial chores, but she was soon selling, and then making, pocketbooks and satchels. After a few months, Nora was earning enough money to provide securely for her parents, and in November 1950, they left Rădăuți and journeyed from Constanța to Haifa on the *Transylvania,* a ship that took Jewish immigrants from Romania to Israel every Sunday. It was a severe trauma for the Stenzlers to leave Rădăuți so abruptly, but Burschi Schachter made them feel welcome and invited them to Kibbutz Shamir for Passover and on other occasions.

Nora and her parents lived in Israel until 1953, when Nora met her husband-to-be, Abraham Wiznitzer, who had come to Israel from Curaçao to visit relatives. He is a direct descendant of the Viznitzer rabbi of Bukovina. They were married two weeks after they met and returned to Curaçao, where they still live. The Stenzlers remained in Haifa for the rest of their lives. Helene died there on January 26, 1970, and Shaje on April 30, 1979.

7. Schloss Tivoli to Camp Rainbow: The Search for a Country

Rita's authorization to stay in Austria was to end the very day she graduated from medical school. As her studies advanced, the need to find a country that would accept her grew more urgent. In 1951, she went to the United Nations' representatives for displaced people to learn more about immigration quotas and visas. One of the UN officials who interviewed her was impressed and sponsored her for an international seminar to be held that July at Schloss Tivoli. There, under UN auspices, diplomats, officials, and students from East and West carried on "magnificent" night-long debates. Ralph Bunche, the eminent black diplomat, who had recently received the Nobel Prize for his work through the United Nations Palestine Commission in bringing peace to the Holy Land, addressed the conference and talked with the students. "Meeting the United States through him changed my perceptions." Several times after the war, Rita's parents had received tickets from relatives for passage to the United States, but her mother refused to go "to that wild country." Rita's own experience of American indifference to the rise of Hitler and the fate of Jews in Nazi camps also led her to view the United States in a negative light.

At Schloss Tivoli, Rita took part in discussions with Soviet officials and generals and became aware, from the dialogue between them and the Western representatives, of the deep divisions and

conflict between the two factions. The participants discussed colonialism, Hiroshima, the United States, and many aspects of world
politics. "But when discussions about world economics came up, I
went out to sing with the French, Italian, and Spanish participants."
One day, the Norwegians, Indonesians, and Dutch asked to see
Rothschild Hospital, which still housed the displaced people. Rita
took them there, but she was so ashamed of belonging to this homeless
group that immediately after their arrival at the hospital she insisted
that they all leave. "A very lovely Norwegian lady put her arm around
me and said, 'I understand.'"

At the Tivoli seminars Rita came to see the ambiguities and
complexities, the lack or a "good" or a "bad" side, in conflicts between
nations. She also came to appreciate more fully the extreme asym-
metries in historical experience between the United States and the
USSR and the power of mistrust in determining the direction of
international relations. Rita seemed to be the only displaced person
at the seminar, and being among people who belonged to a country,
yet were involved in world affairs, was exhilarating to her. The
dialogue "gave all of us wings which extended us beyond our narrow
selves."

Rita is grateful to the UN representative who arranged for her
to attend the seminar at Schloss Tivoli, where the sessions inspired
her not only to an increasingly active search for a country but also
toward the involvement in foreign affairs that suited her gifts. At
Tivoli, characteristically gregarious, she made intense friendships with
people from Indonesia, Norway, Holland, France, Great Britain,
Morocco — as international a mix as her doll collection.

While she was studying medicine in Vienna, Rita began an association
that was to have a great impact both on her choice of career and
future home. Hans Hoff, professor of psychiatry and neurology and
chairman of the department, influenced Rita's decision to enter the
field of psychiatry and eventually immigrate to the United States.

Hoff, of Jewish background, was a young faculty member, probably a docent, when the Nazis took over power in Austria. One day
not long after the Anschluss, his assistant showed up at the clinic
dressed in an SS uniform. When Hoff saw the uniform, he left the
building. The young doctor followed and Hoff turned back and
confronted him. The SS man began to kick him. This took place on

the crest of a hill, and Hoff fell and slipped down the slope. The SS man told him never to "set his dirty Jewish feet" in the clinic again. Hoff escaped to New York City, where he spent the war years. He is remembered by former students at Columbia University as an excellent teacher, especially of neurology. Sometimes he would lecture, in his formal manner, to as few as four students — who might not have been interested in neurology but were only boning up for examinations — as if he were addressing a packed auditorium. After the war, Hoff's brilliance and determination enabled him to regain his position in the Vienna medical school, despite the presence in the department of former Nazis who opposed his return.

Rita first heard Hoff lecture in 1950. She loved his lectures, which were superbly organized and filled with information. "Into these dismal days," Rita wrote in 1983, "a light appeared: Psychiatry. When I started attending the lectures by Professor Hans Hoff, medicine became magnificent, Vienna became more beautiful, my lodgings bearable, and my economic status insignificant. I read day and night and matriculated for the other exams rapidly. I wanted to move on to the psychiatry exam. More importantly, I wanted to become a psychiatrist, a decision which I have never regretted. I remember the day I took my oral exam (all our exams were oral in psychiatry) as a glorious and wonderful day."

As Rita followed Hoff on his rounds, he took an interest in her. Appreciating her aptitude and enthusiasm, he encouraged her to pursue psychiatry as a field. One day he took her aside and said, "Since you are obviously going to be a psychiatrist you might as well go to the United States." Rita told him of her prejudice against that country. Undeterred, he insisted. "You are made for the United States and Austria will kick you out the day you graduate."

Hoff was not a psychoanalyst, but despite a strong biological emphasis and intense use of sedative medication, his approach to psychiatry was dynamic. His lectures on neuroses, in which he explained human conflict, crystallized Rita's decision to go into psychiatry. "The beauty of Hoff was that his lectures in neurology were as exciting as his lectures in psychiatry." These lectures, his exploration of conflict, his help and support to her personally, remain Rita's most important experience in medical school.

Hoff's influence in Vienna continues. Although he died in 1969, his psychiatry texts are still used in courses at the university, and the young doctors still follow Hoff's heavy use of medication. For Rita,

Hoff's interest and advice were decisive. Hoff had spent six years in the United States. With his knowledge, consistent support of her, and clear recommendation, Rita became determined to find her home in America.

✳

As a native of Romania, Rita was faced with small and rigid quotas for the United States. During the fall of 1951, however, she was notified by the Hebrew Immigrant Aid Society (HIAS) that she might be able to obtain an immigration visa to the United States under a new legal provision which gave visas preferentially to certain professionally qualified individuals. There was, however, a hitch: the law would expire before Rita finished her medical studies. A kind woman at the HIAS office delayed processing Rita's visa as long as she could, and Rita herself used a delaying tactic, stealing from her HIAS file the Vienna police report stating she had no police record. With this report the record would be complete, and the prospective immigrant would have to depart. Without it, a further delay became necessary. Finally, in December 1951, Rita was notified that unless she left by the end of May 1952, she would lose her chance to immigrate to the United States.

One year away from her medical degree, Rita began her first journey to the United States. She first had to go to Salzburg in the American zone of Austria to pick up her visa at the U.S. consulate. It was the height of the McCarthy period, and the U.S. consular officer asked Rita a host of unpleasant questions, presented her with a list of students suspected of being spies, and asked her if she knew any of them. "I replied haughtily that I had left Romania in 1945 and Czechoslovakia in 1948 for no other reason than that I wanted the freedom to act upon what my conscience told me and not what a political system dictated me to do. I stood up to leave." Although her answer bore little relation to his questions, the officer was evidently chastened. "He told me to sit down and gave me the U.S. entry visa as an immigrant on the spot."

From Salzburg, Rita traveled by train to Bremerhaven on the north German coast where, with other immigrants, she was to sail to the United States. This group of immigrants turned out to be much different from the ones on the *Galilah*. A large number were German and some were former Nazis. "It did not feel good, and I did not, and do not, experience pride in having tossed my life and fate together with theirs." Some of the Germans with whom Rita spoke knew, or admitted they knew, about the concentration camps of Hitler's Germany. In Bremerhaven, Rita sought a job that would provide her with enough money to return to Vienna in September. In a few days she found a position on the SS *General Hershey,* escorting orphans to the United States. "I don't know whether it was the letter from my professor of psychiatry or my knowledge of languages, but I got the job."

Rita's assignment was to pick up the orphans in Bremerhaven, escort them to New York, and deliver them at the pier to the representatives of their church groups and their new adoptive parents. "It sounded simple. It was not. They were a strange group, these orphans. I knew nothing about them and had not studied their immigration papers, for which I paid a price during immigration processing in New York harbor." The orphans were of different ages and different nationalities, and while some of them had waited around orphanages for years, hoping to immigrate to the U.S., nobody had troubled to teach them English. "I don't remember exactly how many there were, perhaps fourteen, but I felt overburdened because we were ten days at sea on the *General Hershey.*" The Atlantic was very stormy in May, and the ship was built as a troop, not a child, transport. "It seemed that I spent my days escorting the kids to and from the bathrooms on the lower decks, worried about the heavy iron doors which they could not handle. Day and night I heard over the loud-speaker, 'Escort of orphans, children are climbing the deck.' Or 'Escort of orphans, children in unauthorized area.' These were not well-behaved little angels. They were kids who had lost or had never known their parents and had grown up on the streets and in the black market of postwar Europe." The older girls would slip out of the dorm the moment Rita closed her eyes and go to the sailors' quarters, where they were very welcome.

One young boy, Hans, was an accomplished thief who would pick up anything that was loose. "I spent Mother's Day on the *Hershey,* and when I opened my eyes I saw all the kids around my bunk, each standing with a flower in their hand, which the kind captain had given them to give to me. It was my first Mother's Day as a recipient. Little Hans, however, also had a Dresden figurine, which the captain had not given him but which he had picked up from the captain's cabin. When I admonished him for having again stolen, he gave me a lesson in German diction and personal ethics. He said, '*Stehlen heisst sich selbst etwas aneignen'* [To steal means to appropriate something for oneself]. He claimed that since he got the figurine for me, not for himself, this did not represent stealing."

Rita and her charges all ate, standing, in the same dining hall as the sailors. One of the children, a blond, solemn, emaciated girl, never ate, but the food always disappeared from her tray instantly. She had no change of clothes, and on the evening before arrival in New York, as Rita was spiffing up the kids for presentation to their new adoptive parents, she begged this serious little girl to open her suitcase to look for a change of clothes. The girl carried the key around her neck. "Solemnly she, who by now trusted me, opened her suitcase as if it were a precious possession. To my horror, the trunk was full of rotted food, which she had been hiding in preparation for days of hunger."

As the ship approached New York at dawn, Rita took all the children to the deck to see the Statue of Liberty, rising in front of their anxious, curious eyes. "I whispered to each of them in their native tongues the words inscribed on the statue, 'Give me your hungry, your poor.' We had all found a country."

When Rita and the children arrived in New York, they were all questioned by the immigration authorities. Rita was quizzed about the backgrounds of the orphans. In a scolding tone, "they asked me whether I knew about the possibility that the fathers of some of the orphans might have been Nazis or fascists from other countries. I replied that I knew nothing about the backgrounds of these children." Sadly, neither the children nor the mothers of some knew the identity of their fathers. None of this was satisfactory or reassuring to the immigration authorities who nevertheless let Rita move on to face the representatives of the adoption agencies and some of the adoptive parents. Press cameras were flashing to capture the happiness of these orphans on reaching their new country, but the children were crying, tired, excited, bewildered, and uncomfortable in a foreign land. They huddled around Rita. "We had our ten-day voyage in common, and my knowledge of their languages. Our mixture of anticipation and fear of this new big continent could not be captured by the news media with their flashbulbs."

After Rita finally obtained a signature for the last of the children, she faced a new challenge. Four uncles — two of her mother's brothers, Heinrich and Shmuel Abe, and two of her father's, Henry and Irving, residents of Brooklyn, the Bronx, Long Island, and

Manhattan, all met her at the dock. They had immigrated to the United States around 1910 and were complete strangers to Rita. "They looked so different from my aunts and uncles from Rădăuţi. They had an American-Jewish veneer in appearance, language, manner, and perspective. They seemed to have plunged from Rădăuţi to New York without a European transition. The only member of their families who had come to the United States since before World War I, was a huge disappointment to them. They wanted me to be the way they were when they came to the United States directly from Rădăuţi."

But between Rădăuţi and New York, Rita had experienced Mogilev Podolskiy, Storozhinets, Czernowitz, Iaşi, Prague, and Vienna. They had trouble imagining or accepting all this and asked her about the Rădăuţi they remembered, a place that did not exist anymore except in their memories. "They informed me that my plan to go back to finish medical school in Vienna was ridiculous." They thought she should simply get married to a nice Jewish man, whom they offered to find for her, and settle down in a way of life like theirs. "The dissonance between Irving of New York and Uncle Irving of Rădăuţi was almost like the difference between New York and Rădăuţi. No longer the dashing playboy with flamboyant clothes, he was chubby and henpecked by his American-Jewish wife. Only his deep beautiful voice was the same, particularly when he asked me whether his brother Shaje, my father, was still worried about him. He handed me a silver dollar for good luck, which I still have, and a colorfully wrapped box which contained a lovely sweater for me. A fond memory of Uncle Irving in New York was his introducing me to Broadway and Forty-second Street. He remembered that I loved stuffed peppers and found an Italian restaurant where he went into the kitchen to supervise the making of the stuffed peppers they served."

As Rita and her uncles stood on the pier, a controversy erupted between the Stenzler and Wohl contingents as to which family would be her host. Rita settled the issue by accepting the offer of a room at a hotel for immigrants from the HIAS representative who had sponsored her immigration. A terrible hotel in Manhattan, the Breslin was dirty, neglected, and miserable, but it did have one advantage: it was in mid-Manhattan and Rita could walk to Times Square, which seemed to her the center of the world. She was thrilled to watch the sea of people on the streets. "I was fascinated by the different colors of humanity. The department stores — Macy's, Gimbel's, Altman's — were extraordinary for me. I was intoxicated by their displays."

On her arrival, Rita had very little money. One of the Jewish relief agencies loaned her money for rent and food, which she repaid after completion of her internship. She ate mostly in automats. Soon, however, she faced two additional problems. First, she had to earn enough money quickly so she could buy a ticket back to Europe in September to finish her medical studies. Second, even with the money, a new immigrant, by law, could not leave the country for one year. Rita immediately informed the authorities of her intention to return to Vienna to get her degree. A special hearing was set up for her in a round room with a court recorder and many people taking notes.

"The questions addressed to me were fair and related to my motivation for immigration and my studies. I replied truthfully and enjoyed the hearing. I clarified for the authorities that I was a homeless person in Vienna, that I needed a country to which I could immigrate and obtain a permit to work as a physician, but that at the only time when I could get an immigration visa to the United States, I was not yet a physician. The people at the hearing seemed to understand. The only strange thing was that I had to talk to the stenographer present at the hearing in Romanian via an interpreter, even though my English then was nearly the same as it is now." Rita was given a green card, which meant that she had been accepted as an immigrant in the United States and granted special permission to return to Austria for the academic year 1952–1953.

There was still the problem of travel fare, for which help came indirectly. First Rita had an encounter with an intrusive social worker who doled out the meager loan from the relief agency. Once a week Rita was supposed to submit receipts detailing her expenditures in order to get the loan. "I hated these visits. They insulted my dignity. One day, my social worker questioned why I needed, among my incidental expenses, to buy a *New York Times* every day. I turned around, walked out of the office, and never returned. I looked through the *New York Times* I had in my hands, which had precipitated the ridiculous question, found an ad for a physician/counselor and/or nurse at a camp for emotionally disturbed children. I was not a physician, counselor, or nurse, but I assumed correctly that since they had mentioned all three, they would accept an in-between person, and for that I was qualified. I presented myself to the directors of the camp, a Quaker couple, and got the job." For the two weeks in June before camp began, Rita supported herself by becoming a file clerk in the medical records department of Montefiore Hospital in the Bronx. Her dependence on loans from a helping agency in New York "lasted for two weeks and was never to be repeated again."

Camp Rainbow at Croton-on-Hudson, north of New York City, was in a beautiful setting, but the campers were very troubled emotionally. Looking back as a child psychiatrist, Rita realizes that some of the children were psychotic, while others suffered from severe psychosomatic illnesses. "All of them seemed sad and hopelessly entangled in angry, fierce relationships with their parents and siblings. The hardest day at the camp was visiting day for families. It was hard on the kids, their families, and on us, the staff. The encounters between parents and children were mutual exercises in hurting each other. How unlike Rădăuţi it was! That was my first glimpse of American family life."

Rita had one day off each week, which she always took on a weekday because she enjoyed riding the crowded trains into New York. "I loved New York on the working day when I could feel the full pulse of the city." The disappointed uncles came to visit her at the camp. When they saw her working there, they realized further how different she was from what they had been like when they first came to the United States. The uncles seemed to want Rita to be like the girls they remembered in Rădăuţi in 1910 and to look for a Jewish husband. Her interest in troubled children seemed alien to them.

There was further competition between the Stenzlers and Wohls. "When I visited a Stenzler in Brooklyn, the next day I had to visit a Wohl in the Bronx or Long Island to make peace. During the visit they had television sets on, which I'd never seen before, and they stuffed me with all the food that perhaps they wished they could have given to their relatives during the war years. My disappointment matched theirs. They were not like my beloved aunts and uncles from Rădăuţi, for whom I longed. They had spent years worrying about the family they had left behind. Now I was the only one there and I felt as if they wanted to swallow me up and make me into one of them."

Rita plunged into her job with skill and enthusiasm. She was proud when she was able to diagnose appendicitis in a regular tummy-ache customer of the dispensary, although she had had very little clinical experience. When the surgeon in a nearby hospital confirmed the diagnosis and operated on the little boy, her medical reputation at Camp Rainbow was enhanced.

The children visited Rita's dispensary with their cuts and bruises, but primarily with their loneliness, depression, anger, hurts, and longing. "How different they were from the orphans on the boat, who had been hurt by external circumstances but had developed some inner resilience. These kids at Croton-on-Hudson all knew English but had no emotional language to make themselves understood and loved. They had no true sense of their own identities and, therefore, the people around them seemed like shadowy figures to whom one could not reach out.

When she was hired, the camp administrators had voiced some concern that Rita's lack of familiarity with U.S. children and lifestyles would be a hindrance in establishing relationships with these sick children. The opposite turned out to be true. Her lack of familiarity with their family lifestyles was, in a way, helpful. She could enter into relationships with them without preconceived ideas and expectations. The children poured into the dispensary with both their visible and psychological bruises. They wanted, asked for, and received comfort for their hurts.

Rita credits Professor Hoff with "implanting in me a profound respect for the interaction between soma and psyche." The solidity of her family relationships, Rita feels, enabled her to encounter both emotional and bodily suffering without experiencing anew the exacerbation of her own adolescent hurts. "I had a community feeling at Camp Rainbow with both the counselors and the children." Her interaction with the counselors opened a window into U.S. society. Her peers in age, they were nice to her and knew nothing of the world from which she came. They wanted to talk about the concentration camp, which she did not feel inclined to do. "I was bothered by their inordinate need to spend whole evenings talking about interpersonal relationships. That was new to me." Her complaint is reminiscent of that of the heroine of William Styron's *Sophie's Choice*, who, after a day at Coney Island listening to Brooklyn College students analyzing their problems, said, "I hate this type of unearned unhappiness."

When camp was over, Rita had saved enough money for a one-way passage back to Vienna, and, with immigration papers in her hands, "I felt protected. When I boarded the *Queen Elizabeth* to Le Havre, nobody at the pier appreciated its luxury more than I. I compared it with the *General Hershey* and wished that the crossing would take ten days rather than the anticipated four." The four uncles were at the pier to see Rita off. "They were loving and I felt guilty for not having spent more time with them." But some of the counselors, children, and parents from Camp Rainbow were also there, "so again there was no time for the uncles."

When Rita got back to Vienna in September, it seemed different than it had in May, but the change was in herself. She was no longer a displaced person but a U.S. immigrant. "I saw and perceived Vienna through completely different eyes. I had a vital document, which I displayed even when it was not asked for." She rented a room in a pension, not in the worst section of town anymore, but on the Frankgasse near the majestic Gothic Votivkirche and its lovely park. There was even a maid in the pension who laid a fire in the rooms. As Rita prepared for her exam in internal medicine, part of the third rigorosum, she practiced percussion of the heart and lungs on the maid. To her dismay she heard ominous sounds while tapping her back. Rita insisted that she come to the university clinic. Unfortunately, the diagnosis was correct and the woman died shortly afterward of cancer of the lungs.

During the fall and winter of 1952–1953, Rita studied hard for the third rigorosum: Internal medicine, pediatrics, surgery, forensic medicine, public health, ophthalmology, and dermatology. In the late winter, there were two "sensational" events in her life. First, she suddenly received a check from the United States. "I don't remember the amount, but for me it seemed gigantic. It was a return on my income taxes from my summer jobs. At first I did not know what it meant and was suspicious. When I found out that not only had I been permitted to work and earn money two weeks after my arrival as an immigrant, but that from the taxes I had paid I was given back a certain amount, and that the government had mailed this to someone who was completely ignorant of the system, I could not believe it. No government had ever done that for me. My perception until then had been that governments are only 'out to get you.'"

With her refund check, Rita went to Mariahilferstrasse to buy a nice dress. "I bought a green dress, which I remember till this day to the last detail. It was an initiation dress for my new identity. That dress was possible because I now had a country to which I belonged and which belonged to me."

Rita and her friend
Herta Weiss, Prague, 1946

Rita and Nora, Prague, 1946

Rita (fourth from right, standing) with Romanian students
at a youth festival, Prague, 1947

Rita at Camp Rainbow,
Croton-on-Hudson, 1952

Rita at the Café Beethoven in Vienna
on the evening before her last
medical school exam, spring 1953

Rita with waiter at
the Café Beethoven

Rita at her graduation from medical school, Vienna, 1953,
with representatives of the refugee student body

Rita and Allen Rogers
with their son, David,
1955

Rita's parents on
their wedding anniversary,
Haifa, 1965

The second event occurred early in March. Rita was sitting in an espresso bar close to the Votivkirche. A friend, Dr. Theodor Wanko, an assistant to Professor Hoff, walked in with an expression of profound emotion on his face. "He came over and told me, 'Stalin is dead.' The little tables at the espresso bar were very close to each other and people overheard his statement. A hush fell over us. We knew an era had ended. Our coffee cups were getting cold, as for each and every one of us different memories rushed before our eyes. There were visions of snows of the Eastern Front, of train transports with prisoners of war to the East, of people from the occupied territories of Czernowitz and Bessarabia working in the frozen lands of Siberia, and the faces of Ukrainian peasants full of bitter anger at Stalin." Rita and her friends reflected on the effect a single personality can have on the fate of one or many nations. "We all had learned in our own ways how national decision makers can have such a profound impact on the most intimate elements of our personal lives."

On May 13, 1953, Rita Stenzler, nearly twenty-eight years old, graduated from the University of Vienna Medical School. No member of her family was there to attend the ceremony. Herta Korn did what she could to substitute. Because of the date on her permit, Rita had literally to leave Vienna on the day of graduation. While colleagues and friends were helping her pack, a case of champagne arrived. It had been sent by a lawyer, a friend of the Weisses from Czernowitz, Lecku Geller, who, at times throughout the Vienna years, had loaned her "a little pocket money." The gift was as generous as the pretense that he had been "lending" money, since she could not possibly pay it back. Geller hardly knew Rita, but for him, she was *ein Kind von der Bukovina* (a child of the Bukovina).

(In July 1983, on the steps of the same university, Rita watched as the graduating students, among them Herta's niece, Alika, walked out with flowers, just as they had thirty years earlier. Then it had been the displaced students' president who handed her the flowers to carry.)

Rita was supposed to leave from Cherbourg for New York. The relief agency was again lending the money for her fare. She upset them, however, when she insisted that she could not possibly leave for the United States without first seeing her parents and sister in Israel. Rita had not seen her parents since July 1947, when she had visited Rădăuți from Prague, and she had to find money for the trip.

Many Romanian emigrés had settled into business ventures in Vienna. Their financial situation had improved since they had first arrived after the war. These friends got together and loaned Rita the money for her visit to her parents and gave her gifts to take to them.

She traveled by train from Vienna to Naples, where she was to board an Italian passenger ship, the *Pace* (Peace) on its maiden voyage to Haifa. "When I left Vienna that evening, Herta's father, an elegant and dignified gentleman whom I adored, embraced me at the train station and said, 'Frau Kollegin (Mrs. Colleague), we know that Herta has you and you have Herta. That is good for us to know. This is good-bye for good.' And it was. I never saw him again."

Rita was so thrilled when she saw Naples that she almost missed the ship. Indeed, the gangplank had to be relowered for her to board. This, of course, gave her, as so often was true in her life, a special status among the passengers and crew. She became "the one who almost missed the boat." Wearing her new green dress, Rita looked happily at the Bay of Naples. "How marvelous the journey was. I had a medical diploma in my suitcase, first papers as an immigrant to the United States in my pocketbook, and I was finally going to see my parents after six long years."

When the *Pace* landed in Haifa, Rita, with the help of the first officer to whom she had shown their picture, was able to spot her parents. She saw right away that her father's eyesight and upright bearing were gone. "My parents no longer were Shaje and Helene Stenzler of Rădăuţi. They now seemed only *from* Rădăuţi, immigrants who were part of the crowd, no longer the prestigious citizens I had known." However, although Rita's parents were living in their new surroundings under very modest circumstances, their inner dignity and the "grandeur of their spirits" had not diminished. "They approved unquestioningly of my immigration. They never mentioned or scolded me for having left Romania for Czechoslovakia, or Czechoslovakia for Austria, without consulting them. Over and over the message, not in words, but by a display of love, was: 'We want what you feel is best for you.' They made saying good-bye easier."

From Haifa, Rita returned to Italy, then traveled by train to Cherbourg and from there on the *Queen Mary* to the United States. Her cabinmate was a young woman physician from Finland. "I told her about the United States like an old expert. But still I felt my passion for Europe and my connectedness with all its flaws and accomplishments. I also felt that this was my last voyage as a European, that I was now an immigrant since, with my parents' blessing, I had left for the United States 'for good.' I sensed I would always feel defensively American in Europe and strongly European in the United States, feelings which have endured for more than thirty years."

8. America and Psychiatry

On her second arrival in New York, Rita was met by a social worker, assigned to her by the Hebrew Immigrant Aid Society to "help me adjust to the United States." Miss Arnot presented herself "in flat-heeled sensible shoes and a very unfeminine suit and burst onto the scene while I was having farewell drinks with traveling companions at the harbor. She announced that she had studied my file for a year and knew everything about me. Then she told me that she had arranged a straight surgical internship in Albany, that she knew I would become a surgeon, and that we women should stick together." Rita informed her that she was going to take a rotating internship and a psychiatric residency and planned to get married, although she had no one in mind at the time. Friends she had met the preceding year were waiting at the pier, and Rita decided to stay in New York until her internship began, while Miss Arnot headed off for Albany with "my luggage in order to feel she had some hold over me."

Rita began her internship at Memorial Hospital in Albany on July 1. She was on call every other night, earning $50 a month plus room and board. The hospital was located in the downtown urban area. "U.S. life entered my consciousness through the prism of an emergency room." During that hot summer, she went with the police into cheap hotels to pronounce people dead, delivered babies in slum

170·

dwellings where the only furniture was a bed and a television set, and sewed up the wounds of drunks brought to the emergency ward by the police. At first the burly policemen, who looked so different from the ones she had known in Romania, frightened Rita. In Romania if a problem arose, police could always be bribed.

"At Memorial Hospital there were no elegant lectures as in the Algemeinen Krankenhaus in Vienna." There were, rather, very sick patients to care for. "At Memorial Hospital in Albany I got my real degree. The wards and the delivery room were real. There people were not cases but individuals in their naked humanliness. I became a physician. Slowly, I realized how lousy I was at lab work and how good at picking up a Korsakoff syndrome [an organic psychosis associated with alcoholism]. This was the world I came to know during my first year in the United States, my first year in medicine."

Meanwhile, Miss Arnot continued to try to convert Rita to her view that she should become a surgeon. The hospital telephone operators were instructed not to put Miss Arnot through. But "she never gave up." On the rare occasions when she did get hold of Rita, she arranged for her to visit homes with American families, "in order to get me 'adjusted to the American way of life.' It seemed to me that I always got the same menu: steak and strawberry shortcake. At the time, I thought that was all that Americans ate. The casualness of American entertainment never ceased to amaze me. I would walk in and everybody continued doing exactly what they were doing: kids screaming, men, some of whom were physicians, barbecuing, television blasting. I was always told to make myself at home. But I was not at home, and it was impossible for me to make myself at home in an environment which felt so strange."

On the first day of internship Rita met Allen Rogers, a third-year medical student doing a surgical externship at Memorial. Their friendship soon deepened. "I met Allen in the cafeteria of the hospital and remember not only the beige suit he was wearing that day, but also how I couldn't take my eyes off his handsome face, his civilized appearance and manners, and especially his hands. I don't know when I decided in the most private compartment of my existence that this was going to be my husband and the father of my children. I had no doubts. In the past few years Allen has asked how come we were always on call together at Memorial Hospital." Apparently he was not aware that after she met him, Rita worked it out with the chief resident. "We had an arrangement between us, as far as our work

load was concerned: Allen did all the lab work — which interns had
to do at night, and for which I was completely unskilled and incapable
— and for Allen, with delight, I did all the psychiatric consults and
some deliveries."

Allen and Rita's courtship was dictated by the schedule of their
rotating duties. "If I remember correctly I was on twenty-four hours
and off twelve hours. So was Allen. We cherished our little free time
and each other. We had little money but listened to a lot of good
music, which Allen knew, and knows, and loves. We ate in the
cafeteria and in cheap little Chinese restaurants — the dishes we ate
there are still dear to me because Allen introduced them. Our courtship was very private because Allen is a very, very private person."

They were married in the spring of 1954 in Hanover, New
Hampshire, because Allen was doing an externship in family practice
in nearby Lyme with a wonderful country doctor, William Putnam.[1]
Rita flew there on the day of the wedding after having been on call
for twenty-four hours. "From the moment I met Allen, I felt that he
knew who he was, where he belonged, what he wanted, and what
life meant to him. He was and has remained himself under all
circumstances. His dedication to medicine is deeply imbedded in his
devotion to life. Everything which is alive is sacrosanct for him:
flowers, animals, children. Allen loves making things well and making them grow."

By the time Rita completed her internship, just a year after
arriving in the United States, she had found not only a country, but
a profession and a life partner. In the summer of 1954, Rita moved
to Delaware to begin her psychiatric residency at Delaware State
Hospital, while Allen completed medical school in Albany. But in
the winter, now pregnant, Rita moved back to Albany to be with
Allen. Their son David was born in January. The following summer,
with the baby, Allen and Rita settled in Delaware while Allen did
his internship and Rita continued her residency. Her background
helped in certain ways at the Delaware State Hospital. "The superintendent was a Dr. Tarumianz, from Soviet Georgia, I think, who
acted like the czar of the hospital. Coming from a feudal kingdom,
as I did, I accepted his paternalistic attitude toward patients and
staff, and he and I liked each other. I also enjoyed the patients
immensely. It was a big hospital and all the patients from the state
came there, so it was a good place for research and for continuity in
patient care. My only difference with Dr. Tarumianz came up in July

1956, when I told him that I was leaving because Allen and David came ahead of him, the hospital, and my residency."

Rita's other pillar of support at the hospital was Fritz Freyhan, the medical director, who was and remained a very "German" psychiatrist, meticulous, pedantic, and organized. "I felt as if he treated me the way Professor Foreanu had in Rădăuţi lecturing especially to me." With Dr. Freyhan, Rita wrote one of the early articles on the antipsychotic drug Chlorpromazine. Freyhan's Germanic qualities, which were rather frightening to the other residents and ward nurses, were familiar to Rita, and she was able to get along well with him.

The choice of psychiatry and psychotherapy grew out of Rita's ability to recognize and reach out to the authentic qualities of many different human beings. "Through the psychiatric profession one is intuitively connected with people and their innermost niches." For Rita, this is a privilege. At the same time, the invasive aspect, the intrusion upon human privacy that accompanies much of psychiatry, is offensive to her. "How much invading we psychiatrists do when we ask adults about their childhood . . . One of the most misunderstood psychiatric concepts is the notion that telling it all cures."

In Rita's view, a psychiatrist begins as a stranger who brings a foreign personal reality and background to each encounter with a patient. The practice of psychiatry and psychotherapy thus requires "constant translation from one reality into the other." Rita, whose experience has confronted her so profoundly with the impact on the individual of sociopolitical events, believes that "reality" must always include cognitive and emotional understanding of the patient's background and his or her family's history. In psychiatry, "unlike the rest of medicine, I learned about development and pathology, not in order to fit the individual into the mold, but rather to understand how the mold has affected the individual." From this interaction, Rita has built a concept of what she calls "humanliness." "History, social and political background, group allegiance, group hurts, group cohesion or schisms, all increase the dimensions of humanliness." Rita's struggles to survive in the face of threatening historical circumstances have also sharpened her intuitive ability to judge the authenticity and trustworthiness of human communications.

For Rita, psychiatry must empower the individual. In order to heal, the psychotherapist functions as a facilitator, an empathic listener whose caring may itself have a healing effect but whose special effort is to enable other people to find solutions to their dilemmas that work for them. When you work with patients, "only they know what is good for them." People are "degraded" if they are "told what to do for themselves. In my personal book of ethics, you can tell people what to do for you, or for others, but not for themselves. You can only ask them to be true to themselves."

From Delaware, Rita, Allen, and David moved to Kalamazoo, Michigan, where Allen started his surgical residency and the Rogers's second child, Judy, was born on October 16, 1956, "in association with the Hungarian uprising." Allen next took a year of residency in Ann Arbor, Michigan, and Rita continued her training at Ypsilanti State Hospital, where they lived on the hospital grounds. The Ypsilanti years deepened Rita's love of psychiatry. She established close relationships with the hospital superintendent, Dr. Paul Yoder. "He was a real mensch," and they discussed "everything on earth, but never psychiatry." At Ypsilanti Rita helped to put together a lecture series in which distinguished psychiatrists from all over the country presented their work to the residents and staff, and she also developed new collegial relationships that she still cherishes. Also at Ypsilanti, Rita was able to develop a kind of personalized practice on the huge chronic ward where her patients could come, as if to a private office, instead of voicing their physical and emotional ailments and complaints before a group on rounds. It was quite unusual then, and in many institutions still is, for chronic psychiatric patients to be seen by appointment in a simulated private office. Rita turned both the Delaware and Yspilanti state hospitals, and their patients and staffs, into "my communities."

In 1959, Rita and her family moved back to Kalamazoo, where Allen was chief resident in surgery at the Bronson Hospital while Rita worked at the Kalamazoo Child Guidance Clinic and opened a small practice that grew quickly. After completing his residency, Allen was obligated to give two years of military service. Rita, hoping he would be assigned to Europe, was disappointed when he was sent instead to Atlanta, where he served as a captain at Fort McPherson, headquarters of the Third Army. Rita asked her Jewish friends in Kalamazoo if there were any Jews in Atlanta, and they reassured her, "Yes, the synagogue there just got bombed." To assuage her disappointment at being assigned to Atlanta, Rita bought a "southern belle" dress and went South, where, as it turned out, she had a happy time. She enjoyed the gracious lifestyle, "the warmth and intimacy of relationships and the Southern hospitality." Rita and Allen's third child, Sheila, was born in Atlanta on April 28, 1961. From 1960 to 1962, Rita received her child psychiatry training at Emory University, where she was the first fellow in a new child psychiatry division under Dr. Richard Ward, who was born in Beirut. Rita sometimes discussed with him the different ways children grow up in other parts of the world.

At her first parent-teacher conference in Atlanta, Rita was told by David's first-grade teacher that he seemed to "bring the world" into the classroom. That remark pleased Rita, for it reflected her style as a mother. In the Rogerses' home and on numerous occasions in the United States and overseas, I have observed the joy and affection Rita shares with her three children, just as her mother did with her. Whenever she could, Rita took her children with her on her travels, hoping to offset the parochial and ethnocentric perspective that growing up in America tends to create. Rita has introduced to her children the vast and varied world of peoples, places, and experiences she has known. Their chosen professions — David, an international banker in London; Judy, a French teacher in San Francisco; and Sheila, a journalist in New York — reflect the wide stage of Rita's life. Yet each has developed a personal identity and career, deciding where and how to live.

In 1981, my son Kenneth was the beneficiary of this opening up of the world that Rita can bring about for others. Nineteen, a high school graduate, he was floundering a little, unsure of his future direction. Traveling through Eastern Europe when we revisited the scenes of Rita's youth, he was powerfully affected by the poverty and severe strictures under which most people in that part of the world were living. Ken participated in many heated discussions during the trip, arguing sometimes with Rita's perspective on the nuclear issue, U.S.-Soviet relations, and other topics. In large part through this experience, Ken developed a new awareness, an appreciation of the privileges he enjoyed, and a commitment to use his opportunities and talents more creatively. Over the next five years he made significant contributions to the antinuclear movement and to U.S.-Soviet relations, including a booklet for the town of Brookline, Massachusetts, which replaced the evasive civil defense plan with realistic information, and to the co-leadership of three expeditions of American youth to the Soviet Union, culminating in a climb of Mount Elbrus in the Caucasus by a joint U.S.-U.S.S.R. group.

Allen had been determined to practice surgery in California

virtually since childhood, and it was clear that California was where the Rogers family would end up. So in 1960 Rita, having passed the Michigan state medical boards, went to San Francisco to take the California state boards before coming to Georgia to complete her child psychiatry residency. In July 1962, after Allen had completed his military obligation, the Rogerses moved to Redondo Beach, south of Los Angeles. "Southern California was for me in 1962 what it is now: too much of the good things, too much of plenty, too much sunshine, too much recreation, too many cars, too many people, too much newness, and too much of 'anything goes.' There is also too much distance to reach anything. Because I live in Southern California I have a need to "titrate" it frequently with other styles of life, usually with a visit to Eastern Europe, its most opposite. In Eastern Europe there isn't too much of anything. There is hardship, there are short- ages, there are few of the consumer goods, and there people fall back on the only thing that really matters: human relationships and con- nectedness. There things have continued to look very much the same as in my childhood."

Soon after going to California Rita was hired by Pietro Castel- nuevo Tedesco, a psychoanalyst who was chief of psychiatry at the Harbor General Hospital in Torrance, to begin a child psychiatry program. When he started at Harbor, which is one of the affiliated hospitals of the UCLA Medical School system, child psychiatry as a specialty did not exist in the South Bay area. From 1962 to 1968, Rita built the division, recruited several child psychiatrists, and obtained accreditation for the program in 1968. In 1975 she was promoted to clinical professor of psychiatry at UCLA Medical School. From 1968 to 1984, when she resigned in protest over the multiple encroachments of the county mental health system on the child psychiatry division, including budget cuts and transfer of staff posi- tions to the more "cost effective" adult services, Rita was responsible for training virtually all the child psychiatrists in the South Bay area. The bureaucratic depredations felt to Rita like an attack on her family and, thus, finally became intolerable.

One of Rita's great joys in training young residents in child psychiatry has been to help individuals from different backgrounds understand and respect child patients who come from disrupted homes and low-income families, mostly on welfare, many of them undocu- mented aliens. She helps them examine their own identities — as young people with varying personal backgrounds, strengths, limitations, and hurts, as physicians educated in the medical model, and as psychiatric specialists concerned with emotional disturbances of children and their families. Once identified, these multiple dimensions can become resources available for the personal growth and healing of young patients and the people who care for them. Her approach is described in two publications, "A Teaching Drill in Child Psychiatry" and "Gap Between the Psychiatric and Medical Model."[2] In Rita's training program the trainees are required to express the hurts, vulnerabilities, diagnosis, and prognosis of children and their families and to interpret the psychotherapeutic task in three "languages": in everyday human terms to the patient and his or her parents, in acceptable medical language to the referring pediatrician, and in a more sophisticated psychiatric form, as if the trainee were a "visiting professor," when communicating to other psychiatrists.

Many leaders in American child psychiatry have made a concerted effort in the last two decades to turn their discipline into a more scientific medical specialty, but that is not Rita's principal interest. For her, child psychiatry is an opportunity to interrupt a cycle of emotional wounding that began in earlier generations and presents itself through the troubled behavior of a particular child. As each child confronts the developmental milestones that once troubled his or her mother or father, the struggle reawakens the old hurts of the parent. Experiencing once again the past grievances and frustrations, the parent is unable to perceive the child's uniqueness. The parent's care becomes contaminated by her or his unhealed childhood wounds. Rita draws upon the richness of her own child-parent experiences, and the strength she developed through loving communication between grandparents and parents and parents and children, to interrupt patterns of hurtful communication in the families for which she cares. For Rita, the treatment of a troubled child includes empathy for the hurt child in the parents as well. Ever since Camp Rainbow, when Rita first witnessed "mutual exercises in hurting each other," she has devoted herself to transforming them.

In my travels with Rita I have often had the opportunity to see her with children and watch her delight in them. I have seen her, in chance encounters in cities and airports, reach out to mothers with irritable or crying babies and calm a situation through her interest in the struggling pair. She is always ready to comfort children. At the cave of Daniel Sihastru near Putna in the Bukovina, a little girl selling tickets was holding the side of her face. She said to Rita,

"Please don't be angry, but do you happen to have something for a terrible toothache?" Rita put her arm around her and gave her some Tylenol. The relief was immediate, long before the drug could have acted chemically.

Respect for privacy is an important element in Rita's therapy with children. She sees privacy as vital to the mystery and intensity of human experience. To bring forth too much, especially prematurely, is to damage this experience. She uses the Czech word *hmatane,* meaning "to touch or soil," to express this phenomenon. Children, she believes, need to have their developing inner lives protected through the use of symbolism, allusion, and metaphor, lest an adult trespass on the sanctity of the inner self.

Once Rita treated a seven-year-old girl who at the age of four had discovered the dead body of her mother, who had committed suicide. During the course of her treatment her father took her to the cemetery where her mother was buried, a treasured experience for her. "Something big happened and it's mine," the girl announced in the therapy, choosing not to tell Rita just then about the visit. "You're right," Rita said. "It is yours." She did not ask her to talk about her feelings. In emphasizing privacy, Rita is not negating the value of sharing feelings when the timing is right. But most of the time, she feels, it is enough to give a child a sense that the therapist is attuned to his or her feelings without "invading" most private thoughts. Rita guards carefully against the violation of privacy by thoughtless intrusion, a practice that has become commonplace in psychotherapy, in hospital treatment of emotionally troubled patients, and in the culture generally. "The strongest of our emotions belong only to ourselves; even we don't need to channel all of these feelings into words."

In her writing, Rita's focus has been on the relationships among generations, especially the emotional and social forces that disrupt the continuity between parent and child and the part the child therapist can play in repairing the broken intergenerational connections. Raised as she was in a closely knit Eastern European family, Rita has been impressed and disturbed to see how widespread are the fractures of family ties in the United States and the destructive impact of family instability upon children growing up here. The wounds in Rita's own experience — the loss of grandparents and relatives in Mogilev, the separations from her parents culminating in the permanent dislocation of her life upon immigration to the United States

— have made her sensitive to the power of loss and separation in the lives of young people.

These themes of continuity and dislocation run through Rita's papers. She has written on adoption and abandonment, reactions to sibling death, stepparents and stepchildren, divorce, mother-daughter relationships throughout life, depression in adolescence, parenting one's aging parents, assessing parent-child vulnerabilities, and, above all, intergenerational exchange, emotional "contamination," and the transference of attitudes between parents and children. Rita uses an experiential, not theoretical, approach, drawing on her own memories and emotions, as well as clinical examples, to document how, through interactions with their children, parents seek the fulfillment that their own lives have not afforded or to heal the wounds of the past.

In the survival of her parents through World War II, in the opportunity to establish a family of her own in the United States and start a practice of child psychiatry, Rita has been more fortunate than most of those who lived through the war and the Holocaust. She was able to repair the break in generational continuity that was most often the fate of survivors. "The tragedy of discontinuity through immigration means that one never truly belongs and always searches for belonging." To complete the circle, it has been especially important for Rita to have her children know her past.

Rita's collection of dolls, particularly the pregnant ones or the parent-child pairs, seems to express the importance she places on linking generations. The dolls serve to "tie the past to the present," a goal as important to her own life as to her professional work. During an American Psychiatric Association meeting in Detroit, she obtained her first Romanian male doll in 1967 from a museum. He looked just like the Hutuls riding logs down the streams of the Carpathian mountains. He was not for sale. "I told them — I am not sure that I was polite — that I just had to have him. I stayed at the museum all day until closing time, when the ladies, seeing that they could not get rid of me and fearing that I might return the next day, sold me that little doll. He now stands propped up against a wooden Romanian stand in the middle of a group of Balkan dolls in native costume. These treasured figures help bridge the world from my faraway childhood in Rădăuți, Romania, to the present, so-alien world of Palos Verdes Estates, California."

One of Rita's first opportunities to present a paper in child psychiatry provided a heartwarming experience of continuity. The occasion was a joint meeting of the Israeli Neuropsychiatric Society with the American Psychiatric Association in Tel Aviv in May 1965. Her mother attended the lecture. "I don't remember the topic, only that Peter Martin, a psychiatrist colleague [who was also one of her examiners during the specialty boards in psychiatry] introduced me as giving *naches* [a Yiddish expression that might be translated as bringing public pride and joy] to my mother." (The title of the lecture, long since forgotten, was "The Child Psychiatrist's First Encounter with the Parents.")

The strain that the responsibilities of taking care of one's elderly parents places upon the adult's relationship with brothers and sisters and on marriage ties is an important theme in Rita's writings. "The parenting of one's elderly parent exacerbates and revitalizes old sibling rivalries."[3] "The perceptions of the helplessness of one's parents has a direct impact on one's craving for having and being a perfect parent. The relationship to one's children becomes heavily overshadowed by one's childhood. Nurturance cravings in marriage become accentuated and augmented. Weak relationships become brittle and mature relationships can, indeed, become strengthened and more meaningful."[4] Above all, witnessing one's parents' failing health evokes fears of helplessness, loss, and abandonment.

> Witnessing in one's parent the loss of health, loss of control (body, bowel, urine, sight, or emotions) reawakens one's worst fears of body hurt, abandonment, desertion, and loss of love. The childhood fears are suddenly there, overwhelming, overpowering, and bewildering. One wants to stretch out a hand asking for protection and care, like one used to do when one was a small child. However, the person one wants to reach out to, one's parent, is the one who at that moment is reaching out for protection, and one can give that protective parenting only when there are emotional cushions in one's own internal and external realities.[5]

As will be apparent in the next chapter, Rita's appreciation of the tendency of parents to communicate to their children and grandchildren the conscious and unconscious hurts and grievances that have affected their lives also provides the foundation for her work in the field of psychiatry and foreign affairs. Children and grandchildren in various cultures seek "to avenge the injustices, real or imagined, suffered by their parents and grandparents. Besides illustrating the complexities of parent-child communication, the revenge motif is important because it serves to exacerbate international conflicts over many generations."[5]

✳

On November 27, 1981, Chaim Zisman, known in the local Romanian community as "Opapa," died in Los Angeles at the age of ninety-six. Opapa had been the most vital spirit of a large successful family. The Zismans knew all the Romanians of Los Angeles, Jews and non-Jews, and welcomed Rita and Allen as part of their family a few years after the Rogerses arrived in California. They celebrated "every holiday, every wedding, every birth," with joyous parties, good food, singing, and dancing. Rita and Opapa loved to dance together. Opapa's daughter-in-law Lyah, wife of Opapa's oldest son, Iasha, is the soul of the family and Rita's close friend.

Opapa was born in Mogilev Podolskiy in 1885. As a boy of twelve he worked in the same foundry Rita did. Over nearly a century, Opapa experienced immense political upheavals. He suffered the pogroms of two czars and after the Russian Revolution moved to Balti in Bessarabia, which was annexed to Romania in 1918. In the 1960s he was finally able to bring his large family, except for one son who was imprisoned by Stalin in 1941, to Los Angeles after fleeing from Bucharest to Paris and then to Peru. "Throughout all these upheavals Opapa remained true to himself, untouched in his love of life by all the turmoil around him." He danced at his grandchildren's weddings, as joyful as Rita's Zaziu. He arranged successful marriages and placed new arrivals from Romania and Russia in jobs and homes. "When Opapa called to say that one had to find a job for a new immigrant, nobody dared refuse. Nobody refused anything to Opapa.

"I was glad I was at home when Opapa died. It would have been terrible to miss his funeral. We were all there. The rabbi who conducted the services was from Balti. In his eulogy he told us how as a child he had been brought out from the concentration camp in Mogilev Podolskiy to Bucharest, where he stayed in Opapa's home and then later Opapa had paid for his passage to the United States. The rabbi said a personal farewell to Opapa, as only somebody orphaned in childhood says to the one who had been to him like a father and mother. All the children and grandchildren of Opapa were at the funeral, and so was the Romanian colony from Los Angeles. But what was strange was that the funeral and the later services did not seem to be happening in Los Angeles. It was another part of the world. We were all holding hands. We went to the house of Opapa's youngest son and there the rabbi held more services. Afterward, the rabbi and I chatted and discovered that between 1940 and 1941 he had been in Rădăuți. His sister was married to my rabbi, who taught Jewish history and religion there. The rabbi asked me my maiden name. When I told him he said, 'I knew a Stenzler in Rădăuți, a tall man with glasses.' So the rabbi knew my father. At Opapa's funeral it was like it was supposed to be: *haimish,* warm, reminiscent. We were at home. Opapa had remained true to himself and to us even in his death."

✳

People like Rita's Opapa, who connects us with the past through the histories we share and visits to the places where memory once formed, are necessary for our sense of personal identity. We can hold these connections partly through memory, but memory by itself is not enough.

After an official visit to Romania in 1985, Rita asked herself many questions: "A child psychiatrist cannot but ask herself why childhood memories, experiences, and perceptions have such intensity and longevity. Is it because they are new experiences? Is it because children are so egocentric and relate everything that happens around them as being caused by them? Why is our childhood entanglement so much tighter than our later relationships? Why do we carry the shadows of our sibling rivalries into our peer relationships at school and work? And why does the emotional place of our childhood invade all other places of our lives?"

Rita has struggled throughout her adult years in America to hold on to her past with certainty. She speaks and writes frequently of how she is drawn to people who are true to who they are, authentic in themselves. The self of Eastern Europe clashes with the culture of Southern California. Having felt so valued by her parents, Rita seeks to recreate these feelings by being special to others, as she became to Opapa. Sometimes this need creates resentment in those around her. At the core of her sense of self are the good feelings of childhood Rita connects with her mother. "She made me feel special like no one else on earth. And that is why I go back to Eastern Europe — in eternal search for her and how she made me feel." Such searches, of course, can only bring out, or help us rediscover, the connection that must already be established inside.

One way that we try to link the past with the present is through the creation, or re-creation, of a community that replicates the memories of childhood. Clerks at the market in Palos Verdes plaza save special fruits for Rita, whose intimate banter with the saleswomen in the village stores is more characteristic of life in Eastern European towns than in Southern California. "In Palos Verdes Estates, the grocery store, the general store, the bakery, the dress shop, the tennis club, became my little community à la Rădăuţi. Not the inhabitants of Palos Verdes, though. They were different for me and I for them. They moved frequently, they divorced even more often, they were tossed together with no feeling of belonging." In Southern California Rita sometimes feels that she no longer fits in either of the two worlds. The child psychiatry unit at Harbor General Hospital in Torrance, near Palos Verdes, became, under Rita's leadership, "another little family unit where nobody left or transferred." But this, too, was eventually shattered by the realities of California county politics.

Rita even tried to convert a most unlikely community, the American Psychiatric Association (APA), into "a replica of Rădăuţi." Although she had received her psychiatric training in state institutions rather than in more prestigious university teaching hospitals, understood little of American psychiatric politics — at least at first — and was a foreign graduate, Rita soon made a place for herself in the APA. For twenty years she felt "at home" at its meetings and enjoyed the "strong ties" the members had "with each other, their profession, and their organization." Taking the specialty boards in 1962 strengthened her sense of connection with American psychiatry. It "felt like a celebration day, a rite of passage. I enjoyed being examined by my peers in a field which was part of my identity." Peter Martin told her that he gave her the highest score he had ever given a candidate. Rita felt, as in Rădăuţi, cherished and appreciated.

In the APA Rita also appreciated the good food, conversation, and travel and the dedication to this branch of medicine she so loved. "I enjoyed the community of interest in the scientific meetings and the togetherness of the social gatherings." She was touched in 1980 when the APA's medical director, Melvin Sabshin, remarked as they crossed with a group of psychiatrists into Canton in the People's Republic of China, "This must remind you of other crossings." Rita was thrilled when she learned in 1978, on arriving at a meeting in Israel, that she had been nominated to be a trustee at large. She was elected by the national membership and served for three "enjoyable and homey" years. Even the porters at the Dupont Plaza Hotel in Washington, where the trustees stayed, became "my buddies." She was appointed to and chaired numerous task forces and committees, especially those concerned with psychiatry and foreign affairs. Through this organization she was able to form connections with other parts of the world psychiatric community. In 1981, when Rita returned from meeting with Polish psychiatrists in Munich after martial law was instituted in Poland, she was able to persuade the APA to send an emergency cable to the president of the Polish Psychiatric Society. It said, "28,000 U.S. psychiatrists want to express our affiliation and concern with you and all our colleagues in Poland. Please reassure us of your well-being." When Rita was in Cracow in 1983, Adam Szymusik, who had been president of the Polish group at the time, proudly showed her this cable, framed, on the wall of his office.

But in the early 1980s a rift in Rita's relationship with the APA occurred, partly in relation to the nuclear weapons issue. Rita had been chosen in 1977 to chair the APA's task force on the Psychosocial Impact of Nuclear Advances, as it was rather euphemistically named. In 1981, as public anxiety about the nuclear threat intensified, the APA's task force (with "Advances" changed to "Developments") and its report, for which Rita bore the greatest responsibility, became the focus of intense public interest. Rita was troubled about what she felt to be the mixing of professional and political agendas, especially on the part of antinuclear activists inside the APA. The strong media coverage the antinuclear movement was receiving brought the task force into the public spotlight. Always suspicious of causes and public movements, which evoked memories of those she had witnessed and experienced thirty years before, Rita became increasingly uneasy in her role as chairperson of the task force. She was antagonistic toward what she regarded as "naive humanism based on lack of suffering" on the part of several of her American colleagues, including, at one time, this coauthor. Once, in a taxi in Kiev, we argued vehemently, as our teenage children listened, over the meaning of Soviet leader Leonid Brezhnev's warning about the dangers of nuclear weapons at the Twenty-sixth Communist Party Congress. "Now we are really *mish-*

pocheh" (family), she said the next morning. "We have argued in front of the children."

In a letter to me at about that time she wrote,

> Political activism, via nuclear issues [is] Americanism, belief in people power, idealism, humanism, and for us from Rădăuți, political naiveté. We are always shocked about how little U.S. citizens, even the most sophisticated ones, know about the rest of the world, how they assume similarity of political structures, of political systems, ethos, and other ways of life . . . Maybe we resent the naive humanism based on lack of suffering. Maybe also we feel that U.S. citizens consider that any political system is good enough for citizens in other parts of the world and the benefits of democracy a privilege to which only the U.S.A. is entitled.

Rita's Rădăuți background and experience were suddenly in profound conflict with her professional commitments to the APA.

This conflict came to a head when, as a trustee planning the annual meeting in Toronto, Rita opposed part of the program, which she believed was a direct promotion of the nuclear freeze campaign. (Others, including me, believed that this was not strictly the case.) "I objected to its being part of the official scientific program. Because of my objection during a board of trustees meeting, this program was held outside the meeting." Some leaders in the APA, Rita believes, never forgave her. Though "I don't blame them, I frankly felt, and still do, that it was a political abuse of psychiatry to use our professional organization for support of the nuclear freeze campaign. International Physicians for the Prevention of Nuclear War is different. This organization says what it does, what it stands for, and what it believes in. APA also became, for my taste, too much involved in U.S. party politics . . . I don't claim objectivity," she acknowledges. "On the contrary, I'm convinced that my reaction is due to personal, national, and historical perceptions. That the strength of my feelings comes from Rădăuți, Mogilev, Prague, and Yalta cannot be denied."

Most of Rita's Romanian friends in the United States do not even speak of their homeland in their families and certainly do not wish to return with their children. They sometimes ask why she wants to go back to places and times that are associated with so much pain and tragedy. But travel, especially to Europe, enables Rita to feel more complete. Her need is especially strong, she suggests, just because she has become so well integrated in the United States personally, professionally, socially, and financially. She wonders if by coming alone to America, putting the ocean between herself and her family, and marrying an American Christian — "nobody else of the Stenzlers or Wohls ever did such a thing" — she was not betraying Zaziu. "That is perhaps why I carry him so much around in my heart and search for him all over Europe. Zaziu belongs to the tapestries of Eastern Europe, its smells, sounds, heartaches, suffering, and resignation. It is the part of the world in which everything has collapsed except human connectedness."

Despite the harsh conditions in Eastern Europe, Rita loves her trips there. She enjoys "the way the people act with each other, how they smile, how they make deals, the fluidity with which a yes becomes a no and a no becomes a yes. It seems as though the people of Eastern Europe have had not only flexible borders, which have changed regimes and flags, but they have also developed flexibility toward life and people. Things are not seen as black and white, good or bad, right or wrong. There is a constant intertwining between external events and internal realities, a constant shifting and dynamism of perceptions and allegiances." In Eastern Europe, including the USSR, Rita feels once again on intimate terms with her surroundings. Speaking several of the languages, she readily engages people in conversation and enjoys "the caress of caring by strangers." When she visited a Russian psychiatrist who had stayed with her in California in his home, "he recalled his visit to our home and sleeping in David's bed. Moscow and Palos Verdes became linked."

Rita visited Israel most frequently when her parents were living there. "My trips to Israel between 1960 and 1967 endeared Israel tremendously to me. There was the familiarity, tenderness, realness, the Jews from all these lands, their involvement with everything and everybody. I always studied Hebrew on the way. I usually would get to a certain page in my self-teaching book, *Mori* ["My Teacher"], and never beyond it. When I would arrive I would try my reviewed Hebrew on the cab driver and others. The conversation went roughly this way: They would ask me, *"At oleh cahdash?* [Are you a new immigrant?] I would reply no. Then they would ask when I would immigrate to Israel. I would reply that I wouldn't. They would ask why and I would say that my husband, children, and I are happy in the United States. They would reply that Jews cannot be happy anywhere but in Israel. I would reply that my husband is not Jewish. Then silence would fall."

In Haifa, Rita's parents were surrounded by friends and family, and a strong feeling of continuity prevailed. Most of the Rădăuţi Jews who went to Israel settled in Haifa, and the Stenzlers' apartment at 51 Herzl Street became "the Grand Central Station for the Rădăuţi colony." They all shopped on Herzl Street and dropped in at the Stenzlers' for coffee and gossip and traditional Bukovinian treats.

Helene made a cozy, warm home of their modest apartment, filling it with plants and photos of her children and grandchildren. "When, later, Nora and I wanted to buy them a bigger, more luxurious apartment, Mutti refused, even though she had to climb three flights of stairs. She refused to move because Papa was already blind and, on Herzl Street, he had continuous entertainment. He could walk down by himself and was immediately surrounded by acquaintances who would chat with him and accompany him on his errands." Haifa became an extension of Helene's Rădăuţi world. She referred to the city as "my Haifa" and to their new land as "my Israel," and, unlike other members of her generation, she learned Hebrew, which she remembered from the prayers of her father and of her grandfather, who had gone to die in what was then Palestine.

In October 1973, Rita went to Haifa. While there, she helped tend the wounded at the Ramban Hospital during the Yom Kippur War. "I was desperate about Israel, and I felt that I needed to go there to be with my people and my father." At the hospital she recognized Rafi, the nineteen-year-old son of Herbert Schiller, a close friend from Rădăuţi. As a teenager Schiller had been orphaned in the camp at Sargorod. He ate out of garbage cans like a stray dog and was smuggled out of the camp by the underground Haganah and taken to Palestine. Rafi, who had no identifying tag, was lying unconscious at Ramban with shrapnel in his cerebellum.

Herbert Schiller had fought in the 1948, 1956, and 1967 wars of Israel. After Rita had called him, he stood, in his home guard uniform, at the bedside of his wounded son. Rita and Herbert went to Jerusalem to the Western Wall to pray for help. Herbert's wife, Trudi, asked her to go with him so he would drive more carefully. Rafi was transferred to Hadassah Hospital in Jerusalem, where, after a long period of unconsciousness, he received rehabilitative treatment. Especially important for his recovery was the coordinated, caring program administered by Atara Kaplan, chairperson of the Department of Psychiatry at Hadassah Hospital.

Rita seems to meet people from Rădăuți wherever she travels. In Bucharest in 1983 for a Pugwash conference, she visited the Curtea de Argeş (Cathedral of Arges), where the first two Romanian kings are buried. Curtea de Argeş reawakened the memory of the legend of Mesterul (Master) Manole, whose wife's body was supposed to have been built into the walls of the monastery in order to keep them from collapsing. Rita recited the poem commemorating the legend. "Our Romanian hosts recited it with me and our childhood memories became intertwined."

Several days later, Rita was taken to lunch by a physician who lived in an old, traditional home. "The street was romantically lined with trees. The door was opened by the son of the family, who looked and acted like the young characters of Caragiale's novels. They were always sons of *boieri* [landowners], handsome, educated, and gifted, with burning eyes. At least that is how I remember imagining them when I read the novels as a very young girl. The young man, a surgical resident, served us brandy, as the characters of the novelist Caragiale would have done in the homes of their parents. His sister was an artist whose paintings were hanging on the walls and who herself looked like a painting by Grigorescu. While we were eating the delicious lunch, the lady of the house asked me where I was from. When I told her Rădăuți, she stopped with the tureen in her hand and informed me that she, too, had attended Liceul Elisabeta Doamna. We compared ages and teachers and I discovered that my hostess had been one class below me. Suddenly, it was not November 1, 1983, but 1938, and I was flooded with memories from another time and another town and another life."

Sometimes Rita experiences these floods of memory even without leaving home. At Yom Kippur services in a synagogue in Encino, California, "the melodies, the service, and the vitality of the congregation brought longing memories of the little shul, Viznitzer synagogue, in Rădăuți and my grandfather praying *Nileh,* the last prayer of Yom Kippur. The big ornamented, elegant, air-conditioned temple in the midst of the Los Angeles valley was so different from the Viznitzer synagogue and from Rădăuți. I think it is not a question of sights and sounds but the intensity of feelings from childhood."

After a "reencounter" with Romania in June 1985, Rita knew that the world of her childhood, the Rădăuți of the 1930s, had vanished. This time she did not want to see the home she grew up in. "It hurt too much to see it so dilapidated and disgraced. Everyone wore national costumes, for Rădăuți had become a community of peasants. Gone are the urbane Romanians, the Germans, the Jews. The Rădăuți of 1985 has nothing in common with the Rădăuți of my childhood. I was quiet as we ate lunch at the Restaurant Nordic. As I looked out the window, I did not even imagine the silhouettes of my parents, my family, and friends. There was no congruence between my memories and the scenery I saw. I rushed the group to depart from Rădăuți, even though they had gone there for my sake."

I often wonder about Rita's constant struggle to renew her identity. Perhaps for her, and others like her who grew up as members of a minority group in a contested European border area, this struggle is the result of an unconscious perception, beginning in earliest childhood, that however secure one may feel within the family and immediate community, status and security in the larger community are always uncertain. The core of one's identity is established from intimate ties within the family. But personal security and identity are not simply private matters, to be established once and for all. They both continue to be challenged and influenced throughout adult life by wider social and political forces. This awareness of uncertainty is reflected in the "shifting perceptions and allegiances" experienced by Rita, and her conclusion that "the only anchored allegiances" remain to oneself and to the continuity of generations so important in her work.

Rita's place within the community of Palos Verdes Estates became strengthened in a curious way. The original owner of the estate, before it was broken up to create the village of the same name, imported several peacocks, presumably to add some exotic color. The birds remained and have multiplied. They are, of course, beautiful, but they also make a harsh unpleasant noise, leave their droppings all over, and eat some of the residents' favorite plantings. In the autumn of 1985, ten of the peacocks were found dead on one of the village streets, poisoned. The incident led to an evening meeting in City Hall, which Rita planned to attend — her first — "I didn't know there *was* a City Hall." Supporters of the peacocks came to the meeting wearing black arm bands, a symbolic display of grief for the dead creatures. Heated arguments were presented for and against the peacocks. The mayor asked if anyone else wished to speak about the ecological aspects of the controversy, and Rita raised her hand.

She stood up and told of a conversation she had had earlier in the day with a young patient, the one who had lost her mother. The girl was noisy and disruptive, if not disturbed. She had heard about the dead peacocks and the possible solutions for dealing with those that were left, including trapping them and taking them away. "What will happen to noisy children," the little girl asked Rita. "Will *they* be trapped or poisoned?" The peacocks won the night, and Rita's status in Palos Verdes was powerfully affirmed.

9. Psychiatry and Foreign Affairs

Almost everything in Rita's background and personal history prepared her for work in the field of psychiatry and foreign affairs. A child of the Bukovina, especially a Jewish child, could not help but know, even if only unconsciously, the vulnerability of her family's situation. As we have seen, such a child grows up to learn how, through two millennia, her beautiful borderland home has been continually buffeted by the aspirations of surrounding states and of ethnonational groups. "In Bukovina one always lives between."

In Rădăuţi each ethnic group clung to its separate identity. For the Jewish community, even the Romanians were foreigners. From Rita's family's perspective, "it was the non-Jews who were the foreigners in Rădăuţi, who had a 'different' life." When Rita heard from her childhood Romanian friends that they were told that "we kill Christian children" at Passover, she learned early that there were "two worlds which live in the same territory, but which have different belief systems." Among the central objectives of psychiatry and foreign affairs is the identification of such different belief systems in specific international conflicts, to find ways of transcending their distancing, destructive impact.

In contrast to her early experience of differences and political strife is Rita's profound sense of personal security. The certainty of

being loved unreservedly by her parents and other relatives was the foundation for all her later experiences. Until "Hitler's evil arm reached out into the Bukovina," Rita's was a highly protected childhood, "sheltered from all unpleasant things." Though no childhood can be free of conflict, Rita's came as close to being so as any. It is difficult to find evidence of much suffering on Rita's part before anti-Semitism and fascism destroyed her community. Rita's life stands as a challenge to those explanations of the personalities of strong and creative individuals which rely heavily on theories of intrapsychic conflict and strength derived from early hardship.

Her security did not make Rita insensitive to the suffering of others. Her mother's empathy, her sensitivity to the feelings of others, which extended to those who caused suffering, set a lasting example. "How can one hate an adult when one sees the hurt child in him? How can one hate a nation when one thinks of the suffering which breeds such hatred?" In Rita's memories of Mogilev, the acts of kindness and compassion by her parents, the Ukrainian peasants, and even certain German soldiers, rather than hatred of the Nazis, stand out. In later years her mother's example of selfless caring remained a source of strength for Rita. When she was separated from her daughter because of oppressive politics, Helene's "motherly love was such that she sacrificed being with us in order to assure what was best for us."

While Helene lived in relative isolation from the surrounding community, Rita's father was more worldly. He spoke the Romanian language, which Rita's mother never really learned. Rita believes it was his unwillingness to be a "quitter" and abandon his aged parents and other dependent members of his own and his wife's family that made him stay in Rădăuţi as Nazism drew near. "With his keen realism, his instinctual ability to discern between information and propaganda, I suspect that my father really knew and felt what was coming." Shaje, like his wife, was possessed of an unusual degree of empathy, most vividly demonstrated in his effort to rescue the two young German officers whose retreat from Mogilev Podolskiy had been cut off by the Partisans in 1944 ("Bronislav . . . just imagine that you and I are them").

The experiences of each period of Rita's life, beginning in the late 1930s, contributed in particular ways to her eventual involvement with psychiatry and foreign affairs. The breakdown of her precious, protected world was brought home when her father was beaten by fascist anti-Semites in his own town. Mogilev taught her the destructive power of political oppression and the experience of powerlessness as loved ones perished. But it was also the place where an invalid Russian surgeon exhibited special caring and tenderness to her and the victims of German bombing. Memories of this doctor came back to Rita during her later work in the Middle East. "My emotional, impulsive trips to Israel during the 1967 and 1973 wars were no doubt related to the unresolved impact of my helplessness when that wonderful human being needed help so badly for his people and I had nothing beyond motivation with which to help him."

The year after the liberation of the camp at Mogilev Podolskiy, during which the Romanian Jews had no defined status in the Soviet system, further impressed upon Rita the impersonal and arbitrary power of modern nationalism. Wandering stateless through Bessarabia and northern Bukovina, forced to separate from her parents and sister in order to elude the Soviet authorities, Rita experienced, as she would again in Vienna, an assault upon personal identity. Her departures from emerging Communist regimes, beginning in 1945, motivated by her fear of being unable to get out later, led to long years of forced separation from her parents, another characteristic effect of modern nationalisms.

But in Prague, from 1945 to 1948, Rita first experienced internationalism. In her precious Czech interlude participation in international student congresses brought her in touch with people who could look past national boundaries. Her work at the Romanian embassy was her first apprenticeship in psychiatry and foreign affairs as she tried to bridge the language and cultural differences between the Romanian and Italian farmers and the Czech authorities. Translating the realities of one people to another is the foremost task of psychiatry and foreign affairs.

In 1967, in order better to understand American concepts of democracy and history, political science, and international relations, Rita enrolled in a master's program in the Department of Political Science at UCLA, earning her degree in 1969. Although Rita did not know it at the time, her mother was pleased with this development in her daughter's career. In late June 1981, Betty Zeiger, Rita's former Hebrew teacher in Rădăuți, showed us the last letter she had received from Rita's mother. Writing in 1968, Helene expressed her pride in Rita's graduate studies, then ongoing. On seeing the letter, Rita said, "I never knew that my mother fully knew what was going on, [that I] was becoming a psychiatrist who combines political

science and psychology and applies them to international relations."
Later Rita wrote, "It was so typical of my mother to greet me with
her pride in my accomplishments, years later in the deserted town of
Rădăuți." Since 1970, the year of her mother's death, Rita has
"practiced" psychiatry and foreign affairs in many countries. Her most
intense efforts have been concentrated in four arenas of international
conflict: the divided Germanies, the Arab-Israeli struggle, the U.S.-
Soviet relationship, and Poland.

✳

Most of Rita's trips to Germany have been in association with meetings dealing with various aspects of the East-West conflict. In 1983,
for instance, she was invited to East Berlin by the World Federation
for Scientific Workers to participate in a round-table discussion on
"Science and the Qualitative Arms Race," where she presented a paper
on "The Arms Race as a Symptom of Mistrust." Some have been more
purely personal, part of her struggle to reconcile a family background
of German culture, a childhood in which German was the language
spoken at home, and an adolescence steeped in German romantic
writing with the impact of Hitler and the Nazi regime.

Once, on her way to East Berlin from Amsterdam, Rita inves-
tigated the Interflug — East German airline — destinations. The
political schism of East and West became apparent. "From the West
we could come in only via Amsterdam or Copenhagen. But Interflug
was flying only to the USSR, Afghanistan, Syria, Yemen, Ethiopia,
Angola, and Cuba. And yet, how much at home I felt on arrival in
East Berlin. I was greeted at the foot of the steps of the plane by my
hosts, in German, my mother tongue. However, I knew that while
I was being entertained lavishly in the VIP lounge, my luggage was
being searched."

While Rita was being wined and dined in East Berlin, she was
keenly aware that others were not treated this way and thought of
the German people who had been killed trying to escape to the West
over the wall. "I had little, probably very superficial, dialogue with
my conscience about these issues. I justified to myself that a dialogue
has to continue and that I personally could not cut off my connectedness with the people from Eastern Europe. But here it also meant
connectedness with the German people. For very strange reasons I
felt more linked through childhood with the people from the DDR
[East Germany] than I had ever felt with the people from West

Germany — maybe because they looked, talked, and were more like the ones in the German novels I used to read before World War Two."

Through her trips to Germany, Rita tries to understand how Germans regarded the Nazi period and the appeal of Hitler to those with whom she speaks. She found the intellectuals in the DDR more honest about the Hitler period than anyone with whom she discussed the topic in the FRG (West Germany). A geneticist from Leipzig said to her, "'I can remember clearly the first time my mother took me to see and hear Hitler in Leipzig. I had goose pimples. I am sure that had I been the right age I would have become a member of the SS.' This was the first time any German had told me that. I had to ask myself, Had I been a German boy at the right age during Hitler's time, what would I have become?"

A year later Rita attended a meeting in Copenhagen on conventional forces in Europe. Her paper, "Conflicting Perceptions Between the U.S.A. and the USSR," was given as an opening statement. Dreary military discussions followed, filled with debate about "logistics, numbers, hardware, et cetera." "Suddenly a remark made me wide awake. A German general said, 'From my experience as a battalion commander at Stalingrad, I know that . . .' I could not believe my ears. Here was a German general who had fought at Stalingrad sitting around the table with us. I was unable to understand his military talk. But most of all I could not follow it because I was remembering where I had been when this general fought for Hitler's Germany in Stalingrad."

Rita and the general dined together and talked about Stalingrad. He described his experience as a young field officer, losing his soldiers and suddenly finding himself and his surviving 120 men surrounded in the snow. "As he talked, I saw the snow of the Ukraine in front of my eyes. I looked at this elderly German general and I evaluated how very much circumstances can make people friends or foes."

The general talked also about the thrill of being a young officer, heightened by the feeling of belonging to the new master race. "He talked about Hitler's charisma. The former inmate from Mogilev in me was startled by my psychiatric tolerance. But then I realized that, after all, I had been a psychiatrist for thirty years. In the following days I could see how much one remains enriched and burdened by being a psychiatrist. The thrill of being in Hitler's army for a young man I could understand. I worried about the roots of this tolerance.

Deep down, perhaps, a part of me had admired the strong, successful master race."

In Rita's observations we can see the effort of psychiatrists who work in the field of psychiatry and foreign affairs to examine their own motives and watch within themselves the play of personal, historical, and ethnocentric bias. Perhaps the day will come when this degree of self-questioning also becomes the responsibility of diplomats who work in the domain of conflicted international relations. In her published writings Rita has stressed repeatedly the need for the psychiatrist to become aware of her ethnic, ideological, and nationalistic biases and allegiances, conscious and unconscious, so as to avoid overidentification with one group's pain or cause while rejecting the legitimacy of the experience, hurts, or point of view of its adversary. We cannot free ourselves of such biases — they are part of our being. But we can recognize them and resist surrendering blindly to their emotional influence and the tendency to condemn the "other" without knowing his experience or perspective. Blindness to the responsibility of one's own group for creating the conflict at hand may be the most important single obstacle to its resolution. In Rita's words, when seen through the lens of such biases, "favorable actions are a response to the decision-maker's own behavior; unfriendly acts spring from unprovoked hostility."[1]

Rita has been relentless in her struggle to become aware of her own motivations and the objects of her prejudices, which sometimes include other psychiatrists. Her understanding of her own biases and her sensitivity to stereotyping by others came into play in an encounter with a noted American Jewish psychiatrist at a conference in Haifa in 1983. He had chaired a session at which Rita had presented a paper, "The Responsibilities of Psychiatrists: The Dual Loyalties."

"He called my paper psychoanalytic, which it was not. He told me how he hated Germans. He said that not only would he never buy a German car but that he even resents riding in a German car. He said he would never set foot in Germany and that the Nazi criminals must be pursued. In spite of his otherwise brilliant intellectual accomplishments, he failed German and ascribed this to his feelings about what the Germans did to the Jews. He wanted to know whether I had ever been to Germany. I said yes and told him that I did not feel the way he did. He asked me where I had been during the war, and after I told him he asked me reprimandingly whether I felt that one should forget and forgive. I replied that I could not hate a group of people because of their nationality, political belief, history, or present regime. I attempted to explain to him that exhibitionistic displays of revenge and hatred are usually a camouflage for something else. I gave him the example of the Ukrainians who had deserted the USSR forces in 1941 and who, in 1944, in terror as the USSR forces returned, demonstrated their renewed loyalty by slaughtering the horses of the German troops who were caught in their midst.

"This kindly, embarrassed gentleman then asked me whether I was telling him that the Soviets were worse than the Germans. I cringed inside. Here was a noted psychiatrist who at an international conference called Ukrainian deserters 'the Soviets' and who obviously knew nothing about the history of the region. I checked with myself and realized that I did not then or now hate 'these Ukrainians' . . . But my own vindictiveness came across when I said to this breakfast companion that maybe if I had been a Jew who spent World War Two in the United States rather than in a concentration camp, I might also refuse to enter a German-made car, German soil, and so forth. I must confess I felt slightly guilty about this retaliatory attack . . . He did not have the same emotional base in Israel that I did. He had reached out to me and I had retaliated with anger, hitting him where he, a sensitive man, hurt the most."

Rita's reasons for harboring less hostility toward Germans than do other Romanian and Eastern European survivors go deeper than this explanation. To Rita, born in the romantic era of Queen Marie's Romania, German, Russian, and even Romanian political regimes and causes never represented their countries or peoples. In the case of the Germans, toward whom Rita never developed the expected or justifiable hatred, she thought "it has something to do with my mother's profound love of German literature and music. She never identified the German people with their regime." But Rita also never identified "the Russians with communism or the Romanians with the Iron Guard or their present regime." Historical romance, cultural history, and adolescent fantasy seem to have had a lasting, powerful influence on her. Perhaps a sense of history and geography and a broadly cultured upbringing can provide safeguards against narrow ethnic and political prejudice.

✳

Until recently, Rita's most extensive involvement in foreign affairs has been in the Middle East. In 1967, in Tel Aviv, during the Six-

Day War between Israel and her Arab neighbors, Rita heard a Jewish boy of fourteen greet his mother with the words "Our planes shot down five of their planes and all our planes returned safely." "This was the first time I wondered what an Arab boy of fourteen might be telling his mother and himself about the events of the air war on that same day."[2] Thus began Rita's preoccupation with the Arab-Israeli conflict, which would consume much of her personal and professional energy over the next two decades. With her frequent visits to Israel, Rita experienced directly the perpetual loss, grief, and anxiety that has resulted from the conflict between Israel and her Arab neighbors. The focus of Rita's efforts in this arena, as in all her activities in psychiatry and foreign affairs, is on finding ways to interrupt the cycles of violence through which historical enmities are transmitted from one generation to another.

Rita's interest in political conflict in the Middle East may have begun in childhood, when "the Turks" were the enemy and mothers threatened their naughty sons with the specter of Turks coming to get them. The Ottoman Empire had included Romania until the nineteenth century, and tales of the five hundred years of Turkish occupation were still vivid in Romanian families. Mothers had heard stories about Turkish cruelties from their mothers or grandmothers. "If a mother chose to be particularly cruel, she might add that they would cut off his genitalia and turn him into a eunuch." The little Romanian boy of the 1930s would not ordinarily encounter Turks, but he would meet children of Hungarian or Jewish minorities. Rita suggests that the term "Turk" came to represent the "other," or the potential enemy, people with a different language, religion, mannerisms, clothes, and food. Threats handed down over several generations, engendering fear and mistrust, provide a reservoir of images and emotions that may later be mobilized by political leaders and focused upon Magyars, Jews, or whoever the designated enemy may be.

A child who has grown up with such fears may seek to become strong, succeeding against the "enemy" where his parents have failed. Rita has written of this intergenerational dynamic, which may have applications to other conflicts between ethnic groups: "Thus the child turns away from words to actions. Not only does he want to vindicate his elders and gratify their need for revenge, but also he wishes to prove himself stronger than his parents."[3] His parents, devalued by their failure to rout the "enemy," can no longer guide him; indeed, his perception of them as weak inflames his need for action and revenge all the more.

"Into the vacuum created by the parents' diminution steps the peer group and the revolutionary leader. The youngster feels abandoned, lonesome, powerless, and frightened as a result of the loss of his parents as authority figures. He looks for security through overemphasized, overaccentuated peer relationships and conforms rigidly to the peers' pressure for sameness in dress, slogan, and agenda. The revolutionary leader in turn will seek out, use, and abuse the youngster's tremendous psychological hunger for peer relationships and substitute parental guidance."[4]

The struggle between Israel and her Arab neighbors has produced five major wars and countless other episodes of killing in the past forty years. Rita gave the first of her many papers on the psychological dimensions of this conflict at an annual meeting of the American Psychiatric Association in 1968. Entitled "The Emotional Climate in Israeli Society," its companion piece was a paper entitled "The Emotional Climate in Arab Society." In these papers Rita described the preoccupation of each side with the conflict and its resulting emotional toll. Rita also described the clash of conflicting histories: "Israel's nationalism is European; that of the Arab nations has the tone of an anticolonial movement. The conflict between the two groups is intensified because each justifies its claim to territory by an appeal to the history of its people. The alienation of the two groups has had cumulative effects."[5]

Over the following two decades, Rita wrote a number of papers and gave numerous presentations on the Arab-Israeli conflict at local, national, and international meetings, several of which she has helped to organize. At these meetings, in which both Arabs and Israelis participate, Rita, in addition to presenting her ideas, inevitably plays a healing role, translating communications that are missed because of perceptual blinders or detecting and bringing to awareness subtle expressions of hurt, anger, or misunderstanding of which the group may not have been aware.

Rita distinguishes between genuine human contact and "'good will toward mankind,' which most of the time makes those who utter it feel good about themselves and is frequently a psychological disguise under which one hides personal selfishness and pettiness. . . . We people from Eastern Europe are more scared of professed good will than of hard realities. Real contact can eventually establish emotional ties across the economic, political, and psychological barriers between peoples in the Middle East. Historical enmity in our times is not a given which has to be perpetuated. . . . The 'emotional contamination' of the eye exchanges between President Sadat and the Israeli people destroyed in one day an historical enmity which existed in political slogans and had been fueled by four bitter wars."[6] But further peaceful exchanges will require Arab and Israeli leaders who are willing to take the risks necessary to bring them about and face the criticisms at home that they are jeopardizing security or prestige by communicating with the enemy.

In February of 1974, Rita and I and William Davidson participated in a meeting at the State Department on Middle Eastern affairs. In preparation for this meeting, Rita went to Israel in an attempt to understand the emotional climate in Israeli society after the October 1973 war. During this visit, she interviewed several Israeli officials who had been involved in the conflict. Among these was Menachem Begin, then leader of the opposition party. Begin's style of communication, which would in a few years become familiar throughout the world, was demonstrated in his handling of Rita.

"I had written to Begin, as I had to the other officials, to let him know when and where I would be in Israel and the purpose of my trip. While registering at the Tel Aviv Hilton, I received a call. It was from Yehud Kadishai, Begin's personal secretary, who put Begin on the line. 'I have a cold,' said Begin, 'so, you have a choice to come to my apartment here in Tel Aviv now or to meet me in two days at the Knesset for lunch.' I suggested that I call back within two to three days to find out how he was. He interrupted me decisively and said, 'I told you, either you come to my apartment now, or we meet at one o'clock the day after tomorrow in the Knesset for lunch.' I chose the latter.

"When I arrived in the Knesset dining room, Menachem Begin greeted me politely and formally. He was dressed in a dark suit and tie, looking very different from the other Knesset members who wore open shirts and short sleeves. Begin told me what to order and then started the interview by telling me that he knew I had been in Mogilev Podolskiy, that he knew about Rădăuţi and my family. I learned almost nothing about him. I barely got one question in before he began telling me what *Eretz,* (the land of) Israel, meant to him and to the Jews all over the world. He interspersed his oratory with advice about what to eat. (This was done in an almost *yiddishe mame*, Jewish-motherlike tone.) When I left the Knesset after two hours, I had learned nothing about Menachem Begin except that he was passionate about the land of Israel and that he would give his life at a moment's notice for the smallest sliver of it."

In 1976, Rita was invited to Egypt by Tahseen Basheer, then foreign policy spokesman for President Anwar Sadat. Rita found that as a Jewish survivor of World War II whose parents had immigrated to Israel, she faced her first visit to Egypt with considerable apprehension. She was particularly anxious when she discovered that she had been scheduled to lecture at the Al Ahram Institute, which had been established after the Six-Day War to study Israeli policy and strategy.

> My expectations when I came to Egypt were fraught with stereotypes, colored by anxieties, and even expressed in mild psychosomatic symptoms. It was nothing I actually could put my finger on, but, rather, a collection of fears and biases. Little things became important, and I needed to examine them. I would remember Egypt not so much for the grandeur of the pyramids or the smiling faces of the people, but for the knowledgeable person who asked me about Israeli towns. I didn't reply, for two reasons. One was a personal paranoia tinged with aggrandizement: It is dangerous, I thought, to talk about Israel in Egypt. The other was that for the first time I fully understood the intense — and mutual — fixation between Arab and Israeli. The person who questioned me probably had read every book there is on Israel, but he had never seen an Israeli town. Without that kind of reality-testing, fantasy follows one's own needs: It leans on externally supplied bits of propaganda, incorporating them into the mind's distortions. The great similarity between Arabs and Israelis is their preoccupation — and lack of realistic verification of ideas — with one another.[7]

In Cairo in January 1978, I had a chance to watch Rita's skill in establishing personal contact across political barriers. We were both members of a delegation from the American Psychiatric Association, which was following up on Sadat's November 1977 initiative to explore avenues of contact with Egyptian government officials and professionals. Our host at a dinner one evening at the Château Restaurant was Morsi Said el Din, then vice minister of Information. Rita and Morsi discussed whether they had danced the polka together in November 1945, when she had been a medical student breathing the freedom of Prague after the war and he was a young reporter in England, assigned to Prague to cover the student congress. After our visit, Dr. Said el Din went to Jerusalem to take part in political talks as the head of the delegation. Soon after, Rita also went to Jerusalem and invited him to a dinner at the home of her friend Atara Kaplan. Despite the increasingly tense political atmosphere, he accepted.

After checking with the Israeli Foreign Office, which approved, Rita and Atara planned an elegant cocktail and dinner party for January 17. On that very day, President Sadat recalled the Egyptian delegation because Israeli Prime Minister Menachem Begin had insulted Egypt's foreign minister the evening before by calling him "young man" — at least that was the ostensible reason. When Rita and Herbert Schiller arrived at the Jerusalem Hilton to pick up Said el Din, he was surrounded by reporters. Escaping them, he embraced Rita and whispered, "You have to act like a close personal friend, otherwise they won't let me go." The Israeli guard and driver assigned to Dr. Said el Din turned him over to Herbert Schiller, who stretched out his hand and said, "Sir, I want to shake hands with you. I fought against Egyptians in 1948, 1956, and 1967. In 1973, both my sons fought against our neighbors — one on the Suez. The other was severely wounded on the Golan Heights. You are the first former enemy I can shake hands with. Sir, excuse my tears, but they are for your and my comrades fallen in battle."

Prominent intellectuals and physicians were present at Dr. Kaplan's cocktail party. From her house the group went to a restaurant in Jerusalem. Dr. Said el Din's driver then arrived and told him that he must go straight to Ben Gurion Airport in Tel Aviv because the whole political committee was already there, ready to leave for Cairo. Dr. Said el Din left, not having eaten even the first course. The rest of the group no longer felt like eating and "without consulting with each other, we went to the Western Wall. I was not surprised, since I knew that all Israelis and I, too, when in Israel in times of crisis, always run to the Western Wall."

When the small group returned, they watched the television news as Dr. Said el Din boarded the plane and told the reporters that he had experienced splendid hospitality from the Israeli people. On the next day the *Jerusalem Post* reported that the Egyptian political committee was completely surprised by the recall. "As proof they stated that Dr. Said el Din, the spokesman, was having dinner with a Jerusalem psychologist [sic]."

Later that year, Rita, William Davidson, and I sought to develop a research project that would further examine the question "What do we tell our children?" We wished to explore on both the Arab and Israeli sides the ways children are indoctrinated through the societies' schools, public media, and family communications into the ideologies of enmity. But as Rita put it, "We found that this is a topic which closed, hermetically, all doors of inquiry."[8] "Because children constitute the richest resource that a society possesses for the conduct of its future wars, governments may be reluctant to permit the systematic study of the mechanisms whereby their country's young people incorporate the elements of national identity, especially political attitudes, into their emerging group concepts."[9]

Rita's personal relationship to the U.S.-Soviet conflict is complex and deeply rooted. Children and adolescents growing up in the Bukovina were inevitably exposed to communism, one of the totalitarian thought systems in that culturally rich border region. Its simple, universal promise attracted one of her cousins. For Rita, communism blended with the romantic images of czarist Russia.

In Mogilev Podolskiy the Soviets were the longed-for liberators. Yet when they finally came they sent her Ukrainian friends and her first sweetheart to their death, and the mixture of kindness and cruelty demonstrated by the waves of liberating troops was difficult to integrate. The most powerful impression was made by the warm Russian doctor in a Soviet uniform. "This skewed for me always the perceptions of Soviet military officers and their uniforms. Whenever I see a May Day or October Revolution Day parade on television, I experience excitement and a feeling that I was with these men, already saved by them, when the Allies finally landed in Europe. We had talked and waited for it in the factory in Mogilev for years." But her year in Bessarabia and northern Bukovina taught Rita the anxiety and helplessness of bureaucratically imposed statelessness, Soviet style, while in the divided city of Vienna she experienced firsthand the painful impact of the ideological and political struggle of East and West.

Not until she participated in the UN sponsored East-West debates at Schloss Tivoli, however, did Rita learn that it was possible to examine the political conflicts, which, until 1951, she had endured as a relatively helpless subject. Also at Schloss Tivoli, "it became clear that there is no good and bad side in this [the East-West] conflict, but rather that there are irreconcilable differences based on historical experiences and profound mistrust."

In 1977 Rita was invited to be a delegate to the Pugwash Conferences, one of only five psychiatrists to have taken part since the creation of the Pugwash movement by Bertrand Russell, Albert Einstein, and other eminent scientists in 1955. The movement was begun in order to address the threat of mass destruction posed by thermonuclear weapons in the context of "the titanic struggle between Communism and anti-Communism."[10]

At these Pugwash meetings, as well as at congresses of the International Physicians for the Prevention of Nuclear War, task forces of the American Psychiatric Association, and other forums, Rita has explored, with colleagues from the physical and social sciences and other psychiatrists, contributions that psychiatry can make to the prevention of a nuclear holocaust. "The grim bond of nuclear weaponry between the U.S. and the USSR constitutes mankind's most perilous disease," Rita wrote in a paper prepared for the thirty-first Pugwash conference in 1981. In a 1982 American Psychiatric Association Task Force Report, she wrote, "The U.S.-Soviet relationship represents a study in distancing and closeness, promises and unspoken threats, ambiguities and certainties, use and misuse of communication, alterations in patterns of relationship, and avoidance of contact because of an overwhelming, overriding, constant awareness of each other."[11]

The new reality brought about by the altogether unprecedented destructiveness of nuclear weapons and their border-crossing intercontinental delivery systems has eliminated for the United States and the Soviet Union the possibility of creating security *nationally.* Their mutual dependence for achieving security in the nuclear world has been a difficult fact for traditional, power-oriented national leaders to accept. In a series of articles on the Soviet-American relationship, Rita has examined the consequences for each nation's self-image of this unwelcome interdependence and the difficulty of reconciling past and present national self-perceptions and domestic political priorities with radically transformed global realities. "If our world is to survive," she wrote, "a stronger and more realistic tie can and must replace the awesome bond of nuclear weaponry which exists between the Soviet Union and the United States."[12] In addition to her published writings in this field Rita has exercised her "Track II" skills through countless informal contacts with Soviet physicians, scientists, officials, and ordinary citizens.[13]

✳

Among the victims of the East-West conflict, Poland has been of particular interest to Rita. While repeatedly the pawn of indifferent empires, divided and crushed between East and West, Germany and Russia, the Polish people have retained their courage and spirit. Rita remembers Polish officers in Rădăuţi retreating from the Nazis, and the emotional currents growing out of the Stenzler and Wohl families' Polish roots remain strong for her. In 1982, she visited Poland for the first time with her daughter Sheila to attend a Pugwash Conference on Science and World Affairs in Warsaw. August 31, which fell during the conference, was the second anniversary of the Gdansk agreements between Solidarity and the Polish state. Solidarity had announced that there would be massive demonstrations to commemorate the anniversary and protest martial law, which had been declared eight months before. The Polish conference organizers had scheduled an excursion to Tarun, a town rich in medieval monuments and the birthplace of Nicholas Copernicus, to keep the delegates away from the demonstrations. Several of the students, eager to watch the events in Warsaw, resisted going to Tarun. The senior officials of Pugwash were in an awkward position. Although they did not wish to offend their Polish hosts and urged the delegates to join the tour, one of them confided six months later to George Perkovich, executive director of Student Pugwash, "It's what I hoped you would do."[14]

Rita also did not want to be removed from events that powerfully expressed Polish national feeling. She received calls pressuring her to go to Tarun. "But I was with the Poles in the street and didn't want to go under any circumstances." She arranged to be picked up at 10:00 A.M. by a Polish psychiatrist who encouraged Sheila to take photographs from the window of his apartment. Sheila and Rita witnessed the efforts of the Polish government to crush the Solidarity demonstrations.

> While the ZOMO militia [riot police] patrolled the streets with hatred and brutality, the old and young, men and women, boys and girls, stood by the crosses and sang. They sang the Polish national anthem with altered words demanding freedom for Lech Walesa and freedom for Poland. They held the "V" sign for victory (the letter "v" does not exist in the Polish alphabet). As one saw the glow in

their eyes, as one heard the burning anger in their voices against their government, as one witnessed their linkage with each other against those who opposed Solidarity, one became aware that the fingers which show the victory sign represent not a hope for victory, but a human glow of a people's affection for each other and their identity as a people. Against that bond, the government has to send out riot police with tear gas and water cannons. Martial law in Poland had been introduced on December 13, 1981, to break up the Polish people's unity and connectedness with each other. Solidarity was outlawed on October 8, 1982, because martial law did not erase the yearning for freedom. With tear gas and water cannons, the ZOMO police chased the people of Poland off the streets, but the brutality of their own government does not erase the cravings, aspirations, and identity of a people who believe in themselves and their cause.[15]

Sheila was spotted with the camera and someone threw a canister of tear gas through the window. "We were scared the ZOMO police would come upstairs. People came into the apartment from all over the building to protect us in their midst." Rita and Sheila stayed there until late in the evening. When they reached their hotel after walking back through the deserted streets, their Polish hosts were relieved to see them and seemed to understand. "I'm not going to ask you where you've been," one of them said.

On one of the last days of the Warsaw conference, Jeff Leifer, the founder of Student Pugwash, gave a presentation of their past year's accomplishments and future plans. According to Perkovich (Rita disagrees), Leifer usually has to fight for time to give the speech. The audience appears to care little about Student Pugwash, and the subject gets changed quickly. After the speech on this day, however, Rita and Jane Sharp, a British political scientist, asked to be recognized. "I already knew Jane to be outspoken and an ally," Perkovich recalls. "So I wasn't surprised to hear her voice her support. Rita and I had never met. Rita stood up — from the back of the palatial room — and in a loud, accented voice gave a passionate tribute to the importance of Student Pugwash's work. She mentioned explicitly the need to do more. She urged the senior group to give us any support it could. The specifics aren't significant; they weren't what mattered at the time either.

"What mattered was the driving, heartful way Rita spoke. It was her energy. Rita's presence and oratory at that moment made the

Rita and Sheila with Lech Walesa in his apartment,
Gdansk, 1983, with two of her interpreter's children

Rita with Romanian nun and academician
at Curtea de Argeş, in 1983

Rita and
Allen Rogers, 1986

Rita and her son,
David, Berlin, 1982

Rita and her
daughter Sheila at
Pugwash conference,
Björklidden, Sweden,
1984

Rita and her
daughter Judy on the eve
of Judy's wedding, 1986

Rita in Tallinn, Estonian Republic, USSR, 1987

whole picture come into perfect focus. Here was this vigorous woman saying in effect, 'The young people, with no resources, are where it's at, and we can't even recognize it let alone do anything to support them.' The older guys just sat there. Whether it was gender, age, or language, the differences between her and her peers was so patent at that moment that it made me feel awkward. Having expected so little from the senior group, I was not dismayed by their reaction. What was surprising to me was that Rita was part of this group. No matter how her words affected the seniors, we students were excited by them. Her challenge to senior Pugwash and praise of us reflected our own sense of reality. She was looking into the future in a way the others could not. We approached her afterward and thanked her. Later I asked Jeff Leifer who Rita was. 'Who is that lady?' I asked in an amused voice. 'Oh boy,' he said, chuckling. 'That's Rita Rogers. She's got a lot of balls. She's not afraid to tell it like it is, and she loves us.'"[16]

From Rita's point of view "The strains of the conference were immense because General Jaruzelski's government was our host and we were also responsible to the Polish organizers of the conference. A majority of us felt allegiance toward Solidarity, and the leadership of Pugwash acted in a responsible and thoughtful way. They were wise. Young people — the students — naturally would have wanted more political activism. But this would have destroyed Pugwash and the dialogue between international physicists, especially East and West, which was aimed at preventing their technical developments from destroying the world. Yet I supported the students because I thought that they should be heard and understood."

On a second visit, in 1983, Rita and Sheila visited Lech Walesa in his apartment in Gdansk. "It is a very ordinary apartment building. We went there on a Sunday at 1:00 P.M. As we walked up the stairs a very unpleasant looking guy walked down. I remembered thinking that I had never disliked a face as much as I disliked this one. Later, when we emerged from the apartment building, the same man walked up the stairs as we walked down. Ten minutes after that we were stopped by the ZOMO Police, asked for identification, and after twenty anxious minutes permitted to leave.

"When I saw Lech Walesa, I felt comforted. He looked, spoke, and gestured like an Eastern European man. He was chubby, with lots of hair, and bushy eyebrows and sparkling warm eyes. Sitting with him on the couch, I felt as if I had known him for a long time.

I only felt estranged when he went on a long political tirade. Then he sounded like a guru with a message and a mission, and my instinctive abhorrence of political messages and missions for the good of humanity — in his case the workers — made me uncomfortable. Walesa's wife, who met us at the door, seemed much more anxious than he. He had a summons to the police for the next day on his living room table and had come from police headquarters in Gdansk just before we arrived.

"He pointed repeatedly to the ceiling while we talked, indicating that our conversation was being recorded. He talked about the aspirations of Polish workers to have control over their working conditions. He mentioned the immense corruption and political blackmail which had existed for a long time in Poland. He stressed that the Workers Union is not concerned with superpower politics and rivalries, but only with the conditions of Polish workers and their families. His humanliness and warmth came across to us strongly. When the five-year-old daughter of our interpreter said to him before we left, 'I pray for you every night before I go to bed,' he swept her up in his arms, raised her high above his head, and said, 'I and the Polish workers need your prayers.' Before we left I thanked him for his time and apologized for keeping him for two hours on Sunday from his family dinner. He told me, 'I have family in the United States.' I told him we knew about it and that we were reading all about him there. He looked me straight in the eyes and said, 'Please don't stop' [being interested in Poland and its fate]. I knew what he meant, especially when I saw that ugly informer outside his apartment building."

Perhaps Rita's most moving encounter with Poland's anguish occurred earlier, not in Poland but in Munich, in December 1981, while she was attending an international meeting of psychiatrists on, ironically, the subject of identity and society. The conference, which was attended by several Polish psychiatrists, was in session when martial law was declared in Poland.

All the Polish psychiatrists present were members of Solidarity. "Solidarity is our only salvation," one of them said. Solidarity had restored their dignity, a chance to speak freely and enter into a genuine academic life, a give-and-take with colleagues from other countries. By the time Rita met with them, however, they had learned of the declaration. As the bad news came to them through radio and television reports in German, the Polish psychiatrists felt increasingly cut off and isolated. The meeting continued, but for the Poles, political events at home overshadowed the discussion. The West Germans at the conference seemed relatively indifferent. "Martial law in Poland is an internal affair" was their attitude. "We want peace, rapprochement with East Germany, and good commerce with the USSR."[17]

At the end of the conference the Polish psychiatrists knew that they had to return to Poland or jeopardize family members, friends, and coworkers. They faced uncertainty and possible arrest, which they had already heard was the fate of members of Solidarity at home. They felt frightened, but beyond concern for their personal safety, the Polish psychiatrists were disappointed that they could not rely on the West. They felt hurt, abandoned, sold out once again, as at Yalta in 1945. On the snowy night of December 17, they set out for the railroad station to catch a train that would take them to Frankfurt for the flight to their homeland and possible arrest and imprisonment.

Rita identified with these Polish psychiatrists. "A part of me went with them," she wrote, "to their enchained, enslaved land." "Reverberations of personal experiences reawakened many long-buried feelings" about her own encounters with totalitarianism between 1939 and 1948. This encounter "reawakened the pain of having to decide between two worlds and to abandon everything that was familiar for the sake of personal freedom." The fact that this confrontation was recurring on German soil gave it extra resonance. "It rekindled my rage toward the rest of the world that stood by when human freedom was so wantonly and cruelly destroyed."[18] "The bond which I felt with the Polish psychiatrists when they learned about martial law on December 13, 1981, is similar to the bond I feel with the people of Rădăuţi with whom we crossed the Dniester between the Ukraine and Romania in October 1941."

Rita's concern for the fate of Poland arouses little sympathy among her Jewish friends. She is troubled about the Jewish tendency to see the world only from the perspective of "what it means to the Jews" and the difficulty Jews sometimes have seeing beyond their own history of suffering to identify with that of other ethnic groups. When Rita tells Jewish friends and colleagues in the United States, Israel, and Europe about her concern for Poland, they sometimes say, in effect, "The Poles are and have always been anti-Semites. We don't care what happens to them and 'their Pope.'" "I find this approach terribly narrow and unpalatable. I know about what the Poles did to the Jews and would probably do again. But Solidarity is not a Jewish story; it is not for or against the Jews."

＊

Each of us, Rita points out, sees the world through an ethnic prism. The practice of psychiatry and foreign affairs demands a constant effort to be aware of it and understand the prism of our adversaries. In contrast to this effort, international relations are often conducted as a cynical, brutal game. National leaders keep their people focused on outside enemies, fostering distrust and diverting attention from moral shortcomings and failures at home. Corporate leaders profit from the conflict with inflated military contracts, paying little heed to their squandering of the earth's resources or their contribution to the possibility of planetary destruction.

Psychiatry and foreign affairs seeks to humanize the communication among nations. International conflict, Rita believes, "need not be a zero-sum game, but an ongoing process of life wherein different realities and perceptions continuously interact with the subjective memories of the past, the perception of the present, and the visions of the future."

In Rădăuți in 1941, before the Jews were sent by Hitler to Mogilev Podolskiy, Rita and her sister trembled each night while Christian maids and friends circulated between the Stenzler home and the house where Rita's father had taken his father, father-in-law, brothers, brothers-in-law, and other relatives. "Our maid would cry so loudly every evening when she saw my father round up those for whom he took responsibility that we — my mother, my sister, and I — had to comfort her. She always asked, 'Warum?' [Why?]" It is the business of those who are engaged in psychiatry and foreign affairs always to ask "Why?" until the answers begin to come and humankind discovers ways to settle its collective differences without relying on violence and the domination of one people by another.

10. The Alchemy of Survival

We are understandably suspicious of anyone who speaks in an affirmative voice, especially in the political domain. Perhaps this is because we have experienced too frequently the manipulations of leaders who cover murderous intentions with bland, reassuring phrases. We have had all too much of what the Russian emigré poet Joseph Brodsky calls "the positive, 'life-affirming' drivel of official newspapers and radio."[1] Looking back on human history Brodsky suggests that "cynicism is the best yardstick of social progress."[2]

But we cannot be satisfied with this, for to surrender to cynicism and renounce any effort to create a more just, caring, and safer social order will simply smooth the way for leaders who can lull us into accepting mass killing as the norm and risking annihilation for their personal agendas. To be able to resist the paralyzing blandishments and callous policies of contemporary governments, East and West, Communist or capitalist, it is essential to have examples of individuals who have shown that it can be done.

With her collaboration, I have chosen to tell the story of Rita Stenzler Rogers because I believe that her life represents such a model. It is empowering to read of an individual who turned the tables on her own history. Rita was able to survive the depredations of several totalitarian regimes, fascist and communist, and has drawn upon that experience to challenge the political habits of our age. She has been able to transform the vulnerabilities and tragedies of her youth into a resource for creative work at both the individual and international level. Although Rita's talents and opportunities have been unique, her example — I have in mind here both the concepts she has developed and the life she has lived — can be an inspiring one for others. Through her, we learn how to interrupt malignant cycles of hurt and revenge in the political domain, as we also seek to do in psychotherapy, and how not to pass on the threatening or painful influences to which we have been subjected. No other life will repeat Rita's, but lessons from this history might be generalizable, reproducible by design, communicable, possibly in realms as varied as preventive mental health, international negotiations, and public policy.

As I consider the meaning of Rita's life, I confront once more the particular problems associated with telling the story of a living person, especially of a colleague and friend. I face again the subjectivity, the absence of personal and temporal distance that might give a more balanced, perhaps more accurate, perspective. Having been the recipient of Rita's affection and generosity, her largess, for so many years, perhaps I have been insufficiently critical, too willing to see things her way.

At the same time, however, by having worked, really *lived* through so much of the process of creating this book with Rita, I may have been held closer to the actuality of her life. With a hundred years or an ocean between us I might have made Rita a flawless heroine and tucked her tidily into the course of history. But I have come to know her too well for that, and she is honest with herself, persistently self-scrutinizing. While I esteem highly what Rita has been able to achieve, my tendencies toward idealization have been continually grounded by the direct knowledge of her human limitations. My experience with her, as in most intimate associations, is filled with contradiction and paradox. Rita's high level of self-esteem, for instance, which was a major force in her survival, also leads her to expect praise and admiration in a way that can be trying. Her charm, her ability to flatter, her intuition as to what will win over another person, friend or enemy, saved Rita's life on more than one occasion, but the accompanying need to stand out, to be the focus of attention, can be irritating to those who are left in the shadows or not otherwise in a mood to be enthralled.

Robert Rosenstone, writing of his grandfather, another Romanian survivor, has noted how difficult it is to place an individual's life historically. "Most history," says Rosenstone, "has no room for itches; they are far too personal. They belong to individuals. It is best to explain the past without individuals. People are messy, quirky, ineffable. Often they are a downright nuisance, always interfering with well-laid plans and significant projects. It is better to look at history as the events that happen to people. This does away with bizarre quirks and itches."[3]

Most of our book has told a story, describing what one woman was able to make of dangerous or destructive circumstances. This concluding chapter is concerned with *how* she was able to transform, draw upon, transcend — the choice of verb determines how to pose the question — periods of political oppression and tragedy and contribute to our understanding of the sources of human suffering.

Rita started no political movements, championed no specific political causes, put forth no revolutionary theories. Her talents, as she acknowledges, are strongest in the domain of feeling, of intuition and human relationships. While brilliant, she is perhaps too life-loving and undisciplined, insufficiently single-minded, too suspicious of causes and power, to be a political or revolutionary leader. Her influence has been indirect, part of a process, though touching personally the lives of hundreds of people, including several national leaders.

In our effort to understand Rita's life, we are not looking for linear causal relationships, in the way that Freud and his followers applied a model of explanation based on the pathogenic influence of repressed drives and feelings to a variety of clinical and nonclinical phenomena. Even explanations based on a model of conflict, or the psychological transforming of suffering, will not encompass the complex personal and historical realities of such a story. Joseph Brodsky, Nadezhda Mandelstam, and other refugees and victims of Stalin's Russia have questioned the applicability of psychoanalytic ideas — especially in relation to creative responses — to historical situations of extreme stress and social dislocation, times in which there is "too much reality to deal with."[4] "It's an abominable fallacy," Brodsky writes, "that suffering makes for greater art. Suffering blinds, deafens, ruins, and often kills."[5] But suffering can also create a necessity, an occasion. The human strength that enables us to tolerate and transform pain may bring forth possibilities, gifts, personal resources, which might otherwise never have been brought into action.

The multiplicity of forces that weave together to form individual lives and historical events should be plainly evident throughout Rita's story. Single-cause explanations are not only inadequate, they can be dangerously misleading. We have often suffered at the hands of refugees from ethnonational conflicts who, unable to understand the burdens of hurt, guilt, and hatred they harbor within themselves, carry out their hostility and need for vindication in a new political arena in which they can experience greater mastery and power. We are familiar with survivors of the Holocaust and victims of Stalinist and post-Stalinist Eastern Europe, who are governed by the motto "never again," by which they mean exclusive devotion to the nationalistic purposes of Jewish people and Israel or single-minded opposition to communism and the Soviet Union.

Rather than examine the psychological distortions that arise from experience as a victim, refugees often seem to confuse knowledge with feelings, fail to examine their hatred and desire for revenge, and lend their expertise to policies founded on ideological polarities, hostilities, and distrust. Rita's career is an enlightening exception. She accepts the responsibility for looking at her own feelings, impulses, and prejudices and works assiduously to maintain a balanced view. Her past experience of oppression and fear and distrust of the Soviet government does not prevent her from seeing the East-West conflict in its full complexity, with both sides contributing heavily to the destructive interaction.

How has this been possible for her? We begin with the fact that Rita survived the war and escaped, though under difficult circumstances, from three Communist countries. Without physical survival there is no story. Rita has spoken and written of her "zest," drive, or "genetically transmitted" instinct for survival and of her belief — the grandiosity of which she readily acknowledges — that she was meant or entitled to survive. She quotes her mother in Mogilev Podolskiy telling her father, "We will survive and the girls will have beautiful lives." In her blind trust she believed every rumor of repatriation, even when transmitted by known liars. But such statements and memories are recollections after the fact. We will never know how many mothers perished with their children in the concentration camps of Hitler's Europe after assuring them that they would survive.

Rita, as we pointed out, was also very lucky. Czech-born psychiatrist Rudolph Roden, a concentration camp survivor, lists among the basic ingredients for survival "something called luck, and plenty of it."[6] She was lucky, first of all, to have been in Romania, for Antonescu's alliance with Hitler resulted in the joint Romanian-German administration that allowed bribery, which would not have been tolerated in an entirely SS-run camp. Mogilev Podolskiy and other sites in Transnistria to which the Jews of Bukovina were transported were "transition centers," ghettos rather than real German concentration camps, although thousands of Jews died there or were transferred to extermination camps. The fact that she and her immediate family were able to remain together in Mogilev Podolskiy was partly luck and partly owing to Rita's bold initiative.

Beyond luck, then, what were some of the determinants of Rita's survival, both physical and psychological? And how, having survived, was she able to draw creatively from the losses and struggles?

First there is "culture," which is hard to define. I have in mind the sense, which she and her family possessed in abundance, that as Jews of the Bukovina they were connected by language, literature, music, and many traditions to a particular human community, strong and rich. It was a society in some ways unique to the Bukovina but connected with Jewish, Austro-German, and French culture, elite, cosmopolitan, and very much part of Europe itself.

Cultural solidarity strengthened the bonds within the Stenzler family and contributed to the close-knit feeling of the Rădăuți community. The family was able to maintain this cohesiveness to a limited degree even in Mogilev, and Rita has tried to re-create it with varying success wherever she has lived. Rita's love of languages and literature deepened these cultural resources. The luxury of make-believe, which a cultured upbringing can stimulate, may help psychological survival. The capacity to walk through Paris in fantasy, to see oneself as the hero or heroine of novels of faraway countries, or to imagine a cozy family life behind a lighted window can nourish the spirit in harsh times.

It has often been said that Romanians as a people have a special talent for survival. Hannah Pakula, Queen Marie's biographer, wrote, "Geographically defenseless, the Romanians developed an unerring instinct for survival and a high degree of intellectual sophistication."[7] Rita sees these qualities compounded in her background: "There was a certain affinity between the Romanians and the Jews in flexibility toward survival. The Romanians had had centuries of learning that things aren't black and white, not necessarily as written in the book. And the Jews have had centuries of need for survival. They are people who have learned that things today are this way and tomorrow they are the other way."

In Rădăuţi, the sense of community protection strengthened each individual. "There was no doubt as to who we were, and where we were and what we were, neither at home nor in the town." This community strength was not destroyed when the group was deported. The Jews of Rădăuţi somehow managed to stay together more or less as a group in Mogilev, to maintain "the shelter of togetherness."

On an individual level, Rita's strength derived from solid self-confidence. Cherished and praised, not only by her parents, grandparents, and other relatives, but by teachers, friends, and neighbors — "I got a lot of feedback" — Rita grew up believing in herself enough to take the risks necessary for survival.

In this, the example of her parents was also vital. "Both my parents felt very good about themselves." Helene, in addition to her unselfish, loving ways and adoration of Rita, demonstrated throughout Rita's childhood and adolescence her caring, protective feeling toward other people, especially children. The commitment to intergenerational connections, so prominent in Rita's life and work, was exemplified in Helene's devoted and affectionate nature. Shaje was the acknowledged community leader in Rădăuţi and the principal "provider and giver" in his extended family. In Mogilev as well, "he would make arrangements for everybody," helping the group as a whole to survive. It was probably Shaje Stenzler's initiatives in arranging for the secretive, complex supply chain, which itself depended so much on community cohesion and solidarity, that created the opportunity for Rita's family and uncounted others to survive the Mogilev years.

It is not easy to make clear connections between these elements of history, geography, culture, community, and family and what Rita was able to do or become as an individual. The richness of background functions as a resource, a kind of soil that creates possibilities and potentialities. But its forms are unexpected. One might as easily anticipate that a pampered, spoiled child of a bourgeois Bukovinian family of the 1920s and 1930s would succumb to the cruelties of her captors as that she would reveal such grit and daring. Nevertheless, Rita's identification with the strengths of her parents is striking. Most obvious is the presence or authority that enabled her father, already in the cattle car, to refuse to sign the papers surrendering ownership of his store or her mother to prohibit the gynecological examination of her daughters in Mogilev. In Prague, when Rita looked the Austrian consul straight in the eye and announced that she was going to escape to the West, we see her parents' courage emerge in a new form. Such a legacy always has a touch of mystery. Psychiatrists are better at explaining human deficiencies and limitations on the basis of a troubled background than accounting for unexpected strengths.

Behind Rita's self-assurance, we can also discern her beloved grandparents Zaziu and Judith, to whom she was and would always be special, precious, deserving to live. A child who grows up with that feeling has a core of resilience strong enough for a lifetime. It may be that secure, loving early years are the most important element not only in enduring hardship but in resisting the temptation later to use ethnonational hatred as an outlet for personal frustration. Conversely, when the inner sense of self is fragile or uncertain, or the individual suffers from profound self-doubt, ethnonationalistic bias may furnish an alternative, though precarious, means of achieving some sense of personal value or superiority.

When Rita returned to the Bukovina for the first time in thirty-four years, she was shocked to see the changes and to recall what had once been. "But the sight of the trees on approaching Rădăuți healed even that memory. Something was permanent. A soothing congruence between childhood and adulthood occurred. I was the same person as that child decades ago. I had dreamed on that road about the wide, wide world. I now had seen much of that world, and I had seen a changing world and remained the same person. No better, no worse." Brodsky said something similar: "I guess there was always some 'me' inside that small and, later, somewhat bigger shell around which 'everything' was happening. Inside that shell the entity which one calls 'I' never changed and never stopped watching what was going on outside. I am not trying to hint at pearls inside. What I am saying is that the passage of time does not much affect that entity."[8]

A great deal derives from or is related to this sense of permanence and certainty of self. It is the foundation on which much else can grow, including energy, enthusiasm, zest for life, and optimism for the future, all of which Rita has in abundance. This stable core of self-possession made possible the adaptability that allowed Rita to impersonate a foundry worker or learn the Czech language *after* becoming a medical student in Prague. It is also vitally important for a psychiatrist, who must reach out to empathize with the many different worlds of patients without losing the distance and objectivity that depend upon certainty of one's identity. It is equally essential for working in psychiatry and foreign affairs, in which one's ethnic, religious, and nationalistic selves and boundaries must be crossed or suspended to identify with the experiences and hurts of others, without becoming engulfed or lost.

I observed a striking example of this adaptability as Rita was emerging from her journey back in time through Romania, Transnistria, and Prague. Our destination was an American Psychiatric Association conference on "Three Psychological Dynamics of International Conflict: Victimization, Dehumanization, and Historical Enmity" at Mont Pelerin, near Vevey, Switzerland. As members of the American delegation, we were to meet with Israeli and Egyptian psychiatrists, social scientists, and officials to continue work on the psychological roots of the Arab-Israeli conflict. In my notes I wrote, "She shifts over to participating with the Arab-Israeli group as if we never were in Eastern Europe at all. She is fully present here, whereas I have great difficulty making the transition."

Trust in oneself makes possible trust in one's intuitive judgment about others. Several times, knowing whom to trust may have saved Rita's life. "When you have a feeling of trust," she once told me, "you should trust it." So much of psychiatry and foreign affairs depends upon building trust — not blind, but carefully selected areas of trust, which can be nurtured where only mistrust has gone before. Trust is a springboard for the risk taking that was so important to Rita's survival. Successful risk taking in a situation judged to be one of jeopardy is a skill with many elements, including the ability to weigh accurately the potential dangers of a given situation, courage, physical capability, strength of will, and a hard-to-define adventurousness of spirit. But when it involves other people, as in Rita's encounter with guards, soldiers, and diplomatic personnel, the capacity to assess in a moment what can be expected of another person and to trust that judgment is vitally important.

Rita has the gift not only to assess others, but to reach out to them. This talent is basic to her skill as a survivor and as a practitioner of psychiatry, child psychiatry, and psychiatry and foreign affairs, as well as to her capacities as a wife and mother and steadfastness as a friend. Endowed with a wealth of nurturance and love, she has translated these resources into a receptivity to others, a curiosity about their uniqueness, and an ability to enter spontaneously and intuitively into their psychological worlds. Modified as shrewdness in judging and appealing to the vanity of an official or anyone in a position of power and authority, this quality is highly adaptive. In psychiatry and foreign affairs it enables Rita to identify emotional common ground and swiftly bridge political barriers.

At times Rita's diplomatic skills can backfire. When she displays a bit too much of the charming, manipulative quality that served her as a survivor, people can be put off and dismiss her as insincere. But her faithfulness to those who become her friends is unsurpassed in my experience. Herta said, "It is a beautiful part of her character . . . I am astonished sometimes. She has so many acquaintances. She has so many people with whom she is in contact. Nevertheless, she will not forget old friends. She is thankful and faithful; when she is close to somebody she never forgets it."

Rita's knowledge of many languages has been important to her ability to make warm connections with people from all over the world, and her interest in reaching into the worlds of others has, in turn, motivated her love of languages. Before a three-week trip to China, she studied Chinese for several weeks through an immersion course with a tutor and tapes. When she made rounds on the inpatient children's psychiatric unit in Beijing, she was able to interview a four-year-old boy in Chinese, but she soon forgot what she had studied. "It seems to me it is profane to study language this way without penetrating its roots, much less knowing its people."

Love for foreign languages, curiously enough, helped Rita finally pass her driving test in 1979, after years of trying. A combination of poor eyesight, lack of skill, and emotional incompatibility with several instructors made the test very hard for her. After being failed by a young Japanese man who hated doctors, she asked for another examiner. A supervisor who loved speaking French with her took over. He was also fascinated with Nadia Comaneci, the Romanian gymnast. Rapport was established and "he let me pass."

Rita describes language as "a thread" that leads her into the worlds of others, allowing relationships to develop where otherwise they would be difficult. Many times, traveling with her, I have seen faces brighten and conversations begin when Rita speaks with people in their native tongue. But her gift with languages is only one part of her ability to establish human connection, which is her first priority. Through the years of our friendship, I have seen many examples of this ability, small and large.

I've witnessed an empathic private conversation with an irate Egyptian minister who felt insulted by an Israeli's remark; the winning over of a nasty female customs officer who turned out to be an exhausted mother of two children burdened with long hours and too many responsibilities; a conversation with two maids in the King David Hotel in Jerusalem — one from Fez in Morocco who spoke French and the other from Samarkand in Uzbekistan who spoke Russian — in which she helped them convey to each other the beauty of the mosques of Fez and the grandeur of the temples of Samarkand; her participation in his last Yom Kippur service in Tbilisi with a Soviet Georgian Jew who was soon to leave for Israel. In each instance Rita finds a way to establish a human tie, helps to create a climate in which, in some cases, delicate issues can be fruitfully approached.

But Rita's persuasive abilities do not necessarily require knowledge of other people's native language. When she boarded the UNRRA train bound for Prague, she had not yet learned a word of Czech. I asked her how she had convinced the Czech officers escorting the train to give her a uniform. "I talked to them," she replied. "I talked to them the way I talk."

In the end it is impossible to define fully the transmuting of all the resources in Rita's background: culture, history, religious feeling, community, family, and personal strengths. There is always something more, a nameless catalyst, a trace of spirit that completes the alchemy of survival. Discouraged about a project on which we were both engaged, I said that it seemed like a lost cause. "For lost causes," Rita said, "one must work even harder than for winning causes."

Futurists frequently write of the passing of the nation-state. But the power of nationalism has grown in each decade of the twentieth century, as colonial empires have broken up and new nations have formed. For many ethnic groups the passions of nationalism — joining emotional attachment to the idea of a people united in culture and language with the apparatus of state sovereignty — have taken the place of traditional family and religious bonds. For individuals, membership in a nation-state has come to serve essential psychological functions, including protection of life, a sense of belonging and self-worth, and even, for some, an essential definition of personal identity. Furthermore, as political scientist Karl Deutsch has argued, the nation-state is increasingly important, for it is often the only organizational mechanism for getting things done.

At the same time, nevertheless, nation-states threaten human well-being and survival. Vast numbers of people have been murdered by genocidal states, driven from their homelands by war, or decimated by famines, which are themselves often the result of exploitative policies of particular national governments. As nuclear weapons spread to more and more nations, we are all their potential victims along with all other living things on which we depend.

Advanced technologies, in addition to escalating the threat of nationalism, create distance between the mass of human beings and the decisions that affect their lives. Scientific and governmental elite groups, with relatively narrow expertise in specific technologies, have become increasingly remote from the human communities they are expected to serve or protect. Responsibility for national security, based increasingly on secret, arcane information held by the widely disparate groups that comprise the security "community," has become fragmented. Those who conduct foreign policy lose access to essential aspects of the technological system. The special language and acronyms of nuclear weapons systems and other advanced technologies further distance military decision making from political reality and human needs.

In response to this situation, a number of professional and citizen groups are protesting what they perceive to be the increasing danger of nuclear annihilation. But protest by itself does not offer solutions or realistic alternatives. Without knowledge and understanding of the historical forces that give rise to political oppression, especially the emotional appeal of militant nationalism, protest and resistance may lead to the replacement of one tyranny by another. Furthermore, considering the compelling power of nationalism, especially for people who consider themselves politically disenfranchised, hope for change in the relations among nations based on the disappearance of state sovereignty is hardly realistic, no matter how anachronistic some of its elements may seem.

The budding discipline of psychiatry and foreign affairs is attempting to illuminate this dark thicket. Psychiatrists, psychoanalysts, psychologists, anthropologists, negotiation theorists, and academicians from other professional disciplines are working increasingly with political analysts and government officials to change the traditional habits of foreign policy. Rita and I both participate in this work. We are struggling to move beyond the zero-sum mentality in international relations — I win, you lose — toward approaches that lead to the discovery of common ground and shared interests even among adversaries. Our central challenge is to reintroduce thoughtful human agency into foreign affairs, to restore responsibility. When Rita was studying international relations at UCLA, a professor spoke about Human Rights Day at the UN. She startled the class by asking why we need a human rights day. Should the UN not exist "for humans every day of the year?"

On both the individual and the international levels, Rita's central interest has been the interruption of cycles of hatred, violence, and the need for vindication from one generation to the next. During her first trip to Cairo, Rita rode on a *chulupa* along the Nile with a young Egyptian widow, the mother of a three-year-old daughter. Her husband, a pilot in the Egyptian Air Force, had been shot down during the 1973 war. "What do I tell our child?" the woman asked Rita. "I don't want her to hate." They talked of how each might work to break the cycles of vengeance that had characterized relations between Egypt and Israel.

In 1976, Rita met for several hours with Jehan Sadat, the wife of Egypt's president, widowed in 1981 as a result of religious and political hatred. "I saw Madame Sadat in what seemed a bower of roses — they were on her tables; she wore them on her dress. She welcomed me with a gleam in her eyes and an elegant compliment on her lips . . . The lunch lasted five hours. We talked about many things, including birth control. I was impressed with the combination of motherly love and motherly frustration with which she discussed 'our people.' . . . We discovered how close and far we had been in October 1973, both in hospitals with wounded soldiers, but one in Haifa and the other in Cairo."

Mrs. Sadat seemed to Rita much less prejudiced toward Israel than she herself was toward Egypt. "We talked about a letter she had written and I read in the *Jerusalem Post* shortly after the October war. In that letter Mrs. Sadat replied with compassion to the mother of an Israeli soldier killed in the war. She had told President Sadat that she had received that letter and wouldn't it be nice to reply? He told her, 'Yes, you should, when there is not a single Israeli soldier standing on our soil.' She then told him, 'But I have replied already.' For me that was psychiatry and foreign affairs, practiced in a womanly manner. I told Mrs. Sadat that my first encounter with her was that letter in the *Jerusalem Post*." During the October war, Israeli television had depicted Sadat and the Egyptian Army as ferocious enemies. "Suddenly to read Mrs. Sadat's letter pierced my firmly held assumptions and prejudices."

Rita left Cairo at dawn the next day for Israel with renewed confidence that fear and violence between nations could be overcome. When she had arrived in Egypt she fantasized "arrest, hostility, and nameless horrors. I found only embracing hospitality . . . I held on to my presents from Madame Sadat (a picture and a symbolic gift of kohl, the eyeshadow Cleopatra used) to help make the bridge between the two realities, one fearful and prejudiced, the other a yearning for understanding. Egypt made me belong more to my own people. Going there gave me hope."[9]

Milan Kundera, in a novel, asked whether, if man were given new planets to begin again the ordering of his relationships and could draw upon "all the experience they had amassed here," would he do a better job? "Will he be wiser? Is maturing within man's power? Can he attain it through repetition?"[10] Kundera does not answer his questions, nor do we, but perhaps better knowledge of the emotional roots of our political selves is a step toward such maturity.

In this search, our best teachers may be those who have known the beast of extremism but have not become its victims, physically or psychologically. Samuel Pisar, a Polish-born international lawyer who survived Hitler's death camps, once said that he heard the "death rattle of the human species" in Auschwitz.[11] Yet Pisar has devoted himself to building East-West trade and improving Soviet-American relations.

Rita and Pisar and other such teachers share the experience of a besieged human community and its continuity with generations that have gone before. They have committed their lives and example to nurturing and protecting this continuity, the chain of generations that transcends the accidents of history and politics. Rita's grandfather Zaziu, by whom she felt especially chosen, represents for her the spiritual force that links generations. "His bond with what he considered important and holy was extraterrestrial. He belonged to the clouds between heaven and earth . . . I can see him, as if it were today, on holidays, in his white *kittel* [ceremonial robe] and fur-trimmed hat, pacing joyfully in his little house, clapping his hands, singing his passionate Chassidic songs."

Notes

INTRODUCTION

1. Elias Canetti, *Crowds and Power* (New York: Continuum, 1973).
2. Milan Kundera, *The Book of Laughter and Forgetting* (New York: Alfred A. Knopf, 1980), 167.

CHAPTER 2

1. Gregor von Rezzori, *Memoirs of an Anti-Semite* (New York: Viking, 1981), 105–106.
2. Octav Monoranu and Ion Miclea, *Putna: Historical and Art Monument* (Bucharest: Editura Sport-Turism, 1977).
3. von Rezzori, *Memoirs*, 196.
4. "Bukovina," vol. I (London: His Majesty's Stationer's Office, 1920), 13.
5. Ion Nistor, *Bessarabia and Bukovina* (Bucharest: Romanian Academy, Romanian Studies, 1939), 37.
6. Ibid., 43.
7. von Rezzori, *Memoirs*, 245.
8. Ibid., 145.
9. H. J. Bidermann, *Die Bukowina Unter Osterreichischer Verwaltung, 1775–1875* (Lemburg: Druck Von Kornel Piller, 1876), 44.
10. Erwin Massier, Joseph Talskey, and B. C. Gregorowicz, *Bukowina Heimat von Gestern*, 2d ed. (Karlsrühe: Selbstverlag Arbeitskreis Heimatbuch, 1957), 11.
11. Ibid., 249.
12. Bidermann, *Die Bukowina*, 51.
13. R. W. Seton-Watson, *A History of the Romanians from Roman Times to*

the Completion of Unity (London: Cambridge University Press, 1934), 352.

14. Ibid., 349.
15. Henry Kamm, "A Poignant Time for Rumania's Dwindling Jews," *New York Times*, September 26, 1985.
16. Raul Hilberg, *The Destruction of the European Jews*, vol. 2, "Romania" (New York: Holmes and Meier, 1985), 791.
17. Ayse Gursan-Salzmann and Laurence Salzmann, *The Last Jews of Rădăuţi* (New York: Doubleday, 1983).
18. "Rădăuţi" entry, Museum of the Jewish Diaspora, Jerusalem.

CHAPTER 3

1. Martin Gilbert, *The Holocaust: A History of the Jews of Europe During the Second World War* (New York: Holt, Rinehart and Winston, 1985), 217.
2. Anna Ornstein, "The Windows," December 1983. Personal notes sent to family and friends.
3. Raul Hilberg, *The Destruction of the European Jews*, vol. 2, "Romania" (New York: Holmes and Meier, 1985), 777.
4. Ibid., 779.
5. Ibid., 778.
6. Helene Stenzler to Rita Rogers, September 25, 1953.
7. Hilberg, *Destruction*, 787.
8. Balfour Brickner, "In Search of Our Ethical Selves, Rosh Hashanah — 1986/5747." "Pebbles in the Shoes of Our Lives," *High Holy Day Sermons* (New York: Stephen Wise Free Synagogue, 1986), 5.

CHAPTER 4

1. Raul Hilberg, *The Destruction of the European Jews*, vol. 2, "Romania" (New York: Holmes and Meier, 1985), 758–796. According to Hilberg, of the approximately 160,000 Jews who were deported from Bukovina, Bessarabia, and the Dorohoi district across the Dniester, about 51,000, or fewer than one-third, survived. About 25,000 died en route to the Dniester, and 10,000 were killed by the Germans in August 1941. More than 74,000 died of disease or were murdered in the camps and ghettos of Transnistria.

CHAPTER 5

1. Stephen Fischer-Galati, ed., *Romania: East Central Europe Under the Communists* (New York: Praeger, 1957).
2. Ana Pauker (1893–1960), the daughter of a Moldavian rabbi, was a leading figure in the Romanian Communist movement. In 1925 she was arrested, escaped, and spent several years in Moscow working for the Comintern. Returning to Romania in 1934, she resumed her revolu-

tionary activity in Bucharest but was arrested again in 1935 and sentenced to ten years' imprisonment. In 1940 she was exchanged for a Russian-held Bessarabian patriot and returned to Moscow. Finally, in September 1944, she returned to Romania to impose Moscow's will on the country and became a notoriously hated figure. Pauker and other leaders of her faction fell into disgrace and were expelled from their party positions in 1952.

3. Tad Szulc, *Czechoslovakia Since World War II* (New York: Viking, 1971), 13. It is worth noting that among the tens of thousands who were fraudulently accused, arrested, and executed for "Titoism," "Trotskyism," "Spanish veteranism" (having fought with the Loyalists in the Spanish Civil War and therefore having been exposed to "Westernism"), and other bizarre forms of alleged ideological impurity, were many of the Czech Communists who had played leading parts in the communization of Czechoslovakia between 1945 and 1948. Among these was the enterprising Joseph Smrkovsky, who had arranged for Russian troops to be the first to enter Prague. Szulc writes, "In no Communist country, not even Hungary and Poland, have so many key personages moved between power and prison and power again, between disgrace and rehabilitation and disgrace anew. Their startling readiness to accept the sublime heights and the abominable depths and their capacity to rationalize each of their successive fates offer an extraordinary insight into the psychology and the sense of blindly unquestioning devotion of so many Communists to their church-like Party."

CHAPTER 6

1. John Foster Dulles, *New York Times*, May 18, 1955.

CHAPTER 8

1. While working on this book, the authors discovered that the same Dr. Putnam had been John Mack's childhood doctor every summer when he and his family lived across the river from Lyme in Thetford, Vermont.

2. R. Rogers and B. Rasof, "A Teaching Drill in Child Psychiatry," *American Journal of Psychiatry* 132 (1975): 158–163; R. Rogers and B. Rasof, "The Gap Between Psychiatric Practice and the Medical Model," *Comprehensive Psychiatry* 18 (1977): 459–463.

3. Rita Rogers, "Between Generations: A Psychosocial Perspective." Presentation at Symposium: "Self-esteem and Values: Psychosocial and Intergenerational Perspectives, Theoretical and Treatment Implications for Child Psychiatry." Harvard Medical School, Cambridge Hospital, September 14, 1983, 12.

4. Ibid., 20.

5. Rita Rogers, "On Parenting One's Elderly Parent," in *Modern Perspectives*

in the Psychiatry of Middle Age, J. Howells, ed. (New York: Brunner/ Mazel, 1981), 197.

6. Rita Rogers, "The Emotional Contamination Between Parents and Children," *American Journal of Psychoanalysis* 36 (1976): 269.

CHAPTER 9

1. Rita Rogers, "Decreasing Tension and Mistrust Among Nations," Proceedings of the Twenty-seventh Pugwash Conference on Science and World Affairs, Munich, Germany, August 1977 (Geneva: Pugwash Publication, 1978), 427.

2. Rita Rogers, "History of the Committee of Psychiatry and Foreign Affairs," unpublished manuscript, 1984, 1.

3. Rita Rogers, "Between Generations: A Psychosocial Perspective." Presentation at Symposium: "Self-esteem and Values: Psychosocial and Intergenerational Perspectives, Theoretical and Treatment Implications for Child Psychiatry." Harvard Medical School, Cambridge Hospital, September 14, 1983, 26.

4. Ibid., 26–27.

5. Rita Rogers, "The Emotional Climate in Israeli Society," *American Journal of Psychiatry* 128 (1972): 992.

6. Rita Rogers, "Intergenerational Transmission of Historical Enmities in a Changing World." Presented July 17, 1981, at American Psychiatric Association Conference: "Three Psychological Dynamics of International Conflict: Victimization, Dehumanization, and Historical Enmity." Mont Pelerin, Switzerland, July 12–18, 1981, 18.

7. Rita Rogers, "A Day in Cairo: An Exercise in Psychiatry and Foreign Affairs," *Psychiatry Digest*, April 1977, 37–41.

8. Rita Rogers, "Psychiatry's Contributions to Conferences on Science and World Affairs," *American Journal of Psychoanalysis* 41(3) (1981): 269–276, 273.

9. John E. Mack, Foreword to Vamik D. Volkan, *Cyprus — War and Adaptation: A Psychoanalytic History of Two Ethnic Groups in Conflict* (Charlottesville: University of Virginia, 1979), xiv. Quoted in Rogers, "Psychiatry's Contributions," 273.

10. Quoted in Rogers, "Psychiatry's Contributions," 270.

11. Rita Rogers, "Soviet-U.S. Relations Under the Nuclear Umbrella, II," in Report of the Task Force of the American Psychiatric Association on the *Psychosocial Aspects of Nuclear Developments*, Washington, D.C., no. 20, 1982, 26.

12. Rita Rogers, "Soviet-U.S. Relations Under the Nuclear Umbrella, I," Proceedings of the Thirty-first Pugwash Conference on Science and World Affairs. Banff, Alberta, Canada, August 27–September 2, 1981 (Geneva: Pugwash Publication, 1982), 253.

13. "Track II diplomacy" (i.e., outside "Track I" channels), is a term coined by Joseph Montville, a U.S. State Department career foreign service officer who has found that this work makes a valuable contribution to the understanding of international tensions. National leaders who have participated in these efforts have often found that, through firsthand experience with their counterparts in an adversary country, perceptions change and associations are established which continue after the organized meetings are over.

14. George Perkovich, personal communication, November 3, 1986.

15. Rita Rogers, "On Solidarity." Unpublished manuscript, November 9, 1982, 2.

16. Perkovich, personal communication.

17. Rita Rogers, "An Encounter with Polish Psychiatrists," *Psychiatric News*, May 7, 1982, 3.

18. Ibid., unpublished version, February 1982.

CHAPTER 10

1. Joseph Brodsky, *Less Than One* (New York: Farrar, Straus & Giroux, 1986), 15.

2. Ibid., 114.

3. Robert A. Rosenstone, "Chaim Baer," *Partisan Review* 53, 3 (1986): 392–393.

4. Brodsky, *Less Than One*, 21.

5. Ibid., 153.

6. Rudolph G. Roden, "Survivors." Presentation at Research Seminar, "Making Sense of Survival." Institute for the Medical Humanities, University of Texas Medical Branch, Galveston, November 15–16, 1984. Unpublished manuscript, 21.

7. Hannah Pakula, *The Last Romantic: A Biography of Queen Marie of Romania* (New York: Simon and Schuster, 1985), 78.

8. Brodsky, *Less Than One*, 16–17.

9. Rita R. Rogers, "A Day in Cairo: An Exercise in Psychiatry and Foreign Affairs," *Psychiatry Digest*, April 1977, 41.

10. Milan Kundera, *The Unbearable Lightness of Being* (New York: Harper & Row, 1984), 224.

11. Samuel Pisar, personal communication, March 13, 1981.

Index

About the
Authors

JOHN E. MACK, M.D., professor of psychiatry at Harvard Medical School and member of the faculty of the Boston Psychoanalytic Society and Institute, is a child and adult psychoanalyst. In 1977, he won a Pulitzer Prize for *A Prince of Our Disorder: The Life of T. E. Lawrence*. His other books include *Vivienne: The Life and Suicide of an Adolescent Girl*, with Holly Hickler; *The Development and Sustaining of Self-esteem in Childhood*, edited with Steven Ablon, M.D., and *Nightmares and Human Conflict*. Dr. Mack, who is active in applying psychological understanding to international conflict, is also academic director of Harvard's Center for Psychological Studies in the Nuclear Age at the Cambridge Hospital.

RITA S. ROGERS, M.D., clinical professor of psychiatry at the University of California at Los Angeles and child psychiatrist, has served as a trustee of the American Psychiatric Association. A pioneer in the field of psychiatry and foreign affairs, she is especially concerned with the Arab-Israeli conflict, Poland, the two Germanies, and Soviet-American relations. She is a member of the Pugwash Conference on Science and World Affairs and writes extensively on child psychiatry and psychological issues in international relations.